Bonfires of Culture

"Franciscan friars burning traditional books and clothes," from *Historia de Tlaxcala* by Diego Muñoz Camargo. MS Hunter 242, Glasgow University Library. Courtesy of Bridgeman Art Library International.

BONFIRES OF CULTURE

*Franciscans, Indigenous Leaders,
and the Inquisition in Early Mexico,
1524–1540*

Patricia Lopes Don

University of Oklahoma Press : Norman

This book is published with the generous assistance of
The McCasland Foundation, Duncan, Oklahoma.

Library of Congress Cataloging-in-Publication Data

Don, Patricia Lopes, 1952–
    Bonfires of culture : Franciscans, indigenous leaders, and the Inquisition in early Mexico, 1524-1540 / Patricia Lopes Don.
        p. cm.
    Includes bibliographical references and index.
    ISBN 978-0-8061-4049-0 (cloth)
    ISBN 978-0-8061-6048-1 (paper)
    1. Mexico—History—Conquest, 1519-1540. 2. Franciscans—Mexico—History—16th century. 3. Indians, Treatment of—Mexico—History—16th century. 4. Inquisition—Mexico—History—16th century. I. Title.
    F1230.D68 2010
    972'.02—dc22
                                            2009024345

The paper in this book meets the guidelines for permanence and durability of the Committee on Production Guidelines for Book Longevity of the Council on Library Resources, Inc. ∞

Copyright © 2010 by the University of Oklahoma Press, Norman, Publishing Division of the University. Paperback published 2018. Manufactured in the U.S.A.

All rights reserved. No part of this publication may be reproduced, stored in a retrieval system, or transmitted, in any form or by any means, electronic, mechanical, photocopying, recording, or otherwise—except as permitted under Section 107 or 108 of the United States Copyright Act—without the prior written permission of the University of Oklahoma Press.

To my husband, Allen

Contents

List of Illustrations	ix
Preface	xi
Introduction	3
1. The Early Colonial Leadership Dilemma	20
2. The Nahualli: The Trial of Martín Ocelotl	52
3. The Millenarian: The Trial of Andrés Mixcoatl	83
4. The Keepers of the Huitzilopochtlis: The Trial of Miguel Pochtecatl Tlaylotla	111
5. The Tlahtoani: The Trial of Don Carlos of Texcoco	146
Epilogue: The Legacy of the Inquisition in Central Mexico	175
Appendix: Boban Calendar Wheel	193
Notes	203
Glossary	235
Bibliography	239
Index	253

Illustrations

FIGURES

"Franciscan friars burning traditional books and clothes," from *Historia de Tlaxcala* — *Frontispiece*

1. Native painting describing the dispersion of the Huitzilopochtlis — 114
2. Selective genealogy of the Texcocan royal family — 150
3. Humboldt Fragment VI — 187
4. Boban Calendar Wheel — 195

MAPS

1. Spain in Zumárraga's Time — 25
2. Southeast Valley of Mexico and the Puebla Area — 55
3. Northeast Valley of Mexico and the Northern Sierra de Puebla — 85
4. Mexico, Texcoco, and Surrounding Area — 124

Preface

The genesis of this book about Franciscans, Mexican indigenous leaders, and the Inquisition came about in graduate school. My professor of Latin American history, Arnie Bauer, asked our colonial seminar to read about a festival in Mexico in 1539 in the final pages of Bernal Díaz del Castillo's *True History of the Conquest of New Spain*. The festival was a curious but fascinating combination of natives performing prehispanic religious ceremonies and rather wild and drunken Spanish conquerors offering their strange reenactment of great European court festivities. Spanish cultural history, particularly festival history, was my interest at the time, so Arnie encouraged me to interpret the festival for my seminar paper, emphasizing indigenous activities and motivations. While the festival story was something that Díaz del Castillo appended to the book and that had little to do with his triumphal version of the military conquest of Mexico, I soon realized that the festival spoke volumes about the more elusive cultural conquest of the natives. Arnie suggested I submit the paper for publication, and "Carnivals, Triumphs, and Rain Gods: A Civic Festival in the City of México-Tenochtitlan, 1539" appeared in the *Colonial Latin American Review* (1997). Thus, I became an oddity—a seventeenth-century Spanish historian of the court and city whose first publication was about indigenous history in the Americas in the early sixteenth century.

In the course of researching the festival paper, I came across a rich cache of documents: over 250 pages of Inquisition trial proceedings against natives in central Mexico in the late 1530s. I expected to find numerous articles, and perhaps a book or two, using these excellent sources. Alas, there were some interesting single articles and chapters here and there, but nothing comprehensive and nothing particularly recent. Since I was inexorably drawn to Mexico anyway, I reasoned that my seemingly out-of-place background in European cultural history and my training in early modern Spanish history might actually be advantages in tackling these Inquisition transcripts, especially for this very early moment in the history of New Spain. In particular, I was intrigued with the idea of bringing the microhistory methodology often used in the interpretation of European Inquisitions to the analysis of the sources and also to ground the study in current Spanish Inquisition historiography, as well as recent indigenous history in Latin American studies. Plus, I must admit, it was a very attractive idea to demonstrate how much can be learned from Inquisition sources about the individual stories of native leaders in the first generation after the conquest. These men and women have been sorely missing from the corpus of recent work on indigenous history in Mexico because of the lack of indigenous language sources in the early period. The reader will have to say whether I have chosen well and have done these historical actors justice.

There are many people I need to acknowledge in the writing of this book. My colleague and good friend Carolle Carter has helped me greatly by reading drafts as well as the final manuscript. My colonial Latin American history students in fall 2007 read a partial manuscript and honored me with their frankness and encouragement. I also wish to thank my first Spanish history mentor, George Vásquez. I owe a great debt to my doctoral mentor, Paula Findlen, for inspiring in me a pleasure in cultural history and teaching me what I know about it. And, of course, I thank Arnie Bauer and my other Latin American history professor, Chuck Walker, for sparking my interest in Latin American history so many years ago.

Thanks also go to Norman Fiering and the John Carter Brown Library in Providence, Rhode Island, for sponsoring my studies there in fall 2004, and Elizabeth Hill Boone, who helped me connect the Boban Calendar Wheel, an early codex in the library's collection, to the Inquisition trials. She later advised me in my reading of two of the pictorial documents in this book; I thank her for her generous help. I also want to express my appreciation to Bernard Bailyn, Susan Kellogg, and the International Seminar on the History of the Atlantic World at Harvard University for the opportunity in the summer of 2004 to present and defend my chapter on the Don Carlos trial, a most helpful formative discussion. My department and college at San José State University have supported me in several research trips in and out of the country, as has the Program for Cultural Cooperation between Spain's Ministry of Culture and United States Universities in the summer of 2003; I acknowledge their financial help in producing the manuscript. The staffs of the Archivo General de la Nación in Mexico City and the Archivo General de Indias in Seville, Spain, extended their usual fine level of assistance with archival documents for this study. Also, my editor at the University of Oklahoma Press, Alessandra Jacobi Tamulevich, has been of great assistance and support, as have the reviewers of this manuscript. Two earlier versions of chapters in this book have been published. Chapter 2, in its earlier version, "Franciscans, Indian Sorcerers, and Inquisition in New Spain, 1536–1543," appeared in the *Journal of World History* (March 2006). An extended version of chapter 5 appeared as "The 1539 Inquisition and Trial of Don Carlos of Texcoco" in the *Hispanic American Historical Review* (November 2008). I thank the editors of these journals for permission to publish.

BONFIRES OF CULTURE

Introduction

Bonfires in the cultures of Mesoamerica and Spain bespoke similar symbolic goals—to destroy the old order of gods and humans and to summon a new age of fealty and devotion. In central Mexico, the indigenous symbol of conquest and the emergence of a new political and religious regime was the toppled and burning temple of the defeated. The symbolic relationship between military and cultural conquest was so strong that, in the midst of Hernán Cortés's conquest of Mexico, one of his native allies, the city-state of Tlaxcala, burned the royal archives of another city-state, Texcoco.[1] The Tlaxcaltecans wanted to avenge the many previous animosities between themselves and the Texcocans and cared little for Cortés's strategic alliances. Thus, the destruction of the Texcocan library, possibly the finest repository of prehispanic literature in central Mexico, actually symbolized native rather than Spanish triumph.

Europeans also burned books and objects in great pyres to mark critical turning points of religion and conquest in Christian history. After the fall of Granada in 1492, the Catholic Kings, Ferdinand and Isabel, tolerated Muslims practicing their religion but eight years later abruptly changed the policy to forced conversion. To signal the new Christian expectations, in the spring of 1500, Isabel's Franciscan confessor, Cardinal Francisco Jiménez de Cisneros, gathered up and burned copies of the fundamental Islamic text, the Qur'an, in a great bonfire in the central square of Granada. The Muslim converts learned soon enough that the penalty for deviation from Christian law and practice might be an Inquisition trial and the burning of men and women outside the walls of the city.

Therefore, for natives and Spaniards in the colonial city of Mexico in 1535, there was no doubt about the symbolic actions of their bishop, Fray Juan de Zumárraga. Zumárraga went to the remains of the burned-down royal archives of Texcoco and gathered up the last of the pictorial manuscripts, or codices, which the Texcocan leaders had salvaged from the Tlaxcaltecan pillage fourteen years earlier. By that time, the Franciscan confiscation and destruction of native votive objects and manuscripts were nothing new. The Franciscans reported to their brethren in Spain that over the previous ten years, they had "destroyed more than 500 temples of the idols and more than 20,000 figures of the devil which [the natives] adore; they have been torn to pieces and burned."[2] By the mid-1530s, locating a few of these codices was something of an evangelical triumph. One friar reported, "As we have destroyed and burned the books and all that pertains to ceremony or is suspect and threatened them if they do not reveal them, now when we ask for books, if they have them, they tell us they are burned and ask why we want them."[3] Zumárraga nevertheless made a great effort to extract the last few precious documents. Like his Spanish predecessor, Cardinal Cisneros, he took the remaining sacred texts to the marketplace in Texcoco, where the Franciscans had established their first mission in 1523. There he summoned native leaders and commoners and very publicly burned the few remaining tangible symbols of Texcocan religion.[4]

Within months, Zumárraga set up an Inquisition tribunal, hiring lawyers, purchasing a court building and jail, and holding trials to punish both native and Spanish subjects who had strayed from the Christian religion. Beginning in July 1536 and continuing until 1540, with a few trials extending until 1543, the bishop conducted approximately 170 *procesos* (trial proceedings) and informal accusations and inquiries against both native and Spanish colonists.[5] Of these proceedings, sixteen involved indigenous people, including twenty-four men and three women, half of the men being either *nanahualtin* (native priests) or *tlahtoqueh* (speakers or leaders) in communities of central Mexico. The narrative arc of the indigenous procesos grew to a wider net of investigations until the climax of November 30, 1539. On that day, Zumárraga condemned to the stake Don Carlos, the *tlahtoani* (speaker or leader) of Texcoco, for the crime of heretical dogmatism, or leading his subjects away from Christianity.[6] In the year after Don Carlos's execution, the authorities on the Council of the Indies and the Suprema, or Supreme Council of the Holy Inquisition, learned about the details of the case and immediately chastised Zumárraga for overzealousness. In the next two years, Zumárraga dramatically reduced the number of accused brought to trial, and in 1543 the Suprema sent a *visitador* (inspector) to take away the powers of inquisitor general from Zumárraga. Thus, Zumárraga's Inquisition began with burning books and ended with the burning of a human being.[7]

Two questions arise from this dramatic chapter of the early colony and the early Franciscan mission. Why did Bishop Zumárraga believe that he needed to persecute the native leaders with an Inquisition? And why did the authorities in Spain disagree with Zumárraga about the necessity of his Inquisition? A single piece of correspondence from one Franciscan friar to another at the height of Zumárraga's Inquisition alludes to the tangle of motives and interests. Fray Andrés de Olmos had been in the city of Mexico from early 1537 to the spring of 1539 and was privy to the evolving discussions about the Inquisition in the episcopal court and among the Franciscan provincial authorities. On January 2, 1540, as Olmos was conducting his own Inquisition of another tlahtoani in Matlatlan, southeast of the city of Mexico, he learned of Don Carlos's execution and wrote to his good friend Bishop Zumárraga:

> I would hope that they [the baptized natives] are Christians, but the way it is right now, baptism is at risk. It is not surprising, because there [in the Valley of Mexico] where the preaching has been abundant for so many years, you find, well, what you find [referring to the numerous cases of recidivism]. It is not merciful to pay no mind to the public wrongs that they do, because they are disregarding the teaching and baptism they have received, which pains me to the soul. It seems to me that they shower us with compliments, and yet I have not known three nobles who have voluntarily come to the religion and remained faithful to it. It is always May for them and there is no winter. The trees, however, will not turn by themselves, and if they do not experience the seasons, no fruit will be

born. It is always May, yet there has to be a winter and punishment for the things they have committed against their baptism, even if they have to be put into the fire, as Your Excellency is commencing to do.[8]

Olmos was one of the best linguists among the friars and had close relationships with numerous native leaders. Though he notes elsewhere in the letter that the natives thought him "tough," nevertheless, he and other friars believed that he blended an abiding love of the natives with strictness. In this passage, one reads Olmos's real dismay and sorrow that the natives either resisted or were unaware of their obligations as Christians, a situation that in his mind unavoidably pressed the friars and the bishop to harsher punishments.

However, two assertions expressed in the passage are a shade more political. The natives' recidivism and their generally unchristian conduct were undermining the validity of the baptisms that the Franciscans had given them, not only putting baptism "at risk," but "disregarding the teaching" of the friars. In the 1530s, the Franciscan policy of readily baptizing the natives in mass baptisms with little or no religious instruction was constantly under fire from some Spanish authorities and other mendicant orders. As the Franciscans were the sponsors of the hasty entrance of native neophytes into the Christian community, the critics held them implicitly responsible for the ubiquitous recidivism. Thus, it was actually the Franciscan policy of mass baptism that was at risk. Yet, Olmos's passage also reveals the Franciscans' obvious strategy of deflecting the blame for their failures and placing it squarely on the shoulders of the duplicitous, recalcitrant, and resistant native leaders: "they shower us with compliments, and yet I have not known three nobles who have voluntarily come to the religion and remained faithful to it."

After the Franciscans had spent more than a decade investing their hearts, their integrity, and their lives in the mission, the order was beginning to realize that it was climbing a higher hill of native beliefs than it had originally thought. The obvious shortcomings of some of their proselytizing methods, their defensiveness in the face of criticism from their many detractors, and their frustration with the alien cultural ways of the natives led the friars to look to a simpler solution for their missionary dilemmas in the persecution of native leaders. This book, in part, narrates the story of the Franciscan path of suspicion and worry toward Inquisition. Investigating the policy dilemma expressed in Olmos's letter requires us to return to the Iberian Peninsula, where the Franciscans had some experience of the ways of Inquisition among unbeliever populations, ideas which they brought with them to the New World.

By the same token, Olmos's characterization of native leaders as duplicitous must be challenged in light of recent studies of native history. The prehispanic origins of the native leaders' thinking and the early colonial context were critical historical factors. While early native leaders may not have understood the complicated political problems of the Franciscans in the colonial community and the Spanish empire, the native leaders were politically calculating men when it came to reading the politics of their own *altepetl* (community or city-state). They hung on to power tenaciously in the face of many internal indigenous challenges and external Spanish intrusions. Showering compliments on the disruptive and nosy friars to send them on their way was deceptive, as Olmos maintained. But, from the perspective of the indigenous leaders, it was also one of many sensible strategies for maintaining political independence and sustaining the native hierarchy. Not only did it potentially control the presence of the friars in native communities, it clearly demonstrated to potential challengers from below that the leaders could manipulate the Spanish interlopers and preserve "face" in a masculine, contentious culture of leadership.

By closely analyzing the texts of these Inquisition transcripts, reading obliquely through the language of Olmos, other friars, and Inquisition secretaries, we may explore the learning process of the first generation of colonial native leaders as they dealt with the Franciscans in religious matters. Specifically, what was left of native autonomy in the wake of the conquest? Given the presence of the Franciscans, how did the authority of native leaders in religious matters evolve? What were the various risks of resisting, acculturating to, or seeming to acculturate to Christianity? And what patterns emerged in the response by the native leaders to the Franciscans?

FRANCISCANS AND SPANISH INQUISITION
"An alliance with social forces"

In the first four and a half years of his Inquisition, mid-1536 to the end of 1540, Zumárraga held 158 trials against both Spanish and indigenous people. This was on average 35 legal proceedings each year at the height of his Inquisition (1539–40), just short of the pace of the busiest tribunals in the early Spanish Inquisition—the Toledo tribunal had an average of 47 trials per year and the Valencia tribunal had an average of 43.[9] At first glance, Zumárraga's Inquisition was focused on the persecution of Spanish colonists. There were more than 150 trials of Spaniards, which meant that 8 percent of the Spanish and European population of about two thousand in central Mexico at the time were tried. By any measure, this percentage was much higher than any Iberian city would have known in the first fifty years of Inquisition and gives some idea of Zumárraga's resolve to discipline the unruly Spanish settlers. By comparison, all 16 of the indigenous cases were brought by 1540 and represented much less than 1 percent of the estimated two hundred thousand baptized natives of 1535.[10] Nevertheless, the indigenous trials were qualitatively different from the Spanish ones. Though fewer, the native trials targeted mostly leaders, resulted in harsher penalties, increased in intensity over time, and were clearly the cause of the negative reaction in Spain to Zumárraga's Inquisition and tarnished the bishop's otherwise exemplary clerical career.

The few historians who have addressed this chapter in early colonial Mexican history have barely grappled with the interpretative questions of the small but intense series of trials of indigenous leaders. In fact, early Inquisitions of native people have garnered little interest. In *Ambivalent Conquests,* Inga Clendinnen's study of a later native Inquisition of the sixteenth century, Franciscans also dominate inquisitorial decisions but are portrayed as motivated by unique "psychological" peculiarities in the culture of their order. Later work also suggests that their apocalyptic view of the world in the sixteenth century pressured the Franciscans into crisis-oriented measures like the Inquisition.[11] Other colonial Latin Americanists have preferred to focus on the procedural aspects of the Inquisition.[12] Additionally, there has been some suggestion that the early Inquisition was a blunder, because the Spanish lacked sufficient experience in dealing with ethnoplural communities.[13] And some historians have speculated that the notoriety of Zumárraga's Inquisition led the Spanish king, Philip II, to exempt his indigenous subjects from the jurisdiction of the Holy Office decades later in 1571.[14]

This book has a slightly different interpretation of the Franciscans' actions in Zumárraga's Inquisition. While the Franciscans certainly were interested in protecting the reputation of their order, their actions were often guided by Spain's fifty-year experiment with Inquisition and ethnoplural communities in the Iberian Peninsula. The answer to why Zumárraga tried the native leaders, why he persisted in trying them even though he lacked the unqualified support of the government in Spain, and why Philip II eventually removed the natives from Inquisition jurisdiction is much better explained in the context of Spanish history than by analyzing the psychology of colonial groups. The political ebb and flow among the Spanish crown councils, Zumárraga, the Franciscan leadership, and factions of the local Spanish government in the Valley of Mexico were very similar to the interplay of their counterparts in the early Spanish Inquisition, 1480 to 1530.

As one scholar of the Spanish Inquisition, Henry Kamen, has noted, the early Spanish Inquisition was an important political instrument of royal policy, but the policy was not solely dictated from the top down. Rather, the Inquisition was a tool the monarch granted to the local elites in communities of the Spanish Empire in order to make "an alliance with social forces" at the grassroots level. According to Kamen, Ferdinand and Isabel, intending to promote political cohesion and centralization, "accepted this policy because it seemed to ensure stability."[15] In a careful quid pro quo between center and periphery, local elites often called upon the crown to send an Inquisition tribunal to their community to counteract a political opponent or competitor. In turn, the crown received some benefit from the local elites, such as more loyalty, symbolic advantages, or financial support. Over the past thirty years, studies of the various regional Inquisition tribunals in Spain have uncovered similar alliances with key regional civic and cultural leaders. Such alliances underscore the role of the Inquisition as an institution that localized crown interests rather than dictating to communities.[16] However, as Kamen notes, despite the crown's intentions of creating harmony and order with the Inquisition powers at its disposal, its alliance with regional groups often led to the opposite—divisiveness and tension. In the early period of fewer permanent regional Holy Offices and the attendant necessity of appointing roving Inquisition tribunals to distant towns and cities, the crown was wary of what was being done in its name. Sometimes it hesitated to appoint the requested tribunals. On occasion it abruptly withdrew a tribunal from a distant community when it perceived that crown interests were not well served.

Events in 1530s Mexico leading up to Zumárraga's Inquisition demonstrated a similar back-and-forth process. A significant motivator in Zumárraga's request for Inquisition powers was the desire to protect and preserve the considerable Franciscan investment in and early dominance of the New World church in central Mexico against its local detractors. From the perspective of the Franciscans, Zumárraga's Inquisition was simply one more component of their implicit social alliance with the crown, based on the preferences and privileges the order had enjoyed since it first arrived in the Caribbean at the turn of the century. The crown, for its part, expected a good supply of enthusiastic and incorruptible missionaries who would convert the New World natives rapidly, steadily, and completely, and make of the indigenous people reliable and quiet subjects and workers. From the beginning of Zumárraga's Inquisition, the king and royal councils were hesitant about Zumárraga's and the Franciscans' desire for Inquisition power and were concerned about reports of Zumárraga's liberal use of the limited Inquisition power they did extend, until they finally ended his privilege in 1543. In a sense, Zumárraga's Inquisition was the most extensive political claim that the Franciscan Order made on its tacit alliance with the crown. The failure of Zumárraga's Inquisition presaged more ambivalent relations later between the Franciscans and crown authorities.

EARLY COLONIAL INDIGENOUS LEADERSHIP
"Beyond the resistance and collaboration pairing"

Like many historians in recent years, I endeavor in this book to give greater indigenous voice to the development and evolution of native–Spanish relations. Yet I do not downplay the importance of the Spanish conquest and its immediate aftermath in the formation of those relationships, as have recent historians who follow the work of James Lockhart (which tends to concentrate on a later period of central Mexican history).[17] Zumárraga's Inquisition demonstrates that the relationships formed in the conquest and post-conquest periods established enduring assumptions, accommodations, and hierarchies for the colonial period. The trial transcripts, however, are Spanish-language, not Nahuatl-language accounts, and it is a difficult task to discern in them the perspectives of early colonial native leaders. One strategy might be to closely read the trial texts for the behavior and motives of the accused—the resisters to Franciscan proselytizing—thus characterizing one small group of leaders. A more ambitious approach would be to elevate the behavior and language of a range of native leaders, not only the accused, but other leaders who interacted with the native resisters and the Franciscans. By doing so, we illustrate broader patterns of behavior of native leaders—whether resistant to or collaborative with the Spanish—that demonstrate a range of less understood motives and strategies. Individual chapters in this book highlight the four most important trials of Zumárraga's Inquisition, analyzing the actions and words of the accused and other leaders implicated or participating in the trials.

The experiences of the resisters provide the initial focal point of this book, and their strategy of appealing to anti-Franciscan sentiment becomes clear. As previous historians have pointed out, the rhetoric of resistance was tied to the many economic, agricultural, and demographic crises of central Mexico in the 1530s; in response, resisters encouraged a return to native religions. But the individual stories of the resisters demonstrate that economic survival was not the only anxiety that resisters exploited. The resisters were inventive in tailoring their rhetoric to native values as a means of increasing their own popularity. They did not simply insist on a return to prehispanic tradition;

they cut and pasted aspects of tradition to create their own variation on prehispanic religion, usually in direct contradiction to Franciscan teaching in the local community. One particularly rich source of discontent on the part of native leaders was the Franciscan effort to regulate native family life and sexual relationships. According to the trials, resisters tapped into a powerful mix of masculine rebellion and outrage against these new cultural and sexual norms.

On the other hand, some individual leaders and groups of leaders collaborated in the accusation and persecution of the resisters, yet their actions did not represent much sympathy with the Christian faith or the Franciscans. Most acted on a variety of complex intentions that were neither resistance nor collaboration. Yet the motives and strategies of these leaders formed "patterned tendencies" of thinking, perceiving, and acting as they dealt with the Franciscans and the resisters. Following historian William Taylor's recent observations concerning indigenous histories, a major goal of this study is to locate and explain these "patterned tendencies" and "reach beyond the resistance and collaboration pairing of subaltern studies" to a more nuanced understanding of the behavior of early colonial native leaders.[18] Taylor argues persuasively that the objective of colonial indigenous studies should be to get "beyond the idea of freestanding, autonomous subjects in colonial histories to how and why they acted as colonial subjects."[19] In this respect, my interpretation is allied with several recent efforts to provide more nuanced and subtle explanations of the "go-between," the arbiter of relations between colonial rulers and indigenous subjects.[20]

Explaining the how and why of these early colonial indigenous leaders requires an understanding of the context of their prehispanic lives. We must remember that the native leaders of central Mexico (particularly in these trials) were not leaders of hunting-gathering groups. They were city men, leading complex economic and political hierarchies, who had a great deal of experience negotiating a place for themselves among powerful and dangerous adversaries. When they confronted challenges in the early colonial decades, they naturally used this repository of tactical and strategic decision making and values and quickly adapted to the crisis at hand. I maintain that their goal was not to be simple interpreters or mediators for the

Franciscans in the native communities. Rather, it was to preserve real autonomy, as they had known it before the Spanish, a kind of non-aligned, middle strategy between the Franciscans and native challengers from below. Early colonial native leaders were in a life-and-death struggle to be perceived as relevant and needed in their communities. The languages and discourses of these native leaders indicate a range of choices between resistance and collaboration. Leaders could pursue a strategy of hiding votive objects and ignoring clandestine practices in their communities, then quickly turn a native religious practitioner over to the Spanish, depending on the way a crisis played out.

As their patterns of action varied and evolved, they shared one consistent motivation—the maintenance of their political autonomy in order to pursue prehispanic interpretations of personal prestige, masculine self-worth, regional political influence, economic enhancement, and communal social prerogatives. Consequently, they embraced time-honored leadership tactics of concession, redefinition, toleration, threat, and deflection in any given episode on any given day. I refer to this whole range of colonial leadership strategies motivated by political sustainability as the "arbitration of avoidance." Using this strategy, native leaders arbitrated between their two main challengers—on one side, the Franciscans, and on the other, junior nobles and commoners from the lower native hierarchy—and consistently avoided a confrontation between the two worlds.

Why avoidance? Zumárraga's Inquisition took place primarily in the Valley of Mexico but extended somewhat into the highland provinces directly adjacent to the valley. The most important and lengthiest trials took place in the eastern half of the Valley of Mexico and involved communities that were generally thought of as collaborators with Cortés in the conquest. Franciscans formed some of their first missions in these communities in the mid-1520s. Thus, many leaders—though not all—in these Inquisition trials had fifteen years of political and military experience with the Spanish and about ten years of interaction with the Franciscans. If there was an initial enthusiasm for alliances with the newcomers, born of a desire to maintain their own political viability, these less well-informed collaborations were over by 1536. Experienced native leaders close to the center of

Spanish power in Mexico were by this time well aware of Spanish military strength, especially the use of violence.[21] Evidence from the trial transcripts suggests that, in the 1530s, these better-informed leaders had made the calculation of a more effective and self-serving strategy than alliance and collaboration: to keep the Spanish and the traditional native worlds apart and to mediate and arbitrate between them in order to bolster the native leaders' own authority and viability; hence, the "arbitration of avoidance."[22]

THE TRIAL TRANSCRIPTS
"How and why they acted as colonial subjects"

The lack of early sources tends to hide the problems and tribulations of the first generation of colonial indigenous leaders. The most prominent written and spoken language in central Mexico was Nahuatl. In its prehispanic written form, Nahuatl was primarily a pictographic language.[23] Though historians today appreciate the ability of the Nahuatl pictographic system to convey motives and thinking, tlahtoqueh in the 1530s would not have used it to record their actions while the friars were burning almost all native manuscripts.[24] Later, Franciscan ethnographers and legal authorities encouraged indigenous scribes to revive the use of Nahuatl writing, but the scribes tended to produce reports of interest to the Spanish, such as tribute lists, histories, and land survey documents. The earliest of these surviving colonial codices seems to date from the mid-1530s. By the late 1540s the Franciscans had succeeded in alphabetizing Nahuatl and other central Mexican languages, teaching them to young indigenous scribes. We begin to see alphabetized Nahuatl in internal indigenous communication from about the 1550s.[25] In the last twenty-five years, historians of the native peoples of Mexico have begun to rely more upon these indigenous-authored, alphabetized Nahuatl accounts. The later accounts, however, reflect native–Spanish interactions after midcentury, not the early period investigated here.[26]

The best contemporaneous textual evidence of what the first generation of colonial tlahtoqueh were doing and saying as they dealt with the leadership problems of the first two decades of colonial rule are early Spanish-language accounts. For central Mexico, the obvious sources are to be found in Hernán Cortés, *Letters from Mexico* (1519–26), which details his conquest and post-conquest dealings with native leaders; the *History of the Indians of New Spain* by Fray Toribio de Benavente, or Motolinía, one of the Franciscan Twelve, who came in 1524 and wrote circa 1540 about the events he had observed over the previous sixteen years; and the collected correspondence of the Franciscan friars, most particularly of Bishop Fray Juan de Zumárraga, recounting the first fifteen years of the church in New Spain.[27]

The primary sources that underpin this book include a fourth group of Spanish-language accounts that have hardly been used, though they may be the best evidence of the motives, sentiments, and decision making of the colonial tlahtoqueh of the first generation after the Spanish conquest—the trial transcripts of Bishop Zumárraga's Inquisition, 1536–40. The remarkable thing about this collection of sources is that it has been widely available for nearly a century. In 1910, the Mexican government commemorated the one hundredth anniversary of Mexican independence by sponsoring the publication of some of the most prized manuscripts of the Archivo General de la Nación, the national archives in Mexico City. The commission in charge of the project selected the trial transcript of Don Carlos of Texcoco as one of three important manuscripts included in the first volume in 1910 and followed with another thirteen trial transcripts, which compose most of the third volume, published in 1912.[28] The commission seems to have been confident that if the transcripts were readily available, historians would generate a significant body of work on the subject of the earliest Inquisition of the indigenous people of Mexico. However, the transcripts have only inspired a few journal articles and a couple of chapters in a book covering the entire period of Inquisition.[29]

The most obvious reason that the Inquisition sources have not been more widely employed is that the Inquisition extracted information from victims who were under duress. The whole reporting process of an Inquisition serves the message of the inquisitor, not the free communication of the victim's choices and thinking. Thus, validity and reliability are problems. Yet, since the 1970s, historians of early modern Europe have interpreted the cultural world of peasants and marginal peoples through Inquisition sources, because, as in this case, they are sometimes the only contemporaneous, detailed evidence of otherwise obscure people extant. The most frequently used methodology for interpreting Inquisition transcripts of subordinate persons has been microhistory—the close reading and analysis of the language of the accused and accusers in a text, contextualized with whatever else is known about the people and the circumstances of the place and time in which they lived. Although a microhistory of a single individual is not exemplary of all people of a class or group, the study of the individual's motives, interests, and decision making gives us access to the internal logic and cultural references of that individual's world and may provide valuable information about the way of life and thinking of his or her contemporaries.[30]

In this study, we are fortunately able to complete a microhistorical treatment of the native leaders' motives and strategies because of two advantages. First, we have a large number of trial transcript pages and numerous cases in a short time frame of four and one-half years.[31] The total number of published transcript pages, plus those from two unpublished trial manuscripts, is 287. Second, the major cases are congregated in the eastern half of the Valley of Mexico and particularly around the community of Texcoco, providing a density of material in a single cultural situation. Thus, the microhistorical study of these trials can provide a sound reading of native leadership in the urbanized indigenous communities closest to the centers of Spanish power in the early colonial period. Moreover, the sources are detailed and varied enough to allow us to see patterns of leadership in the first generation of colonial native leaders and to explore, as Taylor has said, "how and why they acted as colonial subjects" in a time of Inquisition.

The text of this book can be divided into two perspectives—that of the Franciscans and that of the native leaders—though in parts the perspectives are integrated. The first chapter deals mainly with the Franciscan view, and the four subsequent chapters interpret the native view, not only of the accused but also of natives attempting to lead during the Inquisition. Chapter 1, "The Early Colonial Leadership Dilemma," focuses on Zumárraga and the Franciscan leadership and analyzes their perceptions and expectations of the Inquisition in the early sixteenth century. It takes the reader back to Spain and the negotiation between crown and local communities over the use of Inquisition as a tool in ethnoplural communities. The early problems of the colony in central Mexico, especially the politics of mass baptism, are placed in the context of Spanish inquisitional history. I argue that by treating the Inquisition politically, one better understands why Zumárraga asked for an Inquisition and targeted the native leaders. Conversely, the approach also explains why the Spanish authorities ultimately reacted negatively to the bishop's persecution of native leaders.

The trial of a native priest in the winter of 1536–37 is the subject of chapter 2, "The *Nahualli*: The Trial of Martín Ocelotl." Ocelotl was a stranger to the community of Texcoco, where he had settled after the conquest, and he was a *nahualli* (a native priest believed to have supernatural powers). Ocelotl was a kind of go-between who lost his ability to arbitrate between native and Spanish communities when his religious reputation grew in Spanish circles. Local native leaders were a bit ambivalent in handling him, obviously concerned that his magic powers if turned against them were potentially worse than raising the hackles of the friars. But Ocelotl made the mistake of raising his profile with the friars, and Zumárraga proceeded against him with a show trial. The bishop and friars were soon surprised to learn that native leaders had tolerated Ocelotl's spiritual activities, which had allowed him to minister spiritually to prominent native leaders, acquire a significant fortune, and maintain a wide network of business acquaintances in the native noble community. The trial was the catalyst that led Zumárraga and the Franciscans down a path of further investigation, more intense punishment, and a growing fear of indigenous conspiracy.

After banishing Ocelotl, Bishop Zumárraga found himself dealing with another native priest, who seemed to have taken up Ocelotl's cause. Chapter 3, "The Millenarian: The Trial of Andrés Mixcoatl," examines the 1537 trial of a nahualli who lived in the sierra above Texcoco and at one point claimed to be the reincarnation of Ocelotl. Unlike the more careful Ocelotl, Mixcoatl advocated open resistance against the Franciscans. Mixcoatl's activities were indicative of a network of native nanahualtin in the sierra. As the Franciscans pushed farther from the city of Mexico into the rural and mountainous areas, we see the nanahualtin migrating beyond the mission frontier and adapting native religion to meet the threat of Christianity. We also see that the native leaders who favored Mixcoatl lived mostly beyond Franciscan influence, while the leaders who challenged him had closer ties to Spaniards or friars. Mixcoatl's trial demonstrated that a continuous and firm Franciscan presence was necessary to prevent native peoples from returning to their ancient beliefs.

In chapter 4, "The Keepers of the Huitzilopochtlis: The Trial of Miguel Pochtecatl Tlaylotla," the now quite alarmed Zumárraga began to investigate the testimony of a young native neophyte who claimed that tlahtoqueh in the Valley of Mexico had smuggled sacred bundles, called "Huitzilopochtlis" after the Mexica war god, out of Tenochtitlan during the conquest and were hiding them from the friars in homes and caves around the valley. Zumárraga and the friars tried to unravel the secret of the Huitzilopochtlis in a string of trials in 1539–40, the most important of which dealt with Miguel Pochtecatl Tlaylotla, the last known keeper of the Huitzilopochtlis.

Ultimately, the bishop and his colleagues were unsuccessful in locating the bundles, but the hunt for Huitzilopochtlis created a hysteria that led to episodes of vigilantism and false accusations against native leaders throughout 1539. Evidence presented at the trial suggests that the bundles had been lost long before, and that the native leaders were less interested in preserving the bundles than they were in keeping the bishop and friars from persecuting more of their people. Yet, we see in this trial that the friars' first ethnographic efforts to document native religion in the 1530s were directly linked to unraveling the Huitzilopochtli mystery. Moreover, the friars gained insight from the Inquisition trials that helped them develop a philosophy of diabolism, with which they hoped to teach the natives to fear the nanahualtin and the native leaders.

Zumárraga's Inquisition came to a head with the case discussed in chapter 5, "The *Tlahtoani*: The Trial of Don Carlos of Texcoco." The most famous single Inquisition case of sixteenth-century Mexico began when a young native neophyte reported that Don Carlos had committed heretical dogmatism and was leading groups of converts away from Christianity. Zumárraga turned Texcoco upside down, unsuccessfully trying to locate information about Don Carlos's religious crimes. While evidence suggests that the charge of heretical dogmatism that led to his execution was trumped up, Don Carlos's trial exposed two significant problems for native leaders of the time. One was the dwindling economic support for the royal family, which led to numerous factional struggles that undermined Texcoco's native leadership. The other was the Franciscan challenge to the native leaders' control over family matters in their *altepemeh* (communities or city-states), which ultimately caused a male backlash against the friars and created divisions between elite men and women.

The epilogue, "The Legacy of the Inquisition in Central Mexico," looks at the immediate and long-term legacies of the nearly five years of Inquisition for the Spanish local and imperial government, the Franciscans, and the indigenous communities of the Valley of Mexico. It appears that many immediate precipitating factors ended the Inquisition—the execution of Don Carlos, the confiscation of native property, the fear of instigating revolts in the native communities, jealousy over the power of the Franciscans at royal and viceregal courts, and frustration with Zumárraga's rigid style of leadership. Nevertheless, the Inquisition ended mostly because of general disillusionment. The Spaniards in the city of Mexico and Madrid had developed a consensus that the natives were incapable of being good Christians. Of course, the Franciscans kept their illusions much longer and continued their struggle with the native leaders for the souls of the native common people. The native leaders in the Valley of Mexico, on the other hand, who had no choice but to engage the Spanish and live under their rule, found new means by which to assert their independence in economic and political matters. In religious matters, however, living so close to the bonfire of Spanish power, the native leaders carefully learned to live even closer to Franciscan interpretations of the order of God and humans.

CHAPTER ONE

The Early Colonial Leadership Dilemma

Though medieval Spain had been famously and "uniquely" a society of legal tolerance among Christians, Jews, and Muslims, much of that had changed by the mid-fifteenth century.[1] The Spanish Inquisition, established in 1480, culminated a century of popular agitation against Spain's professed Jews and those Jews who had been baptized, the *conversos*. Monarchs in late medieval times were constantly pressed toward harsher policies against many ethnic and religious minorities, and local agitators, many of them Franciscan, conducted pogroms in the larger cities of the Iberian Peninsula. In the sixteenth century, this same conflicted, ethnoplural society was faced with incorporating still other ethnic peoples in the New World under its government and state philosophy of "one faith, one king." The man at the center of this governing conundrum on both sides of the Atlantic was Bishop Fray Juan de Zumárraga.

Zumárraga characterized his problems with native religiosity in the New World as "novel"; however, like most Spanish leaders in the early colony, his life and mind had been culturally shaped in a late medieval Spain grappling with the same ethnic diversity and tension. These earlier experiences formed the template for his decision making in the Americas. Therefore, to understand Zumárraga's thinking about Inquisition, we must return to Spain and examine the social-historical pattern that led from tolerance to forced evangelization to local conflicts in dealing with unbeliever populations of Jews and Muslims and finally to oppression in the form of Inquisition. In the

New World, the Franciscans did not so much force widespread conversion as offer it without evaluating how much the baptized natives understood. When the natives proved to be shallow converts, other mendicants blamed the Franciscans. Defensively, the Franciscans tried to enforce Christian living by regulating the sexual and family lives of natives, thus confronting the native elite's traditional prerogatives in those areas. The Franciscans interpreted their contest with native leaders over community power as recalcitrance and then heresy, and finally, they targeted native leaders for exemplary punishment in the Inquisition.

THE SPANISH INQUISITION
"Stubborn enemies of Christ"

Zumárraga was born in the province of Vizcaya (Basque Country) in northern Spain in the year 1468, making him twelve years old when the Spanish Inquisition was established in 1480.[2] During his entire youth and adulthood into middle age, the society around him was grappling with the issues of centralized kingship and the effect of unbeliever populations on Spain's national identity and security as a Christian kingdom. The Inquisition had come late to Spain. Jews, Muslims, and Christians practiced a policy of relative tolerance called *convivencia* under the medieval Spanish kings. According to Kamen, "though defections to other faiths were severely punished in Christian law, no systematic machinery was brought into existence to deal with non-believers or those forced converts who had shaky belief. For decades, society continued to tolerate them, and the policy of burning practiced elsewhere in Europe was little known in Spain."[3]

Those conditions began to change following the Black Death of the mid-fourteenth century, when the central Iberian kingdom of Castile, in particular, suffered economically. Grievances between monarchs and cities weakened the state, and civil wars debilitated the legitimacy of the royal family in Castile as well as their royal cousins in the eastern kingdom of Aragon. By the mid-fifteenth century, popular preachers and friars, motivated by an extreme sense of religious reform and bigotry, agitated the urban middle and lower classes into making pogroms and forced baptism campaigns in the Jewish neighborhoods. Though involuntary conversion was illegal in Spain, late medieval monarchs were pressured to accept the contradiction that conversion under threat of death was "voluntary"; the kings allowed many of the pogroms to continue unabated.[4]

Whether forced by physical threat or attracted to Christianity for economic and social advantages, Jews did not necessarily find that conversion to Christianity provided legal protection. The same instigators of pogroms, the most important being the well-known Franciscan friar Alonso de Espina, began to spread rumors of rampant "crypto-Judaism," the secret practice of Jewish faith, arguing that the conversos represented a subversive class with questionable fidelity to the Christian faith.[5] Thus, the mere existence of a converso community was transformed into a "converso problem," and agitators demanded legal remedies—exclusion, restriction, and Inquisition. The last was considered most important, because agitators wanted special legal tribunals that would prosecute the heresy of crypto-Judaism without consulting the local bishops, who were widely considered corrupted by converso bribes and by sympathy with the minority.

With conversos occupying some of the higher offices of his royal bureaucracy, Henry IV of Castile resisted persecuting the conversos. But it was his successor and sister, Isabel, and her husband, Ferdinand of Aragon, who, as they came to power in 1475, embraced the social forces agitating for persecution—or, one might say—brought them under their wing. In 1478, they appealed to the Vatican for the establishment of an Inquisition separate from the 250-year-old Roman Inquisition.[6] According to Kamen, the Roman Inquisition was "active in France, Germany and Italy [but] was never deemed necessary in medieval Castile and made only a token appearance in Aragon."[7] The institution was not particularly popular in Spain and was virtually hated in Aragon, for there was little taste for ferreting out heresy among Old Christians. Monarchs were also suspicious of the Vatican's extralegal incursions into their principalities. What Ferdinand and Isabel proposed, however, was an institution that was more state-oriented in the sense of being tied to and under the auspices of the crown as well as focused on the persecution of conversos.

In his papal bull of November 1, 1478, Pope Sixtus VI specifically gave the Catholic Kings "appointment and confiscation, meaning Ferdinand and Isabel's inquisitors had jurisdiction over heretics," and the kings had jurisdiction over the inquisitors.[8] This effectively ended the ability of Spanish bishops to try individual cases of heresy in their dioceses unless the Catholic Kings specifically authorized it. Instead, the monarchs set up a system of permanent tribunals, or Holy Offices, in the major cities, and these offices in turn sent out local tribunals to smaller communities as needed. While the Vatican retained the privilege of vetoing the monarchs' "appointments, canonical regulations and spheres of influence," Ferdinand and Isabel immediately defied the pope with the creation of a royal council for the regulation of the Inquisition—the Suprema, or Supreme Council of the Holy Inquisition—and continued along an independent path.[9]

The Inquisition founded by the Catholic Kings in 1480 was initially "not concerned with general heresy but the secret practices of Jewish rites" in converso communities.[10] Three-quarters of all the executions that the Spanish Inquisition performed in its long history took place in the years 1480–1500, and its victims were overwhelmingly conversos.[11] The Catholic Kings reasoned that they were dealing with a "national emergency"—the subversive element of alleged crypto-Jews disrupting the harmony of the kingdoms.[12] Historians agree that Ferdinand, in particular, did not share the brand of religious zealotry of reformers like Fray Alonso de Espina. Rather, Ferdinand had politically gauged that the crown and the elites—the majority of the nobility, much of the intelligentsia, and most of the church hierarchy—could better "ensure stability" by making an alliance with the lower, urban classes who were clamoring for the legal remedy of Inquisition for the converso problem.[13] Moreover, Ferdinand had calculated that the Spanish Inquisition would help him accomplish his most important goal: the unification and centralization of Spain's fractious, ethnoplural, multi-religious kingdoms with an idea—Christian purity and fidelity.[14]

Yet, founding an Inquisition had its consequences. The Roman Inquisition had been a solution for Christian unorthodoxy which also ended up persecuting converted Jews. The Spanish Inquisition was a solution to the Spanish converso problem that became a mechanism for persecution of heresy generally. And Ferdinand and his successors were not always able to control the social forces that moved the focus from conversos to other minorities. Naturally, once the inquisitors (many of whom had been pogrom instigators) were given powerful crown support, they chafed to apply Inquisition to all manner of perceived heresies. It was a virtual certainty that they would turn their sights to another unbeliever community recently conquered in 1492, the Muslims of Granada (see map 1). Before the crown and the elite could think through the problems posed in regulating the daily life of the much-larger Muslim communities, the religious agitators near those communities were already arguing for rapid evangelization of Muslims, assuring the development of a "Muslim problem."

Unbaptized Muslims who lived under Christian rule were called *mudéjares*, and baptized Muslims were called *moriscos*. Before the conquest of Granada, the mudéjares were "statistically insignificant" in Isabel's Castile, having gradually become moriscos over the previous four centuries.[15] In contrast, in Ferdinand's kingdom of Aragon, mudéjares lived in separate communities, mostly working as agricultural laborers under the rule of powerful and wealthy Aragonese lords who controlled the Cortes (regional parliament). Thus, mudéjares were tolerated for economic reasons. But with the fall of Granada in 1492, the largest, most concentrated population of Spanish mudéjares was created.

In order to get the Granada Muslims to surrender in 1492 without a major battle, Ferdinand and Isabel offered them terms of capitulation that gave them the right to continue living as mudéjares and not be forced to become moriscos. At first, the Catholic Kings appointed the tolerant bishop of Granada, Hernando de Talavera, who observed the articles of capitulation scrupulously and tried to convert the Muslims with persuasion and education, especially the Muslim religious leaders, or *alfaquíes*. In 1499 Ferdinand and Isabel visited Granada and found much less progress in voluntary conversions than was hoped for. When the monarchs left a few months later, they also left behind the queen's Franciscan confessor and principal minister, Fray Francisco Jiménez de Cisneros.[16] At first, Cisneros summoned the alfaquíes and bribed them with gifts to induce them to lead their communities to a more rapid conversion. When the Muslim leaders proved to be "stubborn enemies of Christ," however, he quickly

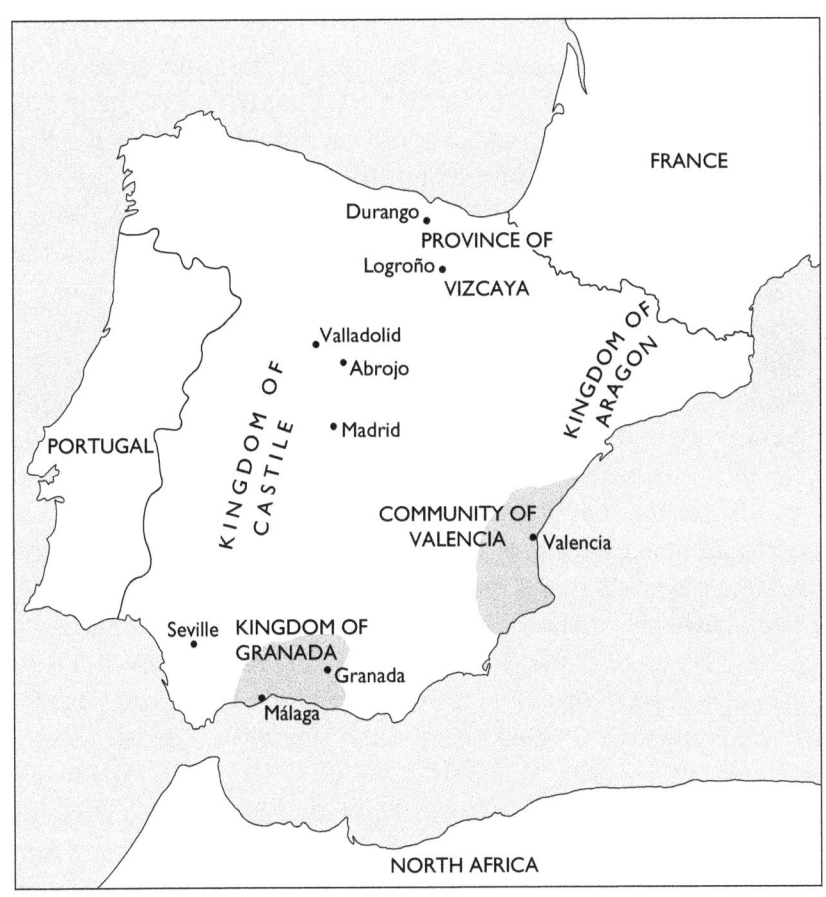

Map 1. Spain in Zumárraga's Time

forced them to convert, occasionally using torture.[17] Cisneros soon boasted to Pope Alexander VI in December 1499 that some three thousand Muslims had been converted, and, it "not being possible to perform the ceremony of ablution with each one, Cisneros resorted to sprinkling the holy water over groups of converts."[18] In addition, "Cisneros had thousands of Arab books publicly burned, excepting only books of medicine, philosophy, and history."[19]

The Granada Muslims soon revolted, at one point attacking Cisneros's home, which sparked a general uprising in communities around Granada in 1500–1501 called the First Revolt of the Alpujarras (the mountainous region of southeastern Spain). Ferdinand and Isabel's armies quickly suppressed the revolt, and Isabel offered an ultimatum to mudéjares in all parts of Castile, including Granada: they could convert immediately or face dispossession of land and property, separation from their children, and expulsion to other parts of Spain.[20]

Spanish concerns about the governance of the Muslim minority were undoubtedly leading to a "morisco problem," but it was more muddled and complex than the persecution of the Jewish conversos. For one thing, the Muslims upon whom baptism was forced were not really crypto-Islamists; they were openly contemptuous of even the most nominal demonstrations of Christianity, spitting in the churches when they were forced to attend mass, ignoring or threatening the evangelists, and cursing Christian symbols.[21] The crown clearly worried about the recalcitrance of these "converts" and the support they could provide to a potential re-invasion from North Africa. Christians were fearful of cracking down on the Muslim community. The Spanish governor, the Count of Tendilla, bristled at the crown's orders to force the moriscos to behave in Christian ways and adopt Spanish customs.[22] Seventy percent of Granada was morisco, and the governor and the Christians lived in constant fear that over-fastidious regulation of the new moriscos' daily lives would provoke another insurrection.

Further, the king could not really bring the harsh legal remedy of Inquisition to bear if he did not have the local Christian elite behind the policy. It was, after all, the civil authority that had to carry out the executions and punishments that the inquisitors would order. Besides, Ferdinand wanted to use the Inquisition to tie the local elites of his various kingdoms to him, not to alienate them. In Valencia, where the mudéjares were 30 to 50 percent of the population, the Aragonese nobility and its powerful Cortes stubbornly opposed any effort to force conversions on their mudéjares. The result was that there was much less uniformity and consensus to the Muslim policy than to the Jewish converso policy.

Even without the opposition of the local elites, the problem for advocates of forced conversion and Inquisition was that they did not have the human resources to go into these large mudéjar or morisco populations either to catechize or to conduct Inquisition at effective levels.[23] Fray Francisco Jiménez de Cisneros, now cardinal, acknowledged as much when he argued in 1500 that the insurgent mudéjares of the First Revolt of the Alpujarras should be "converted and enslaved, for as slaves they will be better Christians and the land will be pacified forever."[24] In other words, if the state did not have the resources to cope, let the slaveholders have the responsibility. Sympathetic with his Aragonese nobles, Ferdinand resisted efforts during his lifetime to force the conversion of the Valencian mudéjares. After the king's death in 1517, Inquisition leaders in Aragon had one last try at the Valencian mudéjares. They managed to persuade Charles V, Ferdinand's grandson and successor, to compel the Valencian Muslims to convert. In 1526, the Valencian alfaquíes quickly responded and extracted a *"concordia,"* a binding legal agreement from Charles V that stipulated that if all the Valencia mudéjares submitted to baptism without incident, they would be free for forty years from any persecution by the Holy Office of the Inquisition. Obviously, the alfaquíes were willing to allow nominal conversion if it allowed them to escape the Inquisition.

Interestingly, Charles V's newly appointed and relatively more tolerant inquisitor general, Alonso de Manrique, readily agreed to the concordia and argued that it was necessary, "since it would be impossible for [the moriscos] to shed all their customs at once."[25] In effect, Manrique acknowledged that forced conversion was creating an unmanageable morisco problem that was too large for the state to handle; thus, it was better to be patient and encourage generational conversions.[26] The Valencia inquisitors, however, regularly ignored the compromises of the state and punished some Valencian moriscos.

But they soon found that Manrique was right. The inquisitors did not have the resources to handle the large population, and their "efforts to keep the Muslims to their nominal Christianity . . . [amounted to] little more than a gesture."[27] Unlike the Inquisition of the conversos and the expulsion of practicing Jews in 1492, both of which effectively suppressed Judaism within a few decades, the Inquisition against moriscos was rarer and less systematic.[28] It was not until the 1560s and a Second Revolt of the Alpujarras that Philip II, Charles V's son, began to furiously persecute the Muslim community, and his successor, Philip III, expelled the Valencian mudéjares in 1609.[29]

The first sixty years of Zumárraga's life coincided with the crucial decades of Spain's invention of a new state identity and these early pangs in the interaction of the state, and later the empire, with unbelievers. In his childhood in the province of Vizcaya in the Basque Country, Zumárraga was somewhat removed from these questions, as there were far fewer conversos and no morisco communities in northern Spain. However, Zumárraga spent most of his adult life between the years 1485 and 1528 in and near the Spanish royal seat of power in Valladolid in the heart of Castile. He was able to closely observe Cisneros, Ferdinand, and Charles V as they grappled with these central questions of state and Inquisition. At seventeen he studied theology at the University of Valladolid. After three years, he took the Franciscan habit in the nearby *convento* (monastery) of Abrojo, and in 1492 he was ordained in the larger convento of San Francisco de Valladolid, which he considered his spiritual home.[30] For the next twenty-three years, Zumárraga followed his lifelong inclination to scholarship by training and educating young Franciscan novitiates in their course of study, known as *studia generalia*, in conventos at Valladolid, Ávila, Segovia, and Palencia.[31] In 1515, he moved up to an administrative career as the superior of the convento at San Francisco de Ávila, and in the early 1520s he became superior provincial of the entire Franciscan administrative province of La Concepción, which included thirty-four conventos in Old Castile.[32] In these various positions of importance and authority in the Franciscan hierarchy, he was clearly aware of debates about conversion and Inquisition and the position held on these matters by various Franciscans, especially the immensely influential Cisneros, the head of his order.

Nevertheless, Zumárraga's only two brushes with adjudications over heresy were in his home province of Vizcaya, and they both dealt with yet another Inquisition target—the heresies of uneducated and credulous Old Christians. At that time, Vizcaya was distinctly divided into two societies. On one side were the leading families like the Zumárragas and their relations, the Larizes and Muntxarazes, and on the other side was a very poorly educated Vizcayan underclass, which was famous throughout Spain for witches, pagan rituals, and unorthodox religious movements. One sixteenth-century inquisitor noted of a visit to Vizcaya, "I found men aged ninety years old who did not even know the Hail Mary or how to make the sign of the cross." For lack of, or poor quality of, priests who ventured there, Vizcaya was "an Indies of unbelief" on the Spanish mainland.[33]

The Vizcayan low nobility served as legal magistrates, civil officers, and mayors, as did Zumárraga's parents and relatives in his hometown of Durango.[34] The Duranguese elite were notably loyal to the crown and the church, but the Vizcayan peasants under them seemed to ignore national institutions in favor of local ideas and loyalties.[35] In the 1440s, Zumárraga's family helped to suppress a religious cult in the famous case of the Fraticelli of Durango. The name "Fraticelli" was applied at the time to a whole class of radical religious sects whose spiritual roots were nominally in the Franciscan movement. As with many religious movements, the early Franciscan Order fractured into diverse interpretations inspired by Saint Francis's life—from those who barely practiced poverty and humility, such as the Conventual Franciscans; to the Observants (favorites of the Zumárraga family), who advocated a moderate but close adherence to Saint Francis's life; to the Fraticelli, the more radical sects that favored schismatic ideas, theocracy, and extreme self-denial.[36] The frequent cultural exchanges between the Vizcayans of southern France and northern Spain seems to have brought a fairly strong Fraticelli movement to Durango in the 1440s. Its leader, Fray Alonso de Mella, wanted to form a theocratic state centered in Durango.[37] The civil authorities (as the Inquisition had not yet been established) tried more than one hundred followers of Mella for heresy and burned thirteen alive. Though a few of Zumárraga's distant relatives seem to have been followers of the Fraticelli leader, his closer relatives served prominently as magistrates in these trials.[38] Zumárraga's conservative family, devoted to the Observant Franciscan mainstream, saw Mella and the Fraticelli as traitors to the Franciscan movement, the Reformed Church, and the Spanish state.[39] These lessons were no doubt impressed upon young Zumárraga and probably influenced his decision to become an Observant Franciscan.

Zumárraga's second encounter with heresy began in 1525, while he was guardian of the convento of Abrojo. As was its custom, the royal family was staying at the royal apartments adjacent to the convento during Holy Week. While there, Charles V had occasion to admire Zumárraga's skill in organizing the visit.[40] More important, the emperor learned that Zumárraga spoke Basque. At the time, in the highlands of Vizcaya, the town of Logroño was troubled by a witch craze. As was typical, the origin of the Logroño witch craze was a French witch, Hendo, who had crossed the border and spread a particularly bizarre version of diabolism among the credulous Vizcayans.[41] Charles V sent Zumárraga to Logroño to try the witches, and Zumárraga took with him his close companion, Fray Andrés de Olmos, who used the experience to make a study of witchcraft.[42] Against the wishes of the local community, Zumárraga attempted to dismiss the accusations against the impressionable young women who claimed to be witches. He ruefully noted of the lower classes in Vizcaya, "I know the people of Durango well—the majority of them have very little judgment."[43] While the trials were going on, the emperor abruptly decided to appoint Zumárraga as the first bishop of Mexico. And so the bishop-elect and Olmos did not see the Logroño witch trials through; instead, in late 1528 they embarked for New Spain.

In the final analysis, what did the historic patterns of conversion of unbeliever populations and Inquisition in Spain imply for Zumárraga as he arrived in the New World? In the social progression from rapid evangelization, to the perception of a "problem" group, to the alliance between crown and local elite, to the application of the legal remedy of Inquisition, there were two obvious stumbling blocks. Both involved the play of power within the local elite. When they did not actively block forced conversions, the local elite argued that the lack of appropriate Christian behavior of the converted was not subversive but due to stupidity or insufficient education. That was the conclusion of Zumárraga with regard to most of the witches of Logroño. When, on the other hand, the local elite became convinced of a "problem"—an ethnic minority it perceived as inherently subversive and conspiratorial—it might decide either that it was unfeasible to apply the necessary educational and legal resources to a large population or that it was economically disadvantageous to persecute certain minorities. Therefore, the "problem" group would be tolerated but monitored, which was the position of the wealthy Aragonese nobles and Inquisitor General Manrique regarding the Valencian mudéjares. There were no stumbling blocks when the local elites widely perceived that the ethnic minority was subversive by intent, small enough to persecute, and in competition with them economically. The early sixteenth-century monarchs, in alliance with local elites, thus usually supported the rigorous Inquisition of Jewish conversos but not necessarily of moriscos or rural Old Christians.

Zumárraga's direct and indirect experiences of Inquisition in Spain carry over to a similarly nuanced position on Inquisition in the New World. From his benign actions as Inquisition judge in Logroño, one is inclined to say that Zumárraga believed the Inquisition necessary to the health of the Christian community but was also aware of the difficulty of policing too closely and too broadly a class of people he thought stupid, uneducated, or inherently amoral. From his perspective and that of many educated Spaniards, the sophisticated conversos deserved the full brunt of the Inquisition, as did the wild Fraticelli leaders, the stubborn alfaquíes of Granada, and the bizarre Hendo, the witch. The credulous and foolish people who followed these leaders, however, probably ought to be spared. His perceptions about unbeliever populations were soon to be tested by the strange underclass of native peoples in the New World.

IXTLILXOCHITL
"Having a hundred gods, they wanted to have a hundred and one"

Looking at the first forty years of correspondence between the Spanish in Spain and the New World, one would not have predicted a "native problem" similar to the converso or morisco problems of Spain. From all quarters, it was argued that the natives were "not Jews or Muslims who had to be forced to accept a religion which their own beliefs held in contempt. They were merely ignorant, misguided people who would soon see the light of reason once the baggage of their old way of life had been swept away."[44] Since 1501, Cardinal Cisneros had been particularly active in sending waves of Franciscans to the Caribbean to establish missions, and the friars reported back that they "found the natives eager for conversion."[45] Conquerors were reporting back news that the natives "would soon be Christian, because they do not have or understand any belief, as it appears."[46] From central Mexico, Hernán Cortés enthusiastically claimed that the natives "would renounce their false beliefs and come to the true knowledge of God; for they live in a more civilized and reasonable manner than any other people we have seen in these parts up to the present."[47] It was obvious in Charles V's instructions back to Cortés in 1523 that the emperor "perceived the Mexicans as capable of rapid evangelization."[48] Zumárraga initially shared these facile assumptions. His first lengthy letter of August 1529 to the Council of the Indies, just eight months after he arrived in New Spain, claimed that the "*señores* [leaders] of New Spain are very loyal vassals of Your Majesty and they have served you very well."[49] He argued that, by contrast, the Spanish conquerors set a "bad example that these newly converted receive." The problem for these observers and for the Franciscans in general was that they misread native action in pursuit of effective alliance with the Spanish as voluntary conversion.

The story of Ixtlilxochitl, the tlahtoani of Texcoco, is an example of this phenomenon. A younger son of the Texcocan royal family, Ixtlilxochitl was obligated to support the indigenous Triple Alliance—Tenochtitlan, Texcoco, and Tlacopan—which governed central Mexico at the time of the conquest. Throughout the conquest, the main partners of the alliance loyally fought against Cortés until their defeat in August 1521. Ixtlilxochitl was the exception; he broke with his royal Texcocan brothers and the alliance in June 1521 and shrewdly joined Cortés in the final assault on Tenochtitlan. In the next few years, Ixtlilxochitl provided tens of thousands of native warriors for Cortés's Spanish–indigenous armies, which roamed central Mexico and reconquered altepemeh that had formerly been subjects of Tenochtitlan.[50] Cortés was so confident of his alliance with Ixtlilxochitl that he placed the first organized group of three Franciscan missionaries in 1523 under the tlahtoani's protection,[51] as well as the second contingent of friars that arrived in 1524, later known as the Franciscan Twelve.

From Ixtlilxochitl's perspective, his protection of the friars, Cortés, and the Spanish soldiers was in accordance with the rules of hegemonic war, politics, and alliance in prehispanic Mexico. According to Ross Hassig, prehispanic hegemons in central Mexico did not militarily hold and administer "conquered" territory through bureaucrats and garrisons in the same manner as European territorial powers. Rather, the goal was a steady supply of tribute from the newly subjugated allies, who were allowed to continue their local governance and cultural traditions with little post-conquest molestation. Prehispanic native allies incorporated each other's tutelary gods and ceremonies into their own traditions to demonstrate respect and fealty. Thus, Ixtlilxochitl "imagined" Cortés and the Spanish "as another altepetl group"—in the words of James Lockhart—as if it were a city-state that had demonstrated its military worth and power in alliance and therefore was deserving of cultural acknowledgement.[52]

In the several years of conquest from 1519 to 1524, before the friars arrived, Cortés had come to understand and accept some of his native allies' notions of the responsibility that comes with alliance. While in 1519 Cortés initially went about throwing down the statues of indigenous gods and destroying temples on his journey to conquer Tenochtitlan, throughout the 1520s he refrained from agitating his indigenous allies with unnecessary insults to their religious practice.[53] Thus, in 1524, one of the Franciscan Twelve, Fray Toribio de Benavente (better known by his indigenous name of Motolinía), assigned to Texcoco, was surprised by the conquerors' tolerance of native religion: "While [the Spanish] were busy building the city of Mexico and making homes and dwellings for themselves, they were content to prohibit public human sacrifices in their presence; but in secret and round about Mexico there were plenty of them performed. Thus, idolatry was left in peace and the houses of the devils and their ceremonies were preserved and their service continued."[54] The religious rituals that

Motolinía saw and the sacrifices he suspected were associated with older, agriculturally based rites and festivities of the weather (especially for the rain god Tlaloc), the harvest, and the hunt. Alfredo López Austin observes that the spiritual understanding of weather and agriculture was similar across central Mexico and represented a *"núcleo duro"*—a core cultural capital of daily, monthly, and yearly rituals and beliefs—that persisted well into the colonial period.[55]

In January 1525, six months after they took up residence in Texcoco, the friars made a dramatic effort to disrupt the religious ceremonies of this "núcleo duro." Motolinía writes, "In Tetzcoco, where the *teocallis* or temples of the devil are most numerous and largest, fullest of idols, and best served by chief priests and ministers, three friars, from ten o'clock at night until dawn, frightened and put to flight all those who were in the abodes and halls of the devils."[56] What the friars found on raids such as these was even more troubling than the fact of the persistence of the rituals. Native leaders such as Ixtlilxochitl, who had allied with the Spanish, had placed in their temples "amongst the idols, the image of the crucified Christ and His blessed Mother, the very images that the Christians [priests who traveled with Cortés] had given them, thinking that they would worship them alone."[57]

In prehispanic times, the Texcocans had placed Huitzilopochtli, the war god of their Mexica allies, at the top of their *cue*, the sacred sacrificial pyramid. To demonstrate political loyalty to Cortés, they now placed there the Christian war gods Jesus Christ and the Virgin Mary and honored their new cult, the Franciscans. However, the pragmatic replacement of the disgraced Huitzilopochtli with more effective Spanish war gods was well beyond the comprehension of Motolinía at the time, and he lamented: "It may have been that, having a hundred gods, they wanted to have a hundred and one." In any case, the Texcocans generally continued with most aspects of their religion except human sacrifice, which Cortés strictly prohibited as a condition of alliance with him.

In October 1524, however, an incident occurred that forced Ixtlilxochitl and probably other native leaders to appear to accede more to the Franciscans in terms of recognizing Christianity, though, again, their responses are better interpreted from a prehispanic native perspective. In order to arrest a rebellious fellow-conqueror, Cortés decided to mount a large expedition that would take him south to Honduras and Guatemala. Fearful of native rebellion in his absence, Cortés took with him the top echelon of the native leaders from dozens of altepemeh in the Valley of Mexico, including Ixtlilxochitl and his older brother, Cohuanacoch, who had led Texcocan opposition against Cortés in the conquest.[58] Unfortunately for all who participated, the disastrous expedition lasted a long and unexpected eighteen months, with most of the Spaniards and natives dying of disease and hardship. Cortés, however, also executed Cohuanacoch, the Mexica leader Cuauhtemoc, and several other prominent native leaders. Ixtlilxochitl and Cortés survived the ordeal, but before their return to the valley in June 1526, native altepemeh in the Valley of Mexico had descended into chaos.[59] The Spanish had appointed *macehualtin* (commoners) to govern in the absence of the tlahtoqueh, and these upstarts boasted that the tlahtoqueh's "rule was already finished and that [the new leaders] and the Spaniards were the lords of the land."[60] When Ixtlilxochitl returned in 1526, he found that many in his family had been murdered, some of his estates confiscated, and what remained of his legitimacy put to the test. At that moment, it was obvious that to retake control of Texcoco he needed an ally, and all of the powerful allies were in the Spanish altepetl.

Given his new wariness of Cortés, Ixtlilxochitl recognized that the only faction within the Spanish altepetl with whom he could establish common cause was the Franciscans, who deplored the rough and blasphemous Spanish conquerors and loudly protested the treatment of the native people. Suddenly, after two years of being politely ignored in Texcoco, the Franciscans had their hands full of "a great number of people [who] came to baptism" with Ixtlilxochitl's encouragement.[61] The Franciscans reported tens of thousands of baptisms with little Christian preparation or instruction and hundreds lining up for the sprinkling of holy water, reminiscent of Cisneros's baptismal campaigns in Granada. Moreover, Ixtlilxochitl agreed to Christian marriages of the elite, and around the same time, he and his wife, Papantzin, were baptized with the Christian names Don Fernando (after the Spanish king Ferdinand) and Doña Beatriz. Seven "comrades," according to Motolinía (or brothers, by some accounts), were baptized and married. Ixtlilxochitl even made his mother offer herself to baptism against her will, threatening to burn her alive if she did not comply with the social graces of his new alliance strategy.⁶²

An even more significant alliance proffer was the architectural accommodation for the Franciscans that Ixtlilxochitl made by building a convent in Texcoco's *tlahtocayotl* (ceremonial center or square, literally "domain of the tlahtoani").⁶³ In the prehispanic period, the tlahtocayotl was not only a spiritual font but also "a pivot of the universe, acting as a magnet drawing all manner of goods, peoples and powers into its space" from the region around it.⁶⁴ The nature of its organization, therefore, was critical to the regional economics and politics of colonial Texcoco. Texcoco's tlahtocayotl contained 400 thousand square feet and was dominated by its *cue* and the teocallis for its principal gods. But it also contained the Texcocan royal palace (which had been ruined in the conquest wars), the residences of important members of the royal family, homes for leading members of the warrior societies and priest cults, the *calmecac* (school for elite children), and the regional market. The control and definition of this space were central to the powerful tlahtoani's symbolic and rhetorical power, as well as to his claim to tribute, both in Texcoco and the region.

The Franciscan convento that Ixtlilxochitl built into his tlahtocayotl beginning in 1526 was a complex containing a church, a monastery, and a large patio surrounded by a wall. According to the most recent research on conventos in Mexico, the initial complexes, at 72 thousand square feet, were about the size of ten tennis courts. This would have displaced about 16 to 17 percent of the area of the tlahtocayotl in Texcoco. The convento housed not only the friars but also Texcocan neophytes who served the friars, and elite children who were required to attend school there.⁶⁵ In a brief time, "the towns that were subject to Texcoco" also began the construction of conventos. Coatepec, near Texcoco, was the site of the "first church outside of the [Texcocan] monasteries."⁶⁶ Motolinía identifies the next circle of outreach as Tepeapulco, Otumba, and Tulancingo, all altepemeh subject to Ixtlilxochitl.

The Franciscans counted the founding of these conventos as triumphs of the Christian message; they even treated Texcoco as a safe base for expansion of the mission.⁶⁷ But it turned out that they were premature in their calculations. After 1526, Motolinía reports no further examples of Ixtlilxochitl's presumed enthusiastic endorsement of Christianity. Rather, the friar notes that after 1526, "three or four years passed in which almost nobody was married, except those who served the friars directly; neither lords, nor gentlemen, nor commoners."[68] If Ixtlilxochitl had wanted more Texcocans married in the Christian church or wanted to signal further support for the Franciscans, it would have happened. But after Ixtlilxochitl got the political upper hand in Texcoco, he grew ambivalent toward the Franciscans, though he sensibly did not openly oppose them and invite Spanish violence into Texcoco.

A telling incident happened in 1532, just before Ixtlilxochitl's death. An unnamed friar, likely Fray Antonio de Ciudad Rodrigo, a member of the Franciscan Twelve, sent one of Ixtlilxochitl's half brothers, Don Carlos Ometochtli, to ask for another royal palace Ixtlilxochitl owned in the Texcocan suburb of Oztoticpac. Fray Antonio hoped to acquire the property for church functions, but he apparently did not feel secure enough in his relationship with Ixtlilxochitl to ask for the palace himself. The wily Ixtlilxochitl, however, understood the game, turned down his half brother, and instead gave the palace to his full brother and chosen successor, Don Jorge Yoyotzin. Yoyotzin was an odd choice for ruler of Texcoco, if support for Christianity was Ixtlilxochitl's aim. Yoyotzin had fought on the side of the Mexica against Cortés in the conquest and was one of Ixtlilxochitl's brothers who were most openly contemptuous of Cortés and all the Spanish.[69]

Why the change in attitude, or at least, in political perspective? As Louise Burkhart has noted, there was a considerable chasm "between the monist, relatively amoral world view of the Nahuas [indigenous peoples speaking the common language of Nahuatl] and the dualist, morally charged world view of the missionaries."[70] Ixtlilxochitl had really never come over to the Christian side, nor is it possible to characterize the Texcocan tlahtoani's activities as cultural syncretism, the blending of Christian and native ideas. Syncretism "implies a resolution of contradictions, a halfway meeting between complementary elements."[71] Like many early colonial native leaders, Ixtlilxochitl did not see Christianity as something to meet halfway; his goal seemed to be to get power back from upstart challengers in his altepetl by moving to a more collaborative stance vis-à-vis the Franciscans, not converting to their religion. Once he forced his internal enemies from below out of Texcoco and again obtained full control with the help of the Franciscans, he quickly moved back to a more middle position. His was a classic strategy of arbitration of avoidance: choosing between a range of leadership choices as the place and time required, always occupying the indispensable middle.

His strategy, however, had its consequences; one might even say it backfired. Between 1526 and 1532, Ixtlilxochitl seems to have recognized the problem he created, and his rueful attitude in the matter of his royal palace points us to the reason his strategy failed. Once constructed, the Franciscan conventos across the eastern half of the Valley of Mexico began to draw in labor, products, and trade from the immediate region, dominating economic activities in the same way as the prehispanic Texcocan central tlahtocayotl had.[72] Soon the Franciscans insisted on the exclusivity of the Christian calendar, objects, and ceremony in the tlahtocayotl near their conventos. It was precisely this regional religious and social power that Ixtlilxochitl had hoped to capture for himself in the first years after the conquest, but now it was shifting to the benefit of the Franciscans.[73] By the time of Ixtlilxochitl's death in 1532, Texcoco's tlahtocayotl was no longer the stage for native religion, nor Ixtlilxochitl's power what it had been when Motolinía arrived in 1524.

While the Franciscans were gathering political strength and influence in the tlahtocayotl, traditional religious practitioners adapted by moving out of the city centers into what Davíd Carrasco has called the "Aztec ceremonial landscape": the suburbs, countryside, mountains, caves, and undergrounds of homes and palaces. By 1532, the Franciscans were becoming increasingly aware of clandestine indigenous worship in these places. As Motolinía notes,

> Now that the friars were thinking that everything was done because idolatry had been abolished in the temples of the devil and the people were coming to learn the Christian doctrine and be baptized, they discovered the most difficult thing of all, and the one that took the longest to destroy. This was that at night the Indians continued to meet and call upon the devil and celebrate his feasts with many and diverse ancient rites, espe-

cially when they sowed the corn and when they harvested it, and every twenty days, which was their month.[74]

Throughout the 1530s, as more Spaniards and friars arrived, the evidence of continued idolatry cropped up, and Zumárraga became more emphatic and disturbed about the evidence of "backsliding." In a letter to the Council of the Indies in 1536, Zumárraga wrote,

> The natives still practice their heathen rites, especially the superstitions and idolatry and sacrifices, though not publicly as they used to do. At night they go to their altars, pyramids, and temples, which have still not been destroyed, and in the center of them they hold the idols in the same veneration that they used to. It is believed that few of the elderly have left their sects or their affection for these things or stopped hiding the many idols, even though we admonish them and threaten them frequently.[75]

The brunt of Zumárraga's suspicions began to fall more and more on the native leaders whom he had praised just a few years before. Though there is no direct evidence of Ixtlilxochitl or his successors overtly protecting these traditional religious activities, the Franciscans knew well that clandestine practices could not have gone on without tlahtoqueh such as Ixtlilxochitl being aware of it. Trial transcripts make it clear that Ixtlilxochitl's colonial successors, if not the collaborators that the Franciscans believed them to be, followed his early strategy of arbitration of avoidance. They tolerated the secret activities to appease the spiritual needs of the community and allowed the covert native and overt Christian spheres of Texcocan life to continue in parallel.

In the early 1530s, Zumárraga began a morals campaign that bypassed the unreliable tlahtoqueh in order to enforce Christian morality in native communities through direct Spanish governmental means. As part of his responsibility as bishop, Zumárraga was appointed Protector of the Indians, which meant that the bishop-elect could send friars into the various altepemeh to investigate the treatment of the natives at the hands of their Spanish *encomenderos* (recipients of a Spanish grant of tribute and labor). In 1532 Zumárraga began to use this power to monitor and punish the natives whose behavior was contrary to Christian teaching. In a move similar to the disciplining of the moriscos and their leaders, Zumárraga sent visitadores into the native altepemeh to check on the Spanish encomenderos. The bishop's written instructions to the visitadores tell them to investigate whether the encomenderos had found out "which natives are unfaithful and gather them and warn them." The encomenderos in these towns were to "make sure that there are no idols, sacrifices, ceremonies, or heathen behavior; that such people be punished and separated from the others." The visitadores were to check if the Spanish and the tlahtoqueh were in collusion to mistreat the macehualtin. Another instruction was for the Spanish to "bring the principal lords to the nearest monasteries of friars on feast days."[76] It is unclear whether Zumárraga was speaking of Christian festivals or the prohibited indigenous festivals that took place every month of twenty days. Either way, the instructions are an indication that the community of friars had begun to view the native leaders as subversive and to classify them as a "native problem." Zumárraga often found himself, like the persecutors of moriscos in Spain, relying too much on a reluctant civil authority to enforce religious edicts.

While idolatry was their greatest concern—and later the subject of the most important Inquisition trials—Zumárraga and the Franciscans increasingly identified the sexual behavior of the native leaders as a defining component of their subversiveness. *Amancebamiento*, an old-fashioned Spanish term for "cohabiting or living in concubinage," was on the accusation lists of twelve of the native trials of the Inquisition and was frequently commented upon in the instructions to the visitadores, as well as the minutes of the Franciscan synods, correspondence between the friars, and all the personal correspondence of Zumárraga. While immoral conduct may have been a lesser religious sin than heresy, it seemed to the friars that evidence of the former implied the probability of the latter.

In some ways, the struggle between the friars and the native leaders on the question of sexual and marital conduct presented a more highly charged power struggle than idolatry. The native elite treated marriage as a secular institution.[77] Sons of wealthy men could take concubines, and nobles could have nearly as many wives as they wanted. The tlahtoqueh had extensive rights to allow, prohibit, or determine unions among commoners and nobles, including administering death to those who were considered adulterers.[78] When Zumárraga asked for "amplification of the authority" of friars to approve or deny indigenous marriages, he usurped the traditional authority of the tlahtoqueh, thus emasculating and insulting them.[79] Even the tlahtoqueh whom the friars considered relatively cooperative resisted this interference, yet the friars stubbornly persisted.

One of the first Franciscans in New Spain, Fray Pedro de Gante, wrote to his brethren in Flanders in June 1529, "The men take many wives, especially the principal lords, who have 400, some 100, 50 or 10 . . . and so [the common men] live miserably cheated."[80] Motolinía describes the impasse that had developed: "The lords had most of the women and would not give them up, nor could the others take them away from them. Neither entreaties, threats, sermons, nor anything else sufficed to make them give up all these women and marry one with the sanction of the Church."[81] By 1536, Zumárraga argued to the Council of the Indies, "There is great necessity to build houses . . . where young girls are cared for who escape the wicked clutches of the caciques and it is necessary that Your Majesty give authority to take daughters five years and older from their homes . . . for the only other remedy is to hang most of the indigenous leaders."[82] Inquisition trial transcripts indicate that the Franciscans forced many elite men to marry women in Christian ceremony against their will, especially in the years 1533 to 1535, in effect creating a community of sinners and contributing significantly to the making of a "native problem."[83]

ZUMÁRRAGA'S QUEST
"Entreat His Holiness to name an inquisitor general"

By the early 1530s, the Franciscan leadership, including Bishop Zumárraga, Fray Andrés de Olmos, and Fray Antonio de Ciudad Rodrigo, were invested in the notion of the indigenous leaders as a problem class. However, as with the "morisco problem" in Spain, Zumárraga had to tread very carefully through a minefield of local colonial politics to gain support for Inquisition. In Valencia and Granada, the Inquisition of mudéjares faced opposition from local elites who feared rebellion, particularly the Aragonese nobles concerned about their own economic welfare. In central Mexico, local opposition came from Spanish settlers and the other mendicant orders. These detractors were concerned about rebellion and economics, but their greater opposition was to Franciscan influence on the monarchy generally and their rapid expansion of power in the New World particularly. Rather than couch their opposition in political terms, however, the detractors argued on ideological grounds, critiquing the natives' capacity for Christianity, especially under the Franciscan policy of mass baptism.[84]

The first Dominican provincial in New Spain, Fray Tomás de Ortiz, opined to the Council of the Indies that, despite the glowing reports the Franciscans were giving the council, "Indians are more stupid than asses and refuse to improve in anything." He hinted that the influential Dominican provincial in Hispaniola, Fray Pedro de Córdoba, agreed with him.[85] Another Dominican, Fray Domingo de Betanzos, who was thought to be in favor of evangelization, created an even greater sensation when he told the council in 1532–33 that the capacity for Christianity of the indigenous peoples of New Spain was doubtful.[86] Others in the Dominican Order, however, such as Julián Garcés, bishop of Tlaxcala, and later, Bartolomé de las Casas, bishop of Chiapas, were vigorous defenders of the indigenous capacity for Christianization. But the comments of a few Dominicans raised a considerable stir about this nagging legal question in Spain.[87] The capacity of the Indians to Christianize was assumed in Alexander VI's "papal donation" of the New World to Ferdinand and Isabel in 1494, in which he gave the Indies to the Catholic Kings because they would convert the indigenous inhabitants. If the natives lacked the capacity to become Christians, the legal ramifications to the crown were troubling, to say the least.

While theological and legal scholars thrashed out the problem in Spain in the 1530s and '40s, the Franciscans' detractors in central Mexico were more concerned about tying ideological concerns to practical outcomes. Franciscans bristled under the Dominican attack, as they "rightly perceived that if the Indians were declared to be lacking the capacity to become Christians (or judged to have little ability to do so) they would be edged out of the responsibilities and unprecedented power they enjoyed in the New World," which was the real goal of the detractors.[88] While the Franciscans and Dominicans argued about the humanity of the natives, other Spanish detractors argued that the native people lacked capacity, because that suggested that they could be enslaved. Some friars were split on the issue but reasoned that, at least, the natives ought to be better educated before baptism.[89]

As with the large morisco community in Valencia, however, extensive education before baptism in New Spain stretched existing evangelical resources. The need to educate the natives counteracted the advantage the Franciscans had gained with their rapid expansion of conventos in central Mexico in the 1520s and '30s, as a quick inventory of the ratio of Franciscans to natives in the mid-1530s demonstrates. The indigenous population of the Valley of Mexico in 1535 was probably around 800 to 900 thousand souls living in fifty major altepemeh and at least a hundred smaller communities (after the smallpox epidemic of 1519–21 and a decline of 5 to 10 percent in the post-conquest population over the next decade). Motolinía reported that by the mid-1530s only eighty Franciscans in total had come to New Spain to serve some or all of the time in the Valley of Mexico. He counted among the eighty, twenty who were not even friars but lay brothers or novices who could not baptize or perform the sacraments. He estimated that twenty more friars had died and another twenty had returned to New Spain.[90] Approximately a third of these eighty men were serving outside the Valley of Mexico at any one time, and at most, only half had acquired the language proficiency to speak directly to the natives. Each Franciscan, capable or not, would have had to serve an average of fifteen thousand people just in the Valley of Mexico. Since the friars served in communities of three, they generally could have a presence in about a third of the fifty major altepemeh in the valley, which was insufficient for direct proselytization of the population.[91] The friars often established a Franciscan convento only to leave it to local caretaking neophytes, returning on important feast days to celebrate mass and preach; thus, the barely indoctrinated were leading the hardly converted.[92]

Even though their resources were small and the recidivism of those they hastily baptized obvious, the Franciscans chose to spend their limited human resources on the administration of mass baptisms of tens of thousands more people rather than the better education of those they had baptized or were about to baptize. In baptizing so many natives, the Franciscans clearly felt obliged to do all they could to save the souls of those who might otherwise have died outside of the church. Many wrote of the horror they personally felt for natives who were carried off by disease and war without benefit of salvation. In their minds, this moral high ground could not be separated from the practical necessity of building the brick-and-mortar infrastructure to make it possible. The most important first step in that process was mass baptism in order to create the spiritually motivated laborers who would construct the convento buildings in the precinct of the tlahtocayotl. The data demonstrate that the rate of baptisms increased at about the same pace as the construction of Franciscan conventos, both of which doubled in the 1530s.[93] The physical existence of the convento also served the institutional interests of the Franciscans against their competitors in the other mendicant orders. A convento allowed the Franciscans to claim the altepetl as part of their exclusive proselytizing territory; other orders did not challenge the territorial marker but simply moved on to other altepemeh to develop mission communities.

Unlike Spain, where higher ecclesiastical authorities regulated where the orders could build conventos, the Franciscan friars arrived in New Spain before any bishops did. The Dominican friars arrived in 1526 but did not have a significant presence until nearly 1530, and the Augustinians arrived in 1533, finally building a convento in 1537. The later-arriving orders were forced into less prosperous and more dangerous proselytizing territories beyond the Valley of Mexico.[94] By the late 1530s, the orders were engaging in a headlong rush to build conventos, forming a haphazard crazy-quilt of missionary territories across central Mexico.[95] Zumárraga's entire tenure as bishop was plagued with complaints about jurisdiction issues and insinuations that he favored the Franciscans. According to some, the mendicant territorial issues had become "more difficult and contentious than those over the encomenderos."[96] Therefore, while the Dominicans' criticism of the Franciscans' mass baptisms and prioritization of expansion over education were valid, the Dominicans' theological arguments about rapid evangelization actually veiled political concerns about the Franciscans' rapid institutional expansion. "Had they been given their own share of the natives to convert," it is doubtful the Dominicans would have raised the larger moral and legal issues of native capacity.[97]

As for the Franciscan response, they could have followed Inquisitor General Manrique's pragmatic solution in Spain, which was to give unbelievers mass baptisms but tolerate their deviations or deceptions until they acculturated over generations. But in the politically and morally charged environment of mendicant rivalry in the 1530s, the Franciscans keenly felt the scandal of the badly behaved natives under their charge. Thus, they tended to obscure the scandal with a vociferous and contentious moral defense of mass baptism and the indigenous capacity for Christianization. For five years, the Franciscans wrote to their advocates in the Vatican, insisting on a papal bull that would assert that the American natives were "fully human." In early 1537 they finally received *Sublimis Deus*, a papal bull in which Pope Paul III stated, "all are capable of [understanding] the doctrine."[98] The "fully human" position, however, was a mixed blessing. The Franciscans had the moral authority to press on with the mass baptisms and the construction of conventos, but now the natives had to be held to the Christian standard expected of any Spaniard.

Holding the natives to the same standards as the Spanish Christians was a daunting task, given the larger number of natives and ubiquity of their unchristian behavior. But the Franciscans pressed on. The use of exemplary punishment of certain sinners, of native dogmatizers, and of amoral nobles was their strategy. The move toward exemplary punishment by Zumárraga and other Franciscan leaders was not new. It mirrored similar thinking in Spain with regard to Old Christians in remote areas of the Iberian Peninsula in the late sixteenth century. As Kamen points out, "Rather than making its sentences lighter because of the low degree of religious understanding in rural areas, the Inquisition [in Spain] increased its punishments in order to achieve greater disciplinary effects."[99] Zumárraga had been disinclined to this reasoning when he was an inquisitor in Logroño in 1527. But in central Mexico he had to adapt to new circumstances. He hoped to end the scandal of the immoral behavior of the natives without having to give up the spiritual and practical benefits of mass baptisms. While he did not fully understand why native recidivism was happening, he needed to reassign blame for the problem from the Franciscan Order to the native leaders.[100] Zumárraga was inclined to spare the native commoners and punish their leaders, whom he viewed more and more harshly as he saw them take advantage of young women, collude with unsavory Spaniards, and support secret indigenous religious practices.[101]

There was also the matter of obtaining local Spanish elite and crown support for an Inquisition, which had been the key political factor in sustaining the legitimacy of an Inquisition tribunal in Spain; Zumárraga demonstrated acute sensibilities in this regard. He could have begun Inquisition trials in the city of Mexico in 1528. The crown had given bishops in the Americas power to try heresies in their jurisdictions. Cardinal Cisneros, the great model of Observant Franciscan leadership, had decided against establishing a permanent Holy Office in the New World, favoring a circumscribed "Apostolic Inquisition" of the colonial bishops; it was one of his last acts before he died in 1517.[102] One can only speculate that Cisneros reasonably believed that the New World was not stable enough for a permanent Holy Office. Furthermore, the advantage of Apostolic Inquisition was that it gave extraordinary powers to try heresy to the very men he was appointing to New World posts, without establishing a high-level bureacracy that might become corrupt and arrogant, as some Holy Offices in Spain had become.[103] For two decades, Cisneros had carefully placed Observant Franciscan missionaries in the New World and named bishops from both Franciscan and Dominican orders, demonstrating "antipathy for the secular orders of the Spanish Church."[104]

Dissatisfied with this limited power, Zumárraga chose not to exercise his Apostolic Inquisition powers for seven long years. Richard Greenleaf has explained this seven-year interregnum by arguing that the bishop wanted to wait for the politically strident climate in the early colony to subside. Indeed, several Franciscan and Dominican friars had compromised the credibility of the Apostolic Inquisition by holding a few dozen highly political Inquisition trials (called the "Monastic Inquisition") in the years 1526–28, abusing the power in order to persecute various political factions in the Spanish community. Zumárraga waited, Greenleaf argues, because he wanted to take the politics out of the institution.[105] The scandalous legacy of the Monastic Inquisition was probably a consideration; however, Zumárraga waited a very long time.

There is, however, another explanation for this hiatus. Evidence in Zumárraga's correspondence indicates that he rejected his limited "apostolic powers" because he believed in the 1530s that the time had come to found an independent Holy Office in New Spain. Such an independent and permanent tribunal would mean he was not subject to the oversight of the regional Holy Office of Seville, as he was in the more temporary post of "apostolic inquisitor." Zumárraga had become wary about oversight from Seville because, through the years, he had earned enemies on the Council of the Indies who were friends or relatives of members of Seville's regional Holy Office. Many on the Council of the Indies were businessmen and traders who agreed with some Dominicans about the natives' incapacity for Christianity and also objected to the heavy influence of the Franciscans in New Spain's government. These men had allies and agents in the city of Mexico and, no doubt, were concerned that Zumárraga might use greater Inquisition latitude and independence to punish their fellows. One of the conditions of the Apostolic Inquisition was that all accused who were convicted had to be sent to Seville for appeal. With this oversight, they could effectively veto Zumárraga's sentences.

So, between 1528 and 1536, Zumárraga refrained from using the more limited "apostolic power" and made several efforts to get a permanent Holy Office into New Spain. He first obtained support for his plan from the highest local colonial authorities—the Audiencia, the governing legislative and judicial tribunal of New Spain, as well as Cortés and, after 1535, the new viceroy, Don Antonio de Mendoza. The president of the Audiencia in 1530–35, Sebastián Ramírez de Fuenleal, bishop of Santo Domingo, was highly supportive of the Franciscan mission and advocated for the Christian capacity of the natives.[106] Ramírez de Fuenleal argued to the Council of the Indies that a separate Holy Office under Zumárraga's control was necessary in order "to combat foreign merchants and corsairs who were coming in increasing numbers to Mexico." Cortés was still general of the Spanish forces in the early 1530s, and he emphasized to the emperor, Charles V, the need for an established Holy Office "to provide order to the land ... because vicious people come here and they are hardly dealt with at present."[107] Although the arguments to the crown did not speak of trying native leaders, when Zumárraga eventually did begin trying natives, the Audiencia, Cortés, and Viceroy Mendoza all supported his decisions.

Unfortunately, their support did not move the Council of the Indies in Seville. Enemies on both sides of the Atlantic had created enough doubt about Zumárraga's decision making and character that the Empress Isabel, Charles V's wife, ordered Zumárraga to return to Spain and consult with her. Zumárraga returned to Spain in 1532–34, but he had little trouble reassuring the young empress of his integrity and leadership.[108] Zumárraga did his best to advocate for the establishment of a separate Holy Office in the city of Mexico. Nevertheless, he returned to New Spain in December 1534 without his much-desired Holy Office or an appointment as inquisitor general. When the Suprema finally sent instructions in the summer of 1535, they simply confirmed Zumárraga's "apostolic powers."[109]

By this time, however, Zumárraga had either grown bolder or more concerned about the threat of the native leaders, or both. When he proceeded with his Apostolic Inquisition, he gave it all the trappings of a permanent Holy Office, paying for jail structures, bailiffs, prosecutors, defense attorneys, a courtroom, notaries, and translators. He asked the emperor to provide him with the *encomienda* (Spanish grant of tribute and labor) of an altepetl, Ocuituco, to help finance this and other projects. His secretaries and officers even referred to Zumárraga as "inquisitor general" and his ecclesiastical court as "Holy Office" in most of the trial transcripts, though they had no such official standing. Even as Zumárraga brought the first cases of his Inquisition, he continued to correspond relentlessly and press for greater latitude in the moral disciplining of the natives.

But he was met with reluctance in Spain. On November 30, 1537, Zumárraga and the other bishops of New Spain wrote to the crown, "Some punishment is necessary, yet Your Majesty has ordered that the adulterous Indians should not be given the lash as is done with the Spaniards. So we have refrained and have ordered our visitadores not to exceed the orders of Your Majesty."[110] As Zumárraga was writing to Spain, Charles V was penning a letter to Zumárraga ordering that cases dealing with the "Indian marriage problem" should be brought to the civil court of the Audiencia for remedy, not to his Apostolic Inquisition.[111] As chapters in this book will reveal, Zumárraga completely disregarded these orders and brought polygamy cases to his docket. In another letter of November 1537, he and the other bishops begged the emperor for the authority "to take extremely rigorous measures against idolatry."[112] But in October of 1538, Charles V was sending directives to the bishops not to submit natives to Zumárraga's Apostolic Inquisition in the city of Mexico but to handle those cases under the ordinary punitive authority of the various bishops in their dioceses—which suggests that Zumárraga may have been encouraging the other bishops to send these cases to him.[113] Obviously, Zumárraga's detractors in the city of Mexico and Seville were preventing him from forging the necessary alliance between crown and local elite that was essential to the rigorous, far-reaching Inquisition that he believed necessary.

Perhaps in frustration, Zumárraga finally took the unusual and somewhat dangerous step of going around the royal court and appealing to the Vatican, probably in hopes that the pope would persuade Emperor Charles V to establish a Holy Office in New Spain. In February 1537, while Zumárraga was trying his second case against a native leader, he sent two young friars to represent him at the Franciscan chapter meeting in Italy, a synod of Franciscan leaders from every part of the world. He gave them written instructions to speak with various leaders in Rome, including the pope. But there were actually two sets of instructions, which suggests that one was official correspondence and the other secret—typical of diplomatic affairs at that time. In both letters, Zumárraga's attitude concerning the value and necessity of indigenous punishment is clear. "As the natives need to be brought to our faith benignly and with love, after they are members of the church it is often necessary to give them some pious punishments, because their natural condition is so slovenly in temporal matters as well as spiritual ones and they are always in need of a spur. They will not come to the doctrine, nor do the things obliged by Christianity, if they are not compelled to do so," he writes in the official instructions.[114] Zumárraga goes on to complain that the Spanish emperor's royal councils were discouraging the friars from using the whip on the natives, and he notes that "the religious come to me complaining" about these impediments to their ability to proselytize. He requests permission "to punish the Indians as a father would for the sins they have committed after their baptisms, and to compel them to follow Christian doctrine."[115] In this official letter, Zumárraga says little about the Inquisition beyond these general sentiments of the necessity of corporal punishment.

The other, secret instructions, however, contain an item 7, which appeals for an independent Holy Office in order to deal specifically with the problem of the recalcitrant native leaders. Zumárraga argues to the pope that the royal councils in Seville have created problems, because it is "inconvenient to have to remit the convicted to the Inquisition in Castile . . . for it is so distant." He argues this, though the records show that he largely ignored oversight from Seville and was already punishing convicted natives locally. Zumárraga directs his representatives to "entreat His Holiness to name an inquisitor general who is not subject to the Inquisition over there [the Holy Office in Seville], only to the pope."[116] The letter implies that, as he was already holding Inquisition trials in the indigenous communities, Zumárraga may have been a little desperate to obtain some higher ecclesiastical support or affirmation for what he was doing, or at least some guidance as to how far he could go: "There is a question about whether it would be appropriate to punish the natives with the usual penalties when they fall into sin, as they are new to the religion and they are not as readily persuaded as others have been over there [unbeliever communities in Spain]. Present this concern and seek a determination as to what manner of penalty can be applied to these [natives]."[117]

The pope did not respond to these pleas and apparently made no effort to persuade Charles V to give Zumárraga the latitude he wanted or a Holy Office. Yet Zumárraga's efforts in this matter are persuasive evidence that he knew very well before he was eventually reprimanded in 1540 that he was treading on dangerous ground. Given the history of the Inquisition in Spain, one could predict that he would lose his Inquisition power once the crown became aware of the consequences of his Inquisition activities in the native communities.

CONCLUSION

The social processes that led Iberian leaders down the path toward Inquisition of ethnic minorities found their parallels in central Mexico in the decade between 1526 and 1536. There were, however, a few differences. Clearly, ethnic minorities in Spain understood the consequences of forced baptism better than native leaders. Thus, the alfaquíes and converso leaders were able to negotiate more effectively with local Spanish elites than their counterparts in the Valley of Mexico, who initially greeted Franciscan evangelism by fitting it into their prehispanic cultural frame of reference and sending the wrong cultural signal to the Franciscans. By the early 1530s, however, leaders in the Valley of Mexico were better informed and more savvy about the shortcomings of alliance with the Spanish. They began to adopt an arbitration of avoidance strategy, keeping the friars at arm's distance politically and culturally whenever possible.

As in Spain with unbeliever communities, the Franciscans responded to the wariness and secretiveness of the native leaders by defining them as a subversive class, categorizing their existence as a "native problem." Historical events and circumstances, however, differed in Mexico, where the primary catalyst for Inquisition was the defense of the Franciscan Order as an institution against a vigorous cultural and intellectual critique. In the final analysis, the Inquisition trials of moriscos and native leaders (unlike trials of conversos) were not sustained, mostly because the Franciscans were unable to forge a strong alliance between themselves and the crown. In each case, local elites in Valencia and Granada as well as in the city of Mexico disrupted the negotiations between center and periphery that were critical to a consensus. In the early days of his Inquisition, Zumárraga's attempt to resolve his dilemma by appealing to the Vatican confirms that he understood his weak position with respect to the crown. But, in the mid-1530s—at the high point of his reputation and power, his Franciscan community under attack, and perhaps, the dream of a true, reformed American church in peril—he emotionally came to believe that the entire Christian mission was at stake and that, whatever his differences with the crown, he could work through those dangerous waters as his Inquisition proceeded.

CHAPTER TWO

THE NAHUALLI
THE TRIAL OF MARTÍN OCELOTL

Martín Ocelotl was probably the most famous *nahualli*—a native priest believed to have supernatural powers—in Mexico before 1540. His fame is owed to his Inquisition trial in late 1536 and early 1537 for idolatry, heretical dogmatism, and concubinage. Historians have dismissed Ocelotl as a "petty native messiah" and a charlatan who "borrowed liberally" from Christian teaching to invent a new kind of native religion for post-conquest times.[1] Other historians have praised him as a respected "high priest" from "a family of important priests or priestesses" who was among the most successful in bartering his spiritual knowledge to native communities after the conquest.[2] He has further been described as a "merchant priest . . . a spokesman of a comfortable milieu . . . representing the interests of the traditional establishment around Texcoco" and leading a "hard-fought offensive against the religion of the invaders."[3] Given the unusual amount of evidence in his trial transcript, sorting out the interpretations of the contradictory Martín Ocelotl is a crucial task for early indigenous historiography. Who exactly was he and what was he attempting to do? More important, what do his activities say about the preaching of the other nanahualtin who roamed central Mexico in the wake of the conquest? Were the nanahualtin new and innovative or reactionary and traditional, as various historians have argued? Also, did Ocelotl's trial change how the Franciscans viewed the endurance of native religiosity at that time?

A few tentative answers can be offered. Ocelotl's spiritual activities, as depicted at his trial, support the findings of recent research in prehispanic and colonial native religion. Prehispanic religious practices were more diverse, fluid, and decentralized than previously assumed. Colonial native religion adapted and persisted long after the conquest and far more readily than the friars understood or perhaps even could cope with. In addition, Ocelotl's trial demonstrated the complex, tentative, and sometimes contentious relations between the tlahtoqueh and nanahualtin such as Ocelotl. The native leaders' exercise of the prudent policy of arbitration of avoidance meant preventing the native priests from crossing paths with the friars. For their part, the Franciscans were aware of the continued practice of native religion before 1536. But the Ocelotl case opened their eyes to the secret interactions of native leaders and native priests in communities where they had thought their missionary work was done.

THE STRANGER
"They held him in much regard and feared him"

When asked about Ocelotl, a local tlahtoani responded that "they held him in much regard and feared him, but he did not know why."[4] In fact, the tlahtoani was aware that Ocelotl was well regarded and feared because he was an unusually talented and powerful nahualli. The exact definition of nahualli has been a little confused in Mexican history, and depending on the region of Mexico where it was practiced, there have been different understandings of the nature of the occupation. The nahualli has often been associated with the power to turn into an animal in order to escape or do harm.[5] The spirit, or *nahual*, of certain chosen individuals was believed to be able to commune with animal spirits. However, this strict association with an animal spirit companion was more typical of cultural groups farther south in the Yucatan or Guatemala. In central Mexico, human transformation into animals was possible, but not a necessary skill of the nahualli. The nahualli (deriving from *"na,"* to know or have knowledge) was expected to predict the future, at the very least, and his or her knowledge was variously associated with weather prognostication and medical matters. He or she was familiar with the magical power of herbs and green stones and was considered to be good at reading patterns in the flow of water or smoke. The nahualli in prehispanic times was both admired and greatly feared.

Ocelotl induced additional wariness because he was an outsider, a stranger to the leaders and people of the eastern side of the Valley of Mexico. It was Ocelotl's foreignness that gave him spiritual advantages but eventually political difficulties as well. The friars knew little about Ocelotl's prehispanic background before they tried him, though they did know a few things about his reputation. For them, he was a shadowy character whom they assumed to be a Texcocan noble of some sort. Fray Antonio de Ciudad Rodrigo, the Franciscan provincial of Mexico in 1536, mentioned at the trial his many dealings with Ocelotl "around three years before," or 1533, a time when Fray Antonio held the position of guardian of the convento in Texcoco. Interestingly, Fray Antonio refers to Ocelotl in his testimony as "Don Martín," though indigenous witnesses do not. It is apparent from the trial that Fray Antonio thought Ocelotl's considerable wealth denoted Texcocan noble status.[6]

The natives, however, knew that Ocelotl was not noble and not even from Texcoco; he had settled there after the conquest, a fact revealed at trial. Ocelotl had told people in Texcoco that he was born in "Chinanta" (Chinantla), a remote mountain town about two hundred miles southeast of Texcoco in the modern state of Puebla (see map 2), and that his father was a wealthy merchant.[7] Moreover, he told one of his servants that his mother was called Eytacli and still lived in Chinantla; she was a *"bruja"* (witch, a common reference to a nahualli) who was "even more powerful than the son." Eytacli consulted with important people and predicted the future of individuals and communities; she received jewels and other valuable goods in exchange for her services.[8]

Indeed, there is evidence throughout the transcript that Ocelotl was practicing the mutually supportive skills—business and spirituality—learned from each parent. Ocelotl testified before Zumárraga in 1536 that he was forty years old, meaning that he was born around 1496, which seems consistent with other facts about his life.[9] He said that he had been baptized in Texcoco ten or eleven years before, or around 1525; thus, he had been peddling goods and prognostications in Texcoco for at least eleven years.[10] Ocelotl's rapid accumulation of

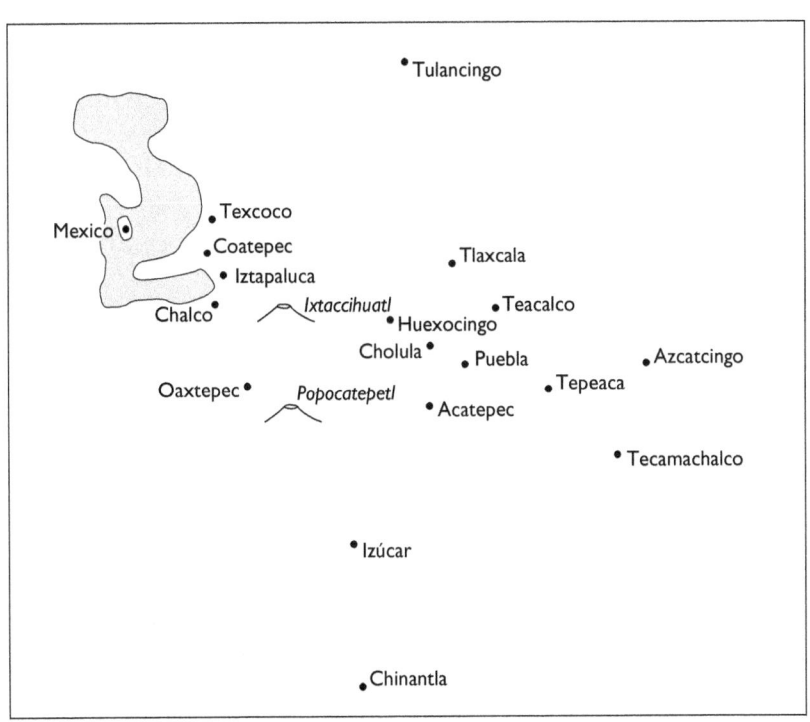

Map 2. Southeast Valley of Mexico and the Puebla Area

wealth by both commercial and spiritual means in a community so distant from his origins and kin demonstrates that Fray Antonio was right about one thing—Ocelotl possessed every bit of the "astuteness" that the friar attributed to him.[11]

Ocelotl was not only gifted with a good nose for business, but he also confidently explored the social gap between the Spanish and native communities as a sort of mediator. The trial revealed that Ocelotl's regular trade and business skills had put him in close contact with the Spanish community. One tlahtoani told a Spaniard that Ocelotl was "ladino," a term that the Spanish used for various natives to suggest that they were fluent in the Spanish language and familiar with Spanish ways.[12] Ocelotl was not above fraternizing with the friars in ways that the natives were not inclined to do. Indeed, Fray Antonio implies in his testimony that he conversed with Ocelotl in Spanish. When he interviewed Ocelotl on "many occasions" in 1533, he said that Ocelotl more or less debated with him, giving "many responses that were witty, like a theologian."[13]

In addition, Ocelotl mediated on behalf of the Spanish with their native servants. Two Spanish officials, one a *corregidor* (local crown official or governor), gave testimony about Ocelotl. When Zumárraga asked Ocelotl at trial if he knew the officials, the nahualli readily responded that he knew both. In the case of one, he had given the Spaniard advice about his servants, and he matter-of-factly suggested that dealing with indigenous servants in the homes of Spaniards was nothing new to him. He also noted that he traded with many Spaniards.[14] Zumarrága assigned him a defense attorney, Alonso de Vargas, who said that "he had many dealings with the man," meaning Ocelotl.[15] Ocelotl had undergone no previous criminal trial, so Vargas probably meant business dealings. Don Juan of Acatepec, a native tlahtoani, claimed to a Spanish witness before the trial that among natives Ocelotl was regarded as "a friend of the Christians."[16] Some native witnesses testified that Ocelotl had assured them that his discussions with them were "with the license of the friars,"[17] and they apparently had no reason to doubt him.

In the trial transcript, even the secretary of the Inquisition, Martín de Campos, identifies Ocelotl as a go-between. In reference to Ocelotl, Campos writes that the "bishop warned the naguatato to tell the truth."[18] "Naguatato" was a corruption of the term *"nahuatlahto,"* which in most of the colonial period meant an interpreter of Nahuatl, the most prominent language in central Mexico.[19] Yet there was also a broader use of the word to mean someone who interpreted and also performed the role of go-between. In a letter to the Empress Isabel in March 1531, the Second Audiencia complained: "In these parts, the naguatatos have been the principal advisors to those who have governed [meaning the encomenderos] and they understand and speak with the Indians and have been the cause of many great problems; as advisors, they have become rich and have many good houses."[20]

Given these interactions, Ocelotl hardly seems a traditionalist hostile to the Spanish. Rather, he seems to have seen himself as a successful manipulator of the Spanish on behalf of native tlahtoqueh whom he hoped to advise and serve. Fray Antonio had been a bit suspicious of Ocelotl's deceptive ways and manipulative behavior. An indication of these worries was that he made Ocelotl marry one of his wives in a Christian ceremony in 1533, and for good measure, forced Ocelotl to swear before the whole community of Texcoco that he would uphold his marriage vows and "not do anything that was against the holy faith."[21] Nevertheless, Fray Antonio did not refer Ocelotl to the Audiencia or civil authorities at that time, as he would have if he were certain that Ocelotl was a nahualli. When Ocelotl was later accused before the Inquisition, the supremely confident Ocelotl argued that his acceptance of the forced marriage and his bargain made years before were being reneged upon. He bitterly complained at trial, as if the friars had gone back on a deal, "I married according to law and left many women that I have and for this I did not hold a grudge."[22]

Ocelotl's propensity to see a mutual relationship with the Spanish and friars—which did not exist on their side—made sense from his perspective. He was an inveterate cultural negotiator in a society that put a high premium on the role. Naturally, he assumed that his ability to communicate with the Spanish was an advantage that gave him prestige in native communities. Anyone could see that he had profited from the Spanish presence. Yet, while he and others believed he was a middleman and a go-between, no one on the native side in 1533 was suggesting that he had acculturated to Spanish ways, as was obvious from his continued practice of native religion. Almost paradoxically, one does not have the sense from the trial transcripts that Ocelotl believed what he was doing and what the friars wanted were contradictory. His intellectual stance is an early example of the tension Louise Burkhart has noted in early colonial society between the relativistic values of the indigenous people and the black-and-white morality of the friars.[23]

After Ocelotl's earlier success as a cultural negotiator, Fray Antonio de Ciudad Real's heightened suspicions about Ocelotl in 1533 changed the situation, especially for the Texcocan leaders. The year 1533 was the middle of the Franciscan morals campaign in the eastern Valley of Mexico, and nobles were learning that their tolerance of Ocelotl, especially their purchases of his spiritual services, could be dangerous to them. The talented negotiator was becoming a liability. The nobles may also have found Ocelotl too independent and perhaps a little too clever for their taste. And as a stranger with no kin and only business ties to Texcoco, he was expendable. In any case, they banished Ocelotl from Texcoco in 1533, about the time he began verbally sparring with Fray Antonio. A Spanish witness, Pedro de Meneses, said the natives told him that Ocelotl left Texcoco when Texcocans tried to "catch" him, possibly in an effort to remove him by force. Neither Fray Antonio nor the Texcocan corregidor, Cristóbal de Cisneros, indicated that they had ordered Ocelotl to be imprisoned in 1533, so we must surmise that the indigenous government and its tlahtoani were acting on their own in trying to catch him.[24] Another witness from outside Texcoco confirmed that Ocelotl left Texcoco in 1533 when he became "very angry" with the people of Texcoco and went to Coatepec, a few kilometers south of Texcoco.[25] The tlahtoani of Oaxtepec, an altepetl farther south, recollected that he had come to know Ocelotl about three years before, meaning about 1533, or the time that Ocelotl left Texcoco.

After Ocelotl's trial, Don Pedro, the native tlahtoani of Texcoco, claimed that he had "banished Martín Ocelotl for certain sins he had committed" six years before.[26] From the other evidence, it is apparent that Don Pedro was referring to the 1533 banishment and that the "sins" Ocelotl committed were more political than spiritual.[27] In the logic of arbitration of avoidance, the Texcocan native government had anticipated the consequences of a potential unhappy meeting of Fray Antonio and the unpredictable nahualli and had nipped the problem in the bud with banishment. Yet Don Pedro had allowed Ocelotl to retain properties in Texcoco, his wife still lived in one of them, and the tlahtoani even protected her and her property rights at a later date. Meanwhile, Ocelotl moved to the southeast periphery of the Texcoco region, the communities of Coatepec, Iztapaluca, and Oaxtepec, to reestablish his businesses and set up a new religious practice. In the three years between 1533, when he left Texcoco, and 1536, when the Inquisition caught up with him, Ocelotl managed to make significant inroads into noble networks and native communities in the surrounding southeastern area and even much farther east into the province of Puebla. His repeated successes raise the question: what were the native spiritual conditions of the colonial Valley of Mexico that provided such opportunities for this nahualli outsider?

We know little of what happened to the vast apparatus of the native priesthood after the conquest—the spiritual specialists, the cults, the temples, and the calmecacs. Most historians note that prehispanic ceremonial activities occupied "a prodigious amount of time, energy, and wealth" in central Mexican altepemeh.[28] Both male and female priests must have numbered in the thousands in the temples. The major altepemeh had temples for many of the gods of the Mesoamerican pantheon, which included gods for artisan groups and for *calpultin* (kin and trade networks in an altepetl). Smaller altepemeh expended many of their goods and services in celebrations of their tutelary or local gods, often to mark locally important dates and events.[29] Native priests provided essential services such as organizing rituals, teaching in the schools, participating in warfare, and also offering "advice on affairs" to the tlahtoqueh and nobility.[30] Their role was considered central to continued existence; therefore, "probably few religious groups in world history have enjoyed more authority in their communities."[31]

What happened to these men and women of the priest class and how did they adapt in the post-conquest period? As Motolinía notes of Texcoco, the native priests continued their services unabated in the years immediately following the conquest, except in the area of ritual human sacrifice. But from about 1527 to 1536, many priests were imprisoned or driven off as the tlahtocayotl was turned over to the friars. Yet, with so many layers of practitioners in the hierarchy who survived and knew no other occupation (and possibly had no property to till or other trade), there must have been many men and women wandering about, willing to adapt and market these spiritual services to someone. Where did they go? Many stayed and simply went clandestine, especially those in lesser or more distant altepemeh that did not warrant a resident friar. Native priests commonly wore black paint all over their bodies to distinguish themselves, but whenever Zumárraga's traveling visitadores were seen in the distance, the native religious men quickly washed off the paint and put away their special clothing.[32] Encomenderos in communities distant from the city of Mexico sometimes knew better than the friars that these quiet subterfuges were going on and did nothing, because they had reached understandings with native tlahtoqueh in exchange for regular tribute. In the 1540s, the Dominicans in Yanhuitlan in the province of Oaxaca actually accused the local encomenderos of making such pacts with the locals.

The bishops acknowledged the problem of clandestine religious activity in the Valley of Mexico communities and recommended tearing down more pyramids and temples—the geographically central spaces of native spirituality. Apparently, Charles V agreed, and he ordered the civil government to tear down more temples and confiscate the property of native priests, though he requested that the friars and the government create "as little uproar as possible," particularly in the taking of property.[33] However, tearing down more of the ceremonial centers merely drove the secret rituals into the broader ceremonial landscape of distant temples, sacred crossroads, pilgrimage routes, and virtually anything associated with water—caves, springs, and mountains. According to Davíd Carrasco, in prehispanic times "there was a constant organic flow from the center of the *altepeme* (city-states), through the *calpultin* (corporative groups in the suburbs) and out into the natural landscape. These paths often led back into the ceremonial centers of local communities."[34] After 1527, it was becoming progressively more difficult to maintain a back-and-forth flow between urban center and natural landscape. Natives were restricted in their ability to bring the symbols of the countryside into the tlahtocayotl.³⁵ Therefore, they had to truncate the traditional patterns and adapt to a more rural and diffuse environment of spirituality. As Carrasco notes, the normal tendency of native religion to act on a "spread-out" ceremonial landscape may have been accentuated under Spanish colonialism.³⁶ The nanahualtin helped native communities and nobles to make these spiritual compromises and adaptations by bringing various brands of spirituality to individual homes and distant locations away from the tlahtocayotl. As rituals did not have the great stages of the tlahtocayotl to work with, different "performances" of native spirituality would be elevated.

What variation of native spirituality did Ocelotl offer that was so easily adapted to the diffuse spiritual environment of colonial times? The trial transcript states that Ocelotl claimed to have been a "high priest" in Chinantla,³⁷ but this seems to have meant very little to the Texcocans. When Zumárraga kept asking the natives if Ocelotl was a *"papa"* (priest), they tended to avoid that categorization. Instead, they responded that he was a "sorcerer" and that he had "lived a long time."³⁸

The trial record of Ocelotl claiming to be a "high priest" is at odds with prehispanic religious hierarchies. Given the fact that his father was a merchant, not a noble, in Chinantla, Ocelotl probably could not have risen to the rank of *quetzalcoatl* (a high priest who came from the nobility). As a young man, he may have attended a calmecac to become a *tlahuitzin*, a cult priest from the commoner class. A quetzalcoatl usually took the role of important counselor and advisor to tlahtoqueh, while a tlahuitzin did not, though the latter still performed significant spiritual duties in the monthly festival calendar. The training for both quetzalcoatl and tlahuitzin could take twenty to thirty years after induction into the priesthood at age fifteen in the calmecac. Each training level required four to five years of service.³⁹ Ocelotl would have been only about twenty-five when the conquest overtook Chinantla. In central Mexico, men were not elevated to high and respected offices until their thirties and in some communities could not even marry.⁴⁰ Therefore, it was probably impossible for Ocelotl to have reached high-priest rank before the conquest, even if the hierarchical standards of the priesthood in remote Chinantla were not as rigid as they were in the Valley of Mexico.

Another telling oddity that casts doubt on Ocelotl's claim to be a high priest was that not one of the twenty witnesses against Ocelotl recalled that he had performed sacrifices of any type anywhere or had offered to do so, even though this was the principal duty of a high priest. The friars were well aware in correspondence from 1531 to 1537 that religious leaders and tlahtoqueh were continuing to perform sacrifices. Even in the 1540s, a visitador to New Spain said that one only had to travel ten leagues outside the capital of the city of Mexico to see a secret human sacrifice.

The first of Zumárraga's trials against natives was of two men, Tacatetl and Tanixtetl, from the community of Tepetepec to the northwest near Tula, a trial that preceded Ocelotl's by just a few months.[41] The accused and accusers in that trial were ethnically Otomi, and through his native Otomi interpreters, Zumárraga learned that Tacatetl and Tanixtetl had been "papas" of the altepetl. They were performing ritual bloodletting on young local men in the community, apparently to rid their community of a drought. When Zumárraga arrested Ocelotl, the bishop clearly assumed that he was one of these native priests trying to continue traditional practices in secret places in the countryside. But while other native spiritual practitioners may have offered these official community services, Ocelotl's services were confined to supernatural activities and not community rituals. He oriented his activities to advising native nobles and tlahtoqueh, and he innovatively crafted ways to fit into the new exigencies of the colonial situation. Ocelotl's spiritual knowledge seems to have drawn from two fonts—his brief calmecac training, possibly to become a tlahuitzin, and, more important, the supernatural learning he gained from his mother, who clearly practiced as a nahualli. Characterizations of the official state cult of the tlahuitzin and the cult of the nanahualtin as respectively "formal" religion and "popular" religion would not be accurate, as H. B. Nicholson explains: "As in most complex religious systems, no sharp line can be discerned between the formal, organized state cult, which served the objectives of the social group as a whole, and the much more magic-dominated type of supernaturalism, which served more private ends."[42] In fact, the high priests of the state cults often enhanced their positions by practicing magic and divination; it is very likely that their advisory functions to tlahtoqueh were predicated as much on their perceived supernatural abilities as on their high status in the state cults.

To understand the motivations of the native leaders, however, we need to look more closely at the prehispanic relationship between the nanahualtin and the tlahtoqueh whom they advised. The nanahualtin's "magic was not an integral part of the mainstream of religious beliefs and practices; it existed, rather, as a subsidiary, parallel system."[43] The artificial distinction drawn in Sahagún's early studies of native culture of the *"naoalli tlamatine"* (nahualli wise man) as either "good" or "bad" is too simplistic. The nanahualtin were prepared to do either type of magic at the behest of their private clients. Sahagún describes the "good" nahualli as "a caretaker, a man of discretion, a guardian." The "bad" nahualli "deludes people"; "he deceives them, he confounds them." The "good" nahualli "never harms anyone," while the "bad" nahualli "is a doer of evil."[44] In fact, the good or bad result of the divination was less important to the natives than the quantity of magic power. The independence and individuality of the nanahualtin implied unpredictability, and their actions indicated unexpected transformative powers in the realm of nature; these characteristics were what commanded the most respect.

The unpredictability of supernaturalism and its practitioners was also its key attraction for native leaders. Nezahualpilli, a grand tlahtoani of Texcoco before the conquest, was an astronomer who had the reputation of a nahualli. In the *Florentine Codex*, Sahagún's indigenous writers note Motecuhzoma's reliance on nanahualtin: "It is said that through these [nanahualtin] Motecuhzoma received life. By them his fate was strengthened; by them he was exalted, and on them he placed the burden."[45] On the uses of divination, Frances Berdan explains: "While the supernaturally-determined fate extended to each individual, at the personal level, one could do a great deal to both predict and influence one's destiny. Here, the realm of divination, magic, and sorcery operated alongside the formal religious system with the two often overlapping."[46] If the individual was the ruler who was also the state, then he would need advice from the nanahualtin. Paradoxically, the anxieties and worries of the tlahtoqueh in the treacherous post-conquest years probably increased their need for the supernatural advice of especially effective nanahualtin.

THE SELF-STYLED ADVISOR
"All that they want to know will be told to them"

Without question, the goal of Martín Ocelotl was a variation on the goal of all prehispanic nanahualtin—to become a desired advisor to the tlahtoqueh by adapting native spirituality to colonial conditions and thus to assist the native leaders in governance. By doing so, Ocelotl reasoned—quite rightly, as it turned out—that he would benefit materially and socially wherever he lived. In two separate and distinct phases before his Inquisition trial, he built and rebuilt two spiritual roles. Before 1533 his spiritual activities were related to the prehispanic god Tezcatlipoca. In 1533–36, after he was pushed out of Texcoco into the area southeast of the Valley of Mexico and the province of Puebla, his spiritual activities were related to the god Mixcoatl-Camaxtli. Ocelotl worked hard to make sure that each role and identity responded to local conditions.

In his first role in Texcoco before 1533, Ocelotl represented himself as part of the god-complex of Tezcatlipoca, the patron god of Texcoco, who rivaled Huitzilopochtli, the Mexica war god, in esteem. For Ocelotl, Tezcatlipoca's additional importance was that he was the patron and favorite of the nanahualtin; he was the "arch-sorcerer, associated with darkness, the night, and the jaguar, the were-animal *par excellence* of the Mesoamerican sorcerer-transformer."[47] Fittingly, "ocelotl" was the Nahuatl word for jaguar. Whether it was Ocelotl's real name did not matter; it was his styling of himself in the manner of Tezcatlipoca that mattered. Tezcatlipoca was quixotic and unpredictable and mixed the dark and evil with the light and good in imaginative ways. Most of all, Tezcatlipoca inspired an unusual amount of fear when compared with older and more primeval gods, such as the rain god Tlaloc. Nicholson has said of Tezcatlipoca that "no deity better expressed the pessimistic, fatalistic Weltanschauung which prevailed in late pre-Hispanic central Mexico."[48]

According to Fray Antonio de Ciudad Rodrigo, Ocelotl either called himself, or others tended to refer to him as, "Tepuele," which Fray Antonio translated as "devil."[49] Actually, "Tepuele" was a corruption of *"telpochtli"* (young man), a pseudonym for Tezcatlipoca. Ocelotl always acted out the most "protean" characteristics of the "young man" god. Tezcatlipoca "presided over banqueting and revelry,"[50] and so Ocelotl invited young manservants of the tlahtoqueh into an underground chamber of one of his houses to have drunken parties.[51] Cristóbal de Cisneros, corregidor of Texcoco when Ocelotl lived there, said that he had conducted an investigation of the nahualli's nocturnal activities. The natives who spied on Ocelotl for the corregidor reported that he went down to Lake Texcoco in the middle of the night, burned incense, said many incantations, and then floated above the rocks; "the devil came and spoke with him for a long time and told him what to do and where to go." After such exhausting adventures, Ocelotl returned to his house and "threw himself on his bed without his wife or others knowing his comings and goings."[52] While Cisneros recounted the story using the word "devil," it is probable that the indigenous spies actually said "Tepuele."

By styling many of his actions closely on the characteristics of Tezcatlipoca, Ocelotl developed a role that evoked a kind of super-nahualli. Sahagún and other friars predictably describe the various talents of the nahualli by forcing them into categories of specialty conjuration. A *quiyauhtlazqui* did rain conjuration, a *tlaolchayauhqui* discerned the sources of disease, other nanahualtin could discover thieves, and most could read omens and the *tonalpohualli* (the sacred calendar). But the early colonial nanahualtin in the trial transcripts did not necessarily recognize these neat categories, and they certainly did not describe their talents as white or black magic the way late medieval Europeans did. Sahagún's own description of the nanahualtin's role model, Tezcatlipoca, as an all-powerful god, tends to contradict these simplistic divisions. Ocelotl, in fact, was thought to have all the categories of powers and used them as Tezcatlipoca did: unpredictably.

Ocelotl's construction of this superior nahualli persona began almost from the time he entered the Valley of Mexico from Chinantla accompanied by perhaps the most famous sorcery legend of the postconquest period—Motecuhzoma's premonition of the coming of the Spanish. In the wake of the Mexica defeat in the conquest (and by association, the defeat of their god Huitzilopochtli), natives in the valley naturally gravitated to stories about omens of this dramatic event. Sahagún's famous book 12 of the *Florentine Codex*, which explains the conquest of Mexico from the indigenous perspective, begins with a series of eight omens that Sahagún's Mexica interpreters agreed in retrospect were clear signs of the end. James Lockhart questions the factual basis of any of the eight omens, supposing that they were "part of native sense-making of the poor leadership" and that post-conquest central Mexico was awash in similar "urban legends."[53] Ocelotl's use of the story of Motecuhzoma's premonition seems to be evidence that some of this urban legend-making was propagated or spread by nanahualtin and other spiritual specialists.

The seventh omen of the *Florentine Codex* states that a fisherman brought a dead crane with an unusual dark spot on its head to Motecuhzoma. The spot appeared to be the image of "people who came as though massed." He "summoned the soothsayers and the sages" (nanahualtin) to explain this omen to him.[54] The story had some basis in fact, in that Motecuhzoma was always consulting with his nanahualtin to explain the omen-filled world of the Mexica. Virtually all natural oddities were brought to his attention for analysis; it was in fact his job as well as the priests'. As with many urban legends that became omens, however, the importance of the massed people only became clear after the events of the conquest.

Ocelotl took the urban legend of Motecuhzoma's omen and claimed it as his own. He stated at his trial that the event took place in 1510 and that Motecuhzoma had invited priests from across central Mexico to explain this vision. The tlahtoani of Chinantla had sent Ocelotl and another nine nanahualtin to Motecuhzoma to explain the omen. Ocelotl said that he had told Motecuhzoma that men "with beards" were coming to invade Mexico. Supposedly, Motecuhzoma became angry at Ocelotl and his colleagues and imprisoned them for a year.[55] That was the version Ocelotl told the inquisitors, but he seems to have told many variations of this story to the natives, changing details as needed. Several natives told witness Catalina López, the indigenous wife of a Spaniard, that when Ocelotl was imprisoned by Motecuhzoma, the nahualli said to the great tlahtoani that "he did not fear him ... because, though [Motecuhzoma] might kill him and tear him into pieces, he would not die nor could he die." According to this version, Motecuhzoma had him killed and ground up his bones, but "Martín rose up before Motecuhzoma as before, healthy and well."[56]

The facts of Ocelotl's biography tend to contradict this story. Ocelotl was fourteen in 1510 and it is unlikely that Motecuhzoma would have listened to him. More important, the indigenous Mexica authors of the *Florentine Codex* record the subsequently famous story of the crane but do not mention anything about men with beards or a pending invasion in connection with the crane omen. And, of course, Motecuhzoma had people killed all the time, but nobody but Ocelotl remembered an incident where someone defied Motecuhzoma and lived to tell about it, let alone resurrected himself before Motecuhzoma. And Ocelotl's resurrection story certainly is infused with a Christian resurrection trope taught by the friars.

But the Motecuhzoma story did several things for Ocelotl's reputation in the colonial period. Since Motecuhzoma's destiny had been defeat, Ocelotl's divination of it and his defiance of Motecuhzoma automatically associated Ocelotl with the winning side in history, suggesting a powerful destiny for Ocelotl. The Motecuhzoma story was like a signature story for Ocelotl. It introduced the stranger from distant Chinantla into the Valley of Mexico lore and spiritual community, and it demonstrated his power of foretelling an event of the utmost consequence, the coming of the Spanish, which was necessary if he wanted to become a spiritual advisor to tlahtoqueh in the valley. The legend of his encounter with Motecuhzoma followed him wherever he went, and he could embellish it as needed, which he obviously did. Finally and most important, the story demonstrates Ocelotl's multiple supernatural powers, which were characteristic of Tezcatlipoca.

Even though the natives called Ocelotl "Tepuele," there is no evidence that he called himself that or "Tezcatlipoca." But he had so allied his own characteristics with those of Tezcatlipoca that his role was something more than a simple priest-cultist of the god. The closest approximation in prehispanic religion was Tezcatlipoca's *ixiptla* (god impersonator). In prehispanic times, an attractive and handsome young captured warrior was selected to be sacrificed during Toxcatl, the annual festival of Tezcatlipoca beginning in late April or early May, at a temple near Chalco in the southeast part of the valley. The selection was made a year before the event, and during that year, the priests would teach the young warrior how to be an ixiptla and play

Tezcatlipoca's flute, conduct himself in the refined, confident way of a god, and finally, behave appropriately on his way to his ceremonial death. Though constantly guarded so that he would not run away, the ixiptla was allowed to go into the marketplaces and whichever house or temple he wanted in order to receive the accolades of the people, as long as he fulfilled the decorum of the god. He was unrestricted in his wanderings, in precisely the same way as Tezcatlipoca. At trial, the witnesses claimed that Ocelotl often roamed the countryside freely and showed up in various altepemeh, seemingly unannounced. When friars traveled about on their *visitas* (inspections), Ocelotl did not defensively rail at the townspeople who attended their sermons, but behaved in the same serene, self-confident manner as Tezcatlipoca. He waved the hesitant natives on and said, "Go, go, I will come later."[57]

Of course, after the conquest, the well-loved, yearlong festivities of Tezcatlipoca could not be performed, which must have induced even more than the usual angst in Texcoco. The quixotic Tezcatlipoca could be serene and the next moment easily "angered" and "annoyed" and capable of terrible retribution. He was thought to be particularly responsible for inducing plagues, and there was no lack of plagues in the 1530s, including a dreadful measles epidemic in Texcoco and the valley in 1531–32.[58] Sahagún wrote down a prayer that the Texcocans offered to Tezcatlipoca on the occasion of a plague, and it reveals the dread the Texcocans felt when trying to appease Tezcatlipoca: "O master, O our lord, O might, O wind, O *mayocoyatzin* [dominator or tyrant], O Titlacauan [another title for Tezcatlipoca], how can thy heart wish it? . . . Will the castigation abate no more, will thy annoyance, thy anger be reversed? Will thy wrath, thy annoyance, no more be placated? Have we perchance just been forsaken?"[59]

The trial transcript does not specify what the frightened natives did for Ocelotl as he walked about, subtly reminding them of their neglect of the unpredictable Tezcatlipoca. But the natives' fear and dread undoubtedly produced plenty of offerings for a pseudo-ixiptla of Tezcatlipoca. Rumors flowed concerning Ocelotl's multiple supernatural skills, which were much in the vein of Tezcatlipoca. One tlahtoani claimed that when Ocelotl "wants to make himself young, he can and, when he wants to be old, he does the same."[60] Various natives claimed that he regularly turned into a tiger, a lion [jaguar], a dog"[61]—one of the more powerful skills of the nahualli repertoire. Stories had it that Ocelotl performed the ultimate transformation when the Texcocans tried to imprison him in 1533. Repeating his purported disappearing act before Motecuhzoma, Ocelotl "evaporated in the grasp of [the Texcocans'] hands and appeared nearby, laughing at them and saying that there were no summons or dispatches for such as he,"[62] a further suggestion of the willfulness and power of Tezcatlipoca.

Using the ixiptla ritual, Ocelotl cleverly blurred the line between man and god. Tetzcatlipoca had omnipresence; "his ritual mirror . . . enabled the god or his priest to 'see all that took place in the world.'"[63] In the book of prayers from the *Florentine Codex*, the prayer to Tezcatlipoca reads: "Thou knowest the things within the trees, the rocks . . . thou knowest that which is within us; what we say, what we think, our minds, our hearts."[64] A couple of different witnesses testified how Ocelotl used a variety of techniques in his divinations that made him seem like a god impersonator of Tezcatlipoca. A Spaniard, Pedro de Meneses, saw Ocelotl in Acatepec, Puebla, with its tlahtoani, Don Juan. Meneses asked Don Juan who the stranger was and he exclaimed, "You don't know him? . . . There isn't much that we say that he does not know."[65] To test the proposition, Meneses later went to Ocelotl, and the nahualli recounted what Meneses and Don Juan had been talking about out of his presence.[66]

The corregidor of Texcoco, Cristóbal de Cisneros, one day tested Ocelotl's powers of divination in the identification of thieves, another nahualli skill. He hid a piece of gold on the person of one of his female servants and claimed to Ocelotl that someone had stolen it. Ocelotl menacingly told the servants that the one who stole the gold must give it to him or, "you already know that I have discovered it and I know everything that you have done in all of your lives."[67] Cisneros said that one of the young women almost hysterically (probably in great fear) called Ocelotl a "devil"; the word she actually used may have been "telpochtli," or Tezcatlipoca. Though Ocelotl never claimed to be Tetzcatlipoca or even his impersonator, one must remember that god-representation was a highly amorphous concept to the central Mexicans. In the indigenous mind, the powerful nahualli *was* in some respects Tezcatlipoca.

After his banishment from Texcoco in 1533, the ever-enterprising Ocelotl created a new role, but this time he tailored his appeal to meet the local religious beliefs of the tlahtoqueh of regions east of Texcoco and beyond to the province of Puebla. Ocelotl moved to a set of houses he owned in a stretch of territory linking three altepemeh—Coatepec, Iztapaluca, and Oaxtepec—all in the southeastern part of the Valley of Mexico. This placed him in close approximation with altepemeh located in the area around the Spanish settlement of Puebla de los Angeles, including Tecamachalco, Tepeaca, and Acatepec, as well as the large urban settlements in Cholula, Huexocingo, and Teacalco. Ocelotl's birthplace of Chinantla was on the southern border of the province of Puebla, over a hundred miles from these highly populated urban centers. But he shared with the people of the far eastern altepemeh "a common Chichimec background."[68] The Chichimecas of the eastern altepemeh were cousins to the Mexica and Acolhua in the valley, sharing the "núcleo duro" of native religion but worshipping a slightly different pantheon associated with the older god Mixcoatl-Camaxtli.

At the apex of the Triple Alliance's power in the early sixteenth century, there had been a tendency for Tenochtitlan and Texcoco "in their immediate spheres of political control . . . [to exercise] . . . a certain loose suzerainty over the priesthoods of tributary communities, even to the extent of occasional direct imposition of cults."[69] But if there was any significant spiritual penetration from the valley before the conquest, Ocelotl's appeals to the Mixcoatl-Camaxtli god complex indicate that the Pueblans had readily reverted to their own spiritual roots after the conquest. Mixcoatl-Camaxtli "especially symbolized the earlier hunting-gathering 'Chichimec' life way."[70] He was as important to the Pueblans as Tezcatlipoca or Huitzilopochtli were to those in the Valley of Mexico. In fact, some historians have suggested that Tezcatlipoca was "probably originally an independent eastern Mexican jaguar-earth god" from the Puebla region.[71]

In order to build a new network of reciprocity with the tlahtoqueh in Puebla, Ocelotl spent the years 1533–36 acting like a representative of Mixcoatl-Camaxtli and attempting to cultivate the Pueblan tlahtoqueh with gift exchanges and weather prognostications. In one incident, Ocelotl sent the servant of Don Juan, tlahtoani of Tecamachalco, to ask Don Juan for some *canutos de colores* (tubes of colors consisting of corn paste, used in the making of votive objects and ritual decorations). When Don Juan sent one hundred canutos to Ocelotl, Ocelotl told the servant, "Go to Don Juan and tell him that I keep these canutos that he has sent me as a gift and . . . tell him to plant a lot of corn and put in a lot of agaves, because hunger will begin soon," referring to impending drought conditions.[72]

Even more telling is a reciprocal exchange with Don Juan in which Ocelotl sent the tlahtoani some cotton with which "Don Juan made 15 *mantas* [capes or blankets] and he sent these to Martín. He said he would keep them as a gift and that he did not want them for himself; instead he wanted them to give to the many who came to see him in the villages."[73] In local relations between superior and subordinate tlahtoqueh, it was very common for the superior to send cotton to the subordinate to make blankets as an obligation and a symbol of obeisance. Ocelotl appeared to be trying to create this dependent relationship with Don Juan, which the tlahtoqueh accepted in order to hear Ocelotl's predictions. The mantas were a precious gift; in colonial times they were used for money. In turn, Ocelotl was giving the mantas to his devotees as a tlahtoani or noble would do in order to ensure their allegiance and maintain their acquaintance for some future favor.

Other Pueblan lords warily tested the new nahualli. At one point, Don Gonzalo of Cachula, near Puebla, made a barter transaction with Ocelotl. Don Gonzalo sent a wood beam needed for the construction of a house, and Ocelotl sent him eight deerskins.[74] The deerskins were obviously intended to reinforce the symbolic hunting associations of Mixcoatl-Camaxtli. But Ocelotl would not allow Don Gonzalo's servants to go away so easily. He insisted, "Stay here for three days and carry a response to your lord."[75] After the servants had spent three days witnessing Ocelotl's hospitality and his interactions with the many people who came and went from his house, Ocelotl sent them along with a message for Don Gonzalo. Don Gonzalo should "plant much corn now and also agaves and prickly-pear cacti because in the next four years there will be a lot of hunger,"[76] meaning that there would not be sufficient rain for the corn. Later, when the same Don Gonzalo became ill, he went to the city of Mexico. Ocelotl went to see him there to give him some medicine and tell him that he had ten more years to live. While there, Don Gonzalo witnessed an old man who came to Ocelotl for a cure and was given two blankets and told, "Take these for when you die, so that you can be wrapped up in them.... You will die within the year." Don Gonzalo, impressed, said that he had heard the man died within the year as prophesied.[77]

Don Luis of Tepeaca, a most important altepetl in the Puebla region with a large Spanish presence, was a harder nut to crack than Don Juan or Don Gonzalo. Around June 1536, Ocelotl had sent a *"convibia fecho,"* or invitation, for Don Luis to come to his house in Coatepec, which would have been a day's journey or more from Tepeaca. Don Luis would not come, but he carefully sent two servants "to see what it was Martín wanted."[78] When the servants arrived, Ocelotl took them into the underground chamber of a house that he had between Iztapaluca and Coatepec, a place he had used on occasion to ensure secrecy. He told them, "I have sent to all the caciques and all the lords of this [Puebla] region that they should plant many fruit trees and agaves and prickly-pear cacti, cereals, and other fruits in their lands, because there is going to be no rain and there will be much hunger and with these things they can maintain themselves, because the corn will not grow."[79] He then gave the servants two mantas and a canuto de colores that was fashioned into the shape of a sword and also some *"suchiles"* (*xochiles,* or flower decorations used in festivities), as well as an oar with "insignias seen on the oars of rowers in Mexico." Then he told them, "tell your lord that these are things from Camaxtli."[80]

Ocelotl was clearly tailoring his message to the leaders of the new locale, and he mixed and matched symbolic connotations. Whereas Tezcatlipoca referred to the history and conquest of the Valley of Mexico, Mixcoatl-Camaxtli was a primeval god, "given to nature in contrast to urban life."[81] Mixcoatl-Camaxtli represented a return to the older gods of rain and harvest, which corresponded to Ocelotl's outreach to the local tlahtoqueh in terms of valuable weather information, the "núcleo duro" that continued into the colonial period. In another get-together at Ocelotl's house, he ended the event by telling the men to "go to your houses and when you arrive, there will be rain because my sisters are coming," meaning the clouds.[82] The sword that Ocelotl had fashioned for Don Luis was an allusion to several interrelated symbols of Mixcoatl-Camaxtli, and 1 Flint was the day sign for both Huitzilopochtli and Mixcoatl-Camaxtli.[83] Mixcoatl-Camaxtli was the guardian god of Quecholli, the *veintena* (twenty-day month) that followed the agricultural season, celebrated the hunting season, and initiated the winter season of warfare in all parts of central Mexico (approximately November).[84] Soldiers fabricated arrows and swords in honor of Mixcoatl-Camaxtli during Quecholli to honor their ancestors, particularly past rulers.[85] In fact, Mixcoatl-Camaxtli had a "stellar affiliation" with Venus, which was associated with warriors and the hunt, and offerings included arrows that were needed to make "cosmic warfare." Thus, Ocelotl's gifts and advice mined the local cosmology.

Obviously, Ocelotl was pressing these nobles hard in order to develop a network of reciprocal patronage. Ocelotl cornered the servants of an unnamed lord from the altepetl of Teacalco, halfway between Puebla and Tlaxcala, and asked them, "Why was he not getting along with me and did not want to obey me nor do one thing that I sent for him to do?"[86] Ocelotl several times told servants to tell the lords and anybody else that "from that time forward, when those of the village want something, they are to come to this house because many in the area had left here satisfied. All that they want to know will be told to them." According to the servant, the residents of Puebla had to go to Ocelotl's house "to hear and to know what they are to do."[87] These servants dutifully returned to the tlahtoqueh with this information. But it seems that three years of network-making were about to be cut short. Before these tlahtoqueh had decided whether to have reciprocal exchanges or direct contact with the strange new nahualli, the Inquisition arrested Ocelotl.

THE NATIVE ALTERNATIVE
"He has the tricks of a dogmatizer"

Ocelotl's eventual punishment—banishment and removal to Spain for imprisonment by the Seville Inquisition—was probably ordained even before his trial began in December of 1536, and the author of his sentence was very likely his old nemesis, Fray Antonio de Ciudad

Rodrigo. On the first day of trial, Zumárraga opined that Ocelotl was "a great danger and impediment to the conversion of the natives."[88] Fray Antonio, the fifth witness against Ocelotl that day, then stated flatly that "he knew [Martín Ocelotl] to be malicious and astute and it was not beneficial to have Don Martín in this territory. Rather, he is a danger to the natives because he has the tricks [*maña*] of a dogmatizer. It would be a service to God that the natives not hear or see him again."[89]

Fray Antonio exhibits a significant influence over Zumárraga's handling of this first, most important Inquisition case. Most accounts of Fray Antonio's character agree with Sahagún's assessment that he was "very fervent in the conversion of souls."[90] Fray Antonio was an austere man who was also politically astute. Not as well educated as some of his colleagues, Fray Antonio was nevertheless sent to Spain by the Franciscan Order in 1528 to persuade Emperor Charles V to stop the enslaving of natives (except in the silver mines) and to recruit nearly thirty missionary friars. He was the most successful recruiter of the early colonial period. In 1536, when Fray Antonio became father provincial, or leader of the Franciscan Order in Mexico, most of his activities suggested a desire to renew the fervor of the Franciscan mission and push the mission boundary beyond the Valley of Mexico. He immediately sent five missionaries to northern New Spain and five more to the South Pacific in 1538, both very dangerous assignments. Zumárraga's new powers of Inquisition and Fray Antonio's elevation to higher office shortly before Ocelotl's arrest came at the point when the integrity of the Franciscans was most in question. It is probable, given the evidence, that the two agreed on an exemplary trial of the "astute" Ocelotl in order to implicitly threaten the recidivist native leaders back to the straight path and, by doing so, perhaps restore the reputation of the order.[91]

Three actions by Ocelotl seem to have captured Fray Antonio's attention and pushed Ocelotl's case into the Inquisition courtroom. The precipitating event was probably Catalina López's report of Ocelotl's curative ministrations to the dying Don Pablo Xochiquentzin, native leader of the city of Mexico. Don Pablo was not of the royal family of Tenochtitlan; however, he had been *zan calpixcapilli* (a nobleman and head of noble calpultin) in the city of Mexico before the conquest. He was the latter of two Aztec nobles whom the Spanish appointed to rule in the city of Mexico after the deaths of Motecuhzoma and his nephew Cuauhtemoc. The Spanish appointed him *cuauhtlahtoani* (indigenous military governor) in 1531 and would only have kept him in that office for five years if they believed they had reason to be confident of his collaboration with them.[92] Several times during Don Pablo's illness, Catalina López had visited Don Pablo's house with beatas from the convent of Saint Isabel in the city of Mexico. In Spain, a beata was someone who had visions and trances in which she communed with God or the Virgin Mary and could therefore act as an intermediary. In essence, she offered a kind of Christian magic, which the Franciscans may have offered to the natives to quell their taste for the indigenous supernatural.

But Ocelotl's activities interfered with these Christian attempts to reeducate the natives. Catalina recounted indignantly that, after several of these visits, she was suddenly refused entrance to Don Pablo's house. She was told that Martín Ocelotl was inside ministering to Don Pablo and that he had told Don Pablo's guards to keep her and the beatas out. Ocelotl had previously ordered the removal of other "curers, who were using Castilian medicine, because they were killing" Don Pablo.[93] Two of Don Pablo's servants told Catalina that Ocelotl had proclaimed that, if Don Pablo survived to the fifth day of his illness, "he will never die." Others told her that Ocelotl had also ordered Don Pablo to give him green stones and rubbed the stones on Don Pablo's back and belly in an attempt to cure him.[94] Catalina López's testimony confirmed that Don Pablo, one of the most powerful native leaders and collaborators in Mexico, had died in the native faith and under the influence of the stealthy Ocelotl. This alone was probably sufficient to bring Ocelotl before the Inquisition.

Ocelotl's recent activities near Puebla, however, were also unsettling to the friars. In the 1530s, the Spanish became alarmed about the supply and communication routes from the city of Mexico to Veracruz. The route from the city of Mexico through Texcoco and Tlaxcala and then on to Veracruz was becoming increasingly dangerous, with indigenous bandits killing several Spaniards. The Spaniards founded the city of Puebla de los Angeles in April 1531 (the first Spanish city not founded on a prehispanic indigenous site) in order to secure a southern route that passed south of the volcanoes on the eastern side of the valley and then on to the Gulf of Mexico.[95] This southern route extended from the city of Mexico through Iztapaluca, Oaxtepec, Puebla, Tepeaca (which the Spanish called Segura de la Frontera), and Tecamachalco, on to Veracruz. As already noted, Ocelotl resided in houses in the first two altepemeh and for three years had been visiting the other three strategic Pueblan altepemeh, trying to build his network of client tlahtoqueh. While the Spanish were concerned about the security of the route in the 1530s and may have been highly suspicious that Ocelotl was preaching along this important route, Ocelotl probably did not see his activities in the same way. The Spanish supply route to the sea was the most lucrative in which to ply his business acumen. Moreover, he shared culture and religion with the leaders of these populous altepemeh; they were his natural clients.

In addition to these pragmatic concerns about Ocelotl's influence with strategic and important tlahtoqueh, there was also the rhetoric that Ocelotl had been relaying to tlahtoqueh through their servants— a strange mixture of indigenous religion and anti-Christian politics, particularly against the Franciscan friars. The "blasphemies," as Fray Antonio called Ocelotl's rhetoric, took place just months before the trial. Evidence of blasphemy, in fact, was the first testimony given in the trial, which indicates that Ocelotl's rhetoric was a primary motivation for the trial.[96] Apparently, from mid- to late 1536, in Ocelotl's meeting with the two servants of the reluctant Don Luis of Tepeaca, Ocelotl had tried to induce Don Luis to have greater contact with him by telling his servants to pass along a warning. Ocelotl apparently told them: "Recently two apostles, with great fangs and other frightful things, were sent by God, and [they said that] the missionaries would become *chichimicli*, which is a very ugly demon."[97] The trial scribe incorrectly wrote the name "chichimicli" for "*tzitzimime*," which the *Florentine Codex* translates as "demons of darkness [who] will come down; they will eat men."[98] The tzitzimime were a somewhat complicated phenomenon that became more complicated through the years as the friars tried to unravel the layered concepts of native religion. It seems from the transcript that in 1536 the friars had not yet learned what tzitzimime were and possibly had not heard anything about them. This would explain why the Inquisition secretary transcribed the word incorrectly and someone, either the witness or the interpreter, had to give a superficial definition of the concept as "a very ugly demon."

Ocelotl's rhetorical manipulations in this important and revealing story of the tzitzimime contain three different levels of significance, some of which the friars understood and some of which only the natives may have understood at that time. First, making "apostles" the harbingers of the warning seems to have been a spontaneous incorporation of Christian symbols and ideas into indigenous religious concepts, comparable to putting Jesus and Mary in the sacred temples. He belittles the friars by making God's apostles come to him, the jaguar, to warn about the tzitzimime, appropriating the preaching power of the friars. He gave the warning apostles fangs or large teeth, which in native religion was the symbol of the jaguar, a zoomorphic feature common to a number of gods, including Mixcoatl-Camaxtli, Tezcatlipoca, and obviously Ocelotl. Ocelotl and these apostles became, more or less, jaguar brothers who opposed the friars.

The second, and more mysterious, manipulation was Ocelotl's adaptation of the supernatural and moral concept of the tzitzimime. The tzitzimime were controlled by the major gods and were presumed to be "stellar demons" that were potentially most dangerous in periods of cosmic uncertainty. The tzitzimime were sent on two occasions. The first was during a solar eclipse, when stars near the sun are most visible due to the moon's blocking out of the sun's rays. It was believed that the stellar demons were attacking the sun, trying to end the world. The other occasion was at the end of the fifty-two-year cycle, when all of the hearth fires were extinguished and re-ignited from the fire created in the New Fire ceremony. Without the "new fire," it was believed that the tzitzimime would descend, eat the humans, and end the world; a new age would begin time all over again.[99] Thus, by making the friars tzitzimime, Ocelotl was signaling to the native leaders that the post-conquest chaos around them was an omen for the end of the world and that the friars were not what they seemed but actually tools of the gods to destroy the world. With such stories passing about, it was not surprising that the friars often reported when they went on their visitas that the natives ran away in fear.

The tzitzimime story, however, had yet a third, powerful moral association that Ocelotl manipulated. The tzitzimime provoked unusual dread because they were women who consumed humans; sometimes they were portrayed as skeletons. They worked at the behest of the more powerful of the male and female gods, including Mixcoatl-Camaxtli and Tezcatlipoca. Spanish friars working with native interpreters often incorrectly conflated the tzitzimime with another frightening female concept, the *mocihuaquetzque*, women who died in childbirth with the fetus unborn, who went about at night looking for a spindle and whorl in order to continue their unfinished womanly work.[100] While native sources drew a distinct line between these separate phenomena of frightening, supernatural female beings, it is interesting that Ocelotl used the feminization of terror as a way to slander the friars. The friars were celibate and dressed in skirts and womanly clothing. For the highly masculine warrior culture of central Mexico, wearing women's clothing was strongly associated with cowardice. Given the recent and unpopular campaign of the friars to force nobles into monogamous marriages, by defaming the friars as tzitzimime, Ocelotl might have been appealing to a male backlash against the policy.

In addition, despite the efforts of the friars to protect the natives from the worst of Spanish colonialism, they still supported the Spanish monopoly on warfare, state violence, and Spanish overlordship, depriving dissatisfied indigenous leaders of the place and respect to which they felt entitled. The native nobility often referred to the friars and their Christian neophytes in the native communities as women or "chickens."[101] The opposite of the chicken was the jaguar, which was symbolically "a predator status *in extenso*," meaning it was widely associated with "aggression, the qualities of strength and fierceness, supernatural protection, and pre-eminent social status."[102] Thus, Ocelotl was juxtaposing the fatal feminine against the lost male prerogatives and status of the tlahtoqueh and other noblemen in central Mexico.

To reinforce this message of masculine assertion against Christian femininity, Ocelotl leveled yet another "blasphemy," according to Fray Antonio. He temporarily housed two servants of the tlahtoani of Teacalco in the underground chamber of his house near Coatepec. He told the servants to go back to their vacillating lord and tell him: "Do you think that you will always be in this law of the Christians? Do you not know that we are born to die and that after we die, we will not have pleasure or rejoicing. Well, why not enjoy ourselves while we live and take pleasure in eating and drinking and enjoying ourselves and sleeping with the wives of our neighbors and take their goods and what they have and give ourselves a good life. We really do not live for anything else."[103] It is debatable whether this bit of hedonistic advice was an extension of prehispanic native religion and philosophy.[104] Some authors have suggested that a "live well and be merry" attitude was prevalent in the early decades when the relentlessly otherworldly Christianity of the friars proved too foreign for indigenous tastes.[105] Indeed, Ocelotl almost seems like the forward flank of that philosophical attitude. However, to the resentful native leaders, Ocelotl's "philosophy" conveyed a politically rebellious and anti-Christian message that many nobles were ready to hear after years of Franciscan interference in their daily lives, sexual relations, and family responsibilities.[106]

Near the end of Ocelotl's trial, after this damning evidence was written into the Inquisition record, Zumárraga shared the trial notes with the Audiencia and Viceroy Mendoza, asking them to affirm his and Fray Antonio's inclination to banish Ocelotl. The colonial authorities heartily agreed: "If [Ocelotl] stayed in New Spain, he could be very dangerous."[107] But the impact of Ocelotl's case on the friars' thinking was not over. Having served a judgment of guilty, the bailiffs were ordered to take possession of all of Ocelotl's properties and goods as a penalty for his crimes. They soon discovered that Ocelotl was a very wealthy man by native standards. Inquisition officers kept uncovering houses, property, jewels, clothing, deerskins, large cargoes of cotton, blankets, pottery, furniture, gold, silver, wood, and untold other objects, as well as numerous slaves. Every time they questioned someone about him, some new valuable or unexpected business connection emerged. Ocelotl was doing business with native traders who owned canoes and transported goods on Lake Texcoco. On several of his wide-ranging properties, he grew what was called "Castilian fruit" (apples, cherries, plums, pears), which probably required him to be in business with Spaniards at some point in order to get the tree stock. The last fifteen pages of Ocelotl's trial manuscript are filled with the tale of the Inquisition bailiff's slow but steady confiscation of more and more worldly goods.[108]

As the bailiffs untangled this embarrassment of riches, the process of confiscation pitted indigenous communities and individuals against one another and against the agents of the Inquisition. When Ocelotl was interrogated about the extent of his estate, he said that he was "owed much gold and silver and clothes and he has a memorial which he can give to His Excellency."[109] As with all things related to Ocelotl, there was probably some truth and some fiction in his memorial about his properties. He no doubt used the opportunity to ingratiate himself with Zumárraga and to get back at some of his native enemies, including those who had testified against him. The Holy Office's officials announced the memorial in the marketplaces on March 2, 1537, but there was apparently no response. The court grew suspicious that the Texcocans, in particular, were holding out. Therefore, on March 8, a week later, an *oidor* (Audiencia judge), Francisco de Loisa, ordered a confiscation demand to be announced in the marketplaces of the city of Mexico and Tlatelolco:

> I want all to know, Spanish or native, especially you, Don Pedro of Texcoco, and all the other nobles of the said town, and the caciques and noblemen of Chalco and Tlamanalco, that Martín Ocelotl has been condemned by this Holy Office of the Inquisition for his crimes to be banished in perpetuity from New Spain and condemned to lose all of his possessions.... To me he has made an account of all the houses, lands, furniture and debts he is owed in these towns.... I order that you are required to call the people of these towns together and each one of you inform me of the goods there that this Martín had ... on pain of the loss of all of your goods ... as well as two years of banishment from New Spain.[110]

The bailiffs followed this up with personal visits to altepemeh in the valley. Don Pedro of Texcoco more or less dismissed the matter with his claim that Ocelotl had been banished from Texcoco years before. The other tlahtoqueh reluctantly gave up a few pieces of property but, to the frustration of the bailiffs, not much else. It seems that many of the tlahtoqueh who had given Ocelotl property for his spiritual services took it back once he was arrested and were determined not to give it to the Inquisition despite many threats.¹¹¹ Some macehualtin began to accuse the tlahtoqueh of hiding goods, and other tlahtoqueh seemed to take advantage of their accused colleagues' predicament. The goods confiscated in Oaxtepec were in the care of its tlahtoani, Don Juan, who had been friendly with Ocelotl but then gave testimony against him.¹¹² At one point, the Inquisition prosecutor told Bishop Zumárraga that the goods in Oaxtepec "are outside the control of the Holy Office and not in its care and keeping, and there is danger and detriment to the Holy Office in this arrangement,"¹¹³ noticing that Don Juan of Oaxtepec was probably using his authority in the matter to take back his prior gifts to Ocelotl, as did other leaders. In fact, the confiscation from February to June 1537 seems to have built resentment and opposition much greater than any unhappiness about the persecution of Ocelotl.

Thus, the local native leaders' strategy of arbitration of avoidance in the difficult case of Ocelotl seems to have passed through three phases. First, the leaders were attracted to Ocelotl's useful supernatural powers; then, on Ocelotl's arrest, they quickly pulled away; and finally, they came back around and made common cause with Ocelotl as he became a victim of Inquisition confiscations and Spanish greed. If the Spanish had truly wanted the natives not to see and hear of Ocelotl again, they would have been better served by taking him away and leaving his properties in the native communities. By following Spanish Inquisition law to the letter, Zumárraga made a grave political mistake. In one stroke, he violated the natives' strong sense of communal property and entitlements and associated the Franciscan friars with the many previous encomendero abuses of the postconquest period.

CONCLUSION

Before the conquest, Martín Ocelotl aspired to be a priest with a possible side practice as a nahualli. The disruptions of the conquest encouraged him to move to the sophisticated centers of the Valley of Mexico and build a reputation as a businessman and a powerful nahualli. As López Austin says of prehispanic nanahualtin, "the profession of magician was divided into various specialties, and the social position, reputation, and fear magicians inspired varied . . . in regard to personal ethics."[114] Thus, Ocelotl's imaginative conflation and blending of native ideas in the post-conquest, even his incorporation of Christian elements, were of a piece with the individuality and creativity of nanahualtin before the conquest. Ocelotl had been able to escape detection for a long time because he stayed focused on the internal network of the tlahtoqueh and appealed to their interests and needs rather than those of the commoners. Unfortunately for him, once the Spanish understood more, his success in working with powerful tlahtoqueh gave his case urgency and quickly brought him down. It would be some time before the Franciscans could fully understand the imaginativeness of Ocelotl's ideological adaptations of native religion. In 1537, they were more impressed with his accumulation of wealth from native tlahtoqueh. Their appraisal of the evidence in Ocelotl's trial indicated to them that the surviving native nanahualtin and tlahtoqueh needed each other. The trial contributed to a growing belief, particularly among Zumárraga and his closest associates, that in order to eradicate the former, they would have to deal harshly with the latter.

CHAPTER THREE

The Millenarian
The Trial of Andrés Mixcoatl

In July 1537, within a few months of Ocelotl's banishment from central Mexico, another nahualli came to the attention of the Inquisition. Andrés Mixcoatl was accused of sorcery by Don Juan of Xicotepec, a prominent tlahtoani of a major altepetl in the sierra northeast of the Valley of Mexico. Over the next month, Don Juan tracked Mixcoatl down, captured him, and brought him in from the sierra to the city of Mexico. The evidence in the Mixcoatl case strongly suggests that this nahualli had surpassed Ocelotl's activities by mounting an anti-friar movement with millennial overtones among the commoners in the sierra. Mixcoatl's activities are detailed in a lengthy report for the Inquisition compiled by Fray Francisco Marmolejo of the Franciscan convento at Tulancingo. Marmolejo's report of August 1537, which constitutes most of the transcript, includes informal interviews with some two dozen commoners and minor leaders, mostly living in remote villages of the Sierra de Puebla.

Historian Serge Gruzinski's well-known analysis of Mixcoatl's case argues that there were class differences between Ocelotl's and Mixcoatl's cases that reflected early colonial native society. In Gruzinski's interpretation, Ocelotl was of the elite and secretly allied with nobles, while Mixcoatl was a plebian hero attempting to lead a millennial revolt of the highland macehualtin.[1] I view Ocelotl, Mixcoatl, and the other nanahualtin as a class of spiritualists who were not particularly well allied with either nobles or macehualtin. They were independent and individual agents (though they often relied on one another) who were embraced or discarded by the nobility whenever the strategy of arbitration of avoidance required. Yet, while the nanahualtin were in a precarious position, their powers were often highly attractive to nervous nobles as they tried to appease the macehualtin without upsetting the friars. Sometimes the nanahualtin succeeded spectacularly in appealing to the local politics of native leaders and the spiritual needs of the commoners; at other times, they could be careless and over-confident, like Mixcoatl, and fail. Success or failure usually depended on the extent to which the presence of a Christian mission influenced the actions of surrounding indigenous leaders.

THE SIERRA
"All were guilty of believing in this Andrés"

Fray Francisco Marmolejo pinpoints the area of Mixcoatl's greatest influence as about seventy-five square kilometers in the northern Sierra de Puebla, which forms a remote mountainous nexus among the four modern states of Mexico, Hidalgo, Veracruz, and Puebla (see map 3).[2] He claims that in these mountains, "all were guilty of believing in this Andrés." According to Marmolejo's report, in the months before his capture, Mixcoatl was holding court in a series of small communities in a triangle that lay between the relatively large altepemeh of Tulancingo, Huauchinango, and Xicotepec in the old Texcocan imperial hinterland.

The people of this region had been tied to the Valley of Mexico in the prehispanic era through economics, political hegemony, and shared religion. They were the descendants of waves of immigrants who had entered central Mexico since about 1000 C.E. When the Toltec civilization, which dominated central Mexico from its capital in Tula in 900–1200 C.E., expanded its empire into the Sierra de Puebla in the eleventh and twelfth centuries, they pushed the earlier inhabitants, the Totonacas, farther north, moving Nahuatl-speaking Toltecas into the Sierra de Puebla, along with the Toltecas' allies, the Otomi. After the fall of the Toltec capital of Tula, migratory groups along the northern border of the Toltec empire, the Chichimecas, moved into the valleys of central Mexico in two migrations, adopting the Nahuatl language and

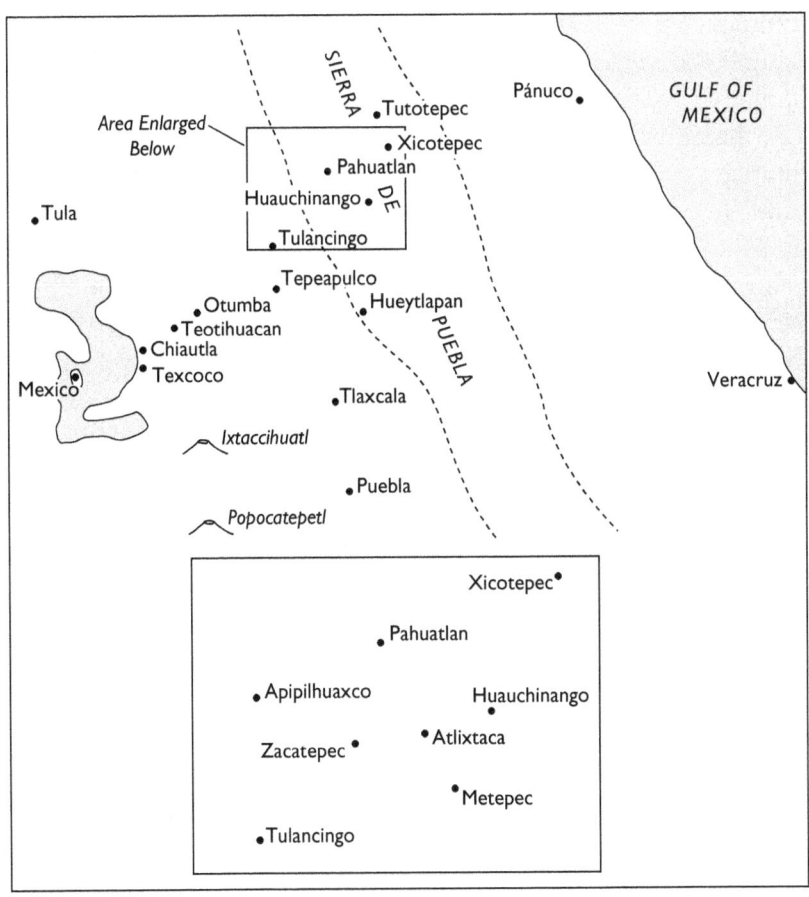

Map 3. Northeast Valley of Mexico and the Northern Sierra de Puebla

Toltec urban ways. First, there were the Chichimecas who had settled in the Puebla-Tlaxcala area in the northern Sierra de Puebla. They were part of the cultural group that Ocelotl appealed to shortly before his arrest. Then, there were the Chichimecas who had settled in the Valley of Mexico, the most important group being the Acolhua, who founded their capital in Texcoco. The Texcocans extended their influence into the far northern part of the Sierra de Puebla, the region where Mixcoatl would later preach. Thus, the sierra people of this remote region spoke Nahuatl, the language of the Toltecas, but also their earlier languages— Totonac, Tepehua, and Otomi.[3]

By the mid-fifteenth century, the sierra was connected to the Triple Alliance primarily through the Acolhua city-state of Texcoco. The famed Texcocan leader of the early Triple Alliance, Nezahualcoyotl, had brought many altepemeh of the northern Sierra de Puebla under his tributary control and had used the region as a staging point for further conquests into the Pánuco region along the Veracruz coast.[4] He also conceived of the northern sierra and the area north of Texcoco as his personal fief, a bulwark of rule against the increasing power and influence of his more powerful partners in the Triple Alliance, the Mexica.[5] A well-traveled road took Nezahualcoyotl's armies through the old Acolhua hinterland of Teotihuacan and Otumba to the area around the pilgrimage site of Tepeapulco and then Tulancingo, thence through Huauchinango and Xicotepec, the two major altepemeh in that part of the sierra. His son Nezahualpilli, with the further assistance of the Triple Alliance, completed the conquest of many of the major altepemeh in the sierra, including the particularly difficult conquests of Tutotepec and Pahuatlan farther to the north. Nezahualpilli brought Nahuatl-speaking Chichimecas from Texcoco into the sierra to continue the cultural synthesis of the sierra and the valley.[6] Tulancingo, Huauchinango, and Xicotepec were ruled by tlahtoqueh who were members of the council of fourteen Acolhua rulers who advised Nezahualcoyotl and Nezahualpilli.[7]

The sierra people, though remote, were definitely part of the Nahuatlized Chichimec culture, though the Spanish conquest would alter the politics of the region.[8] Just before the conquest, Nezahualpilli's son Ixtlilxochitl held Otumba as his northeast capital and took Tulancingo, but in the Spanish conquest the ambitious leader had lost control of the rebellious Tutotepec and other altepemeh. After the conquest, with the help of his ally Cortés, Ixtlilxochitl tried to gain the whole of the northern sierra back, but it was the Spanish rather than he who got the major benefits of these arduous campaigns. As noted in chapter 1, Ixtlilxochitl rapidly lost political leverage and tributary control in the Texcocan hinterland to a succession of Spanish conquerors who received the major altepemeh and the surrounding local communities in encomienda. The area's government became a bit fractured. Tulancingo was given in encomienda in the 1520s and '30s to the conquistador Francisco de Terrazas.[9] Huauchinango was given in encomienda to Alonso de Villanueva. The militarily sensitive area of Xicotepec was provided with a corregidor, a crown official who tended to be closely tied to authorities in the city of Mexico, in the early 1530s.[10] Therefore, the density and quality of Spanish government varied according to the personality of these various rulers. As Zumárraga notes on many occasions, these Spanish officials were sometimes not inclined to waste their resources on policing adherence to Christian doctrine among their indigenous tributaries.

More important to the Christian effort was the distribution of conventos and friars assigned to them, as the friars could proselytize in the immediate areas around the conventos and monitor surrounding altepemeh through visitas. However, the *pueblos de visita* (towns the friars visited infrequently to administer the sacraments) were only as good as the quality of the proselytization and the frequency of the friars' visits. The rest of the time, they depended on *mandones* (native neophytes who instructed others) to monitor the recent converts. The Franciscans had managed to establish a convento in Tulancingo and one farther south in Tepeapulco, from which they could send visitas.[11] But farther into the sierra, at Huauchinango and Xicotepec, the friars had little or no consistent presence. The spread of the Franciscan mission into the sierra in the 1530s may have been constrained by the pressure Zumárraga was receiving from the other mendicant orders to reserve nearby proselytizing territories to them. Eventually, in 1543, it was the Augustinians who finally founded a convento in Huauchinango; much later, in the 1570s, Xicotepec finally received a lay parish.[12]

Thus, in the 1530s, the various indigenous leaders in the northern Sierra de Puebla were largely released from their prehispanic tributary and political obligations to Texcoco and were left more or less to their own devices in dealing with various Spanish colonial authorities and each other. Very likely they knew more about the Franciscans from word of mouth than from actual experience. Therefore, the nanahualtin could operate more freely in the sierra, and there was evidence that some of the native leaders in the sierra initially welcomed Mixcoatl as one who could help them with their many weather- and crop-related difficulties.

Even in the best of times, conditions for raising crops in the sierra were difficult. In the colonial period, with depopulation from disease, Spanish disruption of markets and trading networks, and finally, volatile weather conditions, the simple people of the sierra desperately sought spiritual relief in the magic powers of the nanahualtin.[13] Unable to do much about the consequences of the colonial intrusion, the tlahtoani of Huauchinango, his *achcauhtin* (barrio leaders), and the leaders of surrounding altepemeh tried to mediate with the gods, whether clandestinely or openly, on behalf of the macehualtin. Unfortunately, the 1530s were the beginning of decades of erratic weather. While rain and drought patterns differed from region to region in central Mexico, overall weather conditions are indicated by tree-ring data from the northern plains of Mexico. During the period from 1529 to about 1532, central Mexico suffered from low precipitation, followed by a year or two of heavy rain around 1533–34. Ten years of terrible drought followed, with overabundance of rain in 1545, again followed by three decades of what climatologists have called the "megadrought" of the mid-sixteenth century, one of the worst in North American history.[14] While Andrés Mixcoatl was not of the sierra, he understood its agricultural and economic needs and stood ready to provide remedies, in his own version of the persistent "núcleo duro" of ritual practice.

Mixcoatl seems to have made his spiritual journey through the northeast of the Valley of Mexico and into the sierra in two phases. The first phase began at his birthplace in Chiautla, an Acolhua altepetl in the Valley of Mexico.[15] Chiautla was practically a suburb of Texcoco— the religious and political heart of the Nahuatl-speaking Chichimecas in the Acolhua territory—thus, Mixcoatl could be characterized as a sophisticated valley cousin to the sierra people. Mixcoatl seems to have been younger than Martín Ocelotl. Though we have no evidence that they were acquainted, trial testimony suggests that he at least knew of Ocelotl's reputation and ideas and that he looked up to Ocelotl in a way that suggests relative youth. We may estimate that Mixcoatl was in his early to mid-thirties at the time of his trial. If that estimate is correct, he would have been in his teens at the time of the conquest, certainly aware of most aspects of prehispanic religion but perhaps not as well schooled in supernaturalism as Ocelotl. While Ocelotl was subtle and careful to preserve ritual practice—even as he blended in new concepts and ideas—Mixcoatl took a more haphazard approach that served his most immediate economic and political interests. Because Mixcoatl was young in 1526–28, when the official cults in Chiautla were crumbling, his spiritual training was probably no more than memories and experiences of clandestine practices in the countryside combined with a vivid imagination.

He owned property in Chiautla as well as in Texcoco and lived in Chiautla continuously until the mid-1530s. He testified to Zumárraga that he had been baptized in Chiautla five years before, or around 1532, about the time the friars were busily extending the Franciscan mission into the Acolhua territory.[16] He claimed to have listened to the Christian doctrine frequently from the "disciples, the young boys that they had there who preached and said to stop with the idols and idolatries and believe in God and other things." Mixcoatl admitted, however, that "he stopped doing anything that they [the neophytes] told him" at least three years before.[17]

As with Ocelotl, it was highly unlikely that Mixcoatl took any of the Christian doctrine seriously from the beginning. Shortly after the Texcocan leaders drove Ocelotl out, the tlahtoani of Chiautla, who was closely connected to the leadership in Texcoco, banished Mixcoatl from his altepetl in late 1533 or early 1534. Why? Mixcoatl had allegedly told a witness: "That lord [in Chiautla] always had many quarrels with me. He claimed that, in the church service when they say that there is only one God, I said in its place that the first commandment is to throw God into the fire and the second is to beat him with sticks."[18] Mixcoatl never affirmed or denied that he had spoken against Christianity in Chiautla, but the evidence suggests that he was drawing too much attention to himself, especially after the scandal of Ocelotl. Though it is not entirely conclusive, the fact that Ocelotl,

Mixcoatl, and other nanahualtin were being driven away from the larger altepemeh and into the small towns of the sierra indicates that the friars were having some success with the visitas policy. Primarily, the visiting friars put the resident tlahtoqueh on notice about the political dangers of allowing unrestrained prehispanic religious practices in their altepemeh. Gruzinski has suggested that the tlahtoqueh in Texcoco and Chiautla were part of a zealous "Christian party" advocating for the friars and trying to oppress the nanahualtin.[19] Instead, as has been seen, Don Pedro of Texcoco had allowed Ocelotl to retain properties and continue doing business near Texcoco, and the trial evidence indicates that the tlahtoani of Chiautla allowed Mixcoatl to keep his goods and property, both in Chiautla and Texcoco.[20] Thus, the banishment of Ocelotl and Mixcoatl around 1533–34 looks more like a case of arbitration of avoidance than the zealous Christian conversion of the nobility.

In any case, the nanahualtin tended to just move up the road slightly beyond the Franciscan presence. Mixcoatl told Zumárraga that, after his banishment in 1534, he had moved northeast of Texcoco just short of the sierra, where he offered spiritual services, weather prognostication, and medical advice. His destinations included an altepetl near Otumba called Tepezcuco; another in the northern reaches of the modern state of Tlaxcala called Tepeyahualco; a very important large altepetl near Texcoco called Tepetlaoztoc; the sacred pilgrimage site of Tepeapulco; and the place where the Franciscans established their convento, Tulancingo.[21] Mixcoatl's wanderings in these northeastern altepemeh were contemporaneous to the Franciscan advance into the northeast valley up to the sierra in the early 1530s. One of the first Franciscans to open up this territory to the Franciscans was Fray Andrés de Olmos, who went directly to its spiritual heart in Tepeapulco to establish a mission in 1531–32.[22] Mixcoatl's presence there, like Ocelotl's in the southeastern Valley of Mexico, was a further indication that nanahualtin were moving ahead of the Franciscan vanguard (or at least trying to get ahead of it) to preach on their own terms.

By the summer of 1537, according to Marmolejo's report, Mixcoatl had moved into a second phase geographically and was plying his skills mainly in a group of remote altepemeh between Tulancingo, Huauchinango, and Xicotepec (see inset, map 3). The Franciscans in

Tulancingo did not seem to be aware of Mixcoatl's presence in the northern sierra until Don Juan of Xicotepec confronted Mixcoatl and another nahualli, named Tlaloc, in the marketplace of Copila in June 1537. Don Juan suspiciously "asked him who he was and why he did these things."[23] Mixcoatl and Tlaloc claimed they were summoning better weather for the macehualtin of Copila, and in short order Don Juan sent his men to arrest them. Mixcoatl and Tlaloc managed to get away, and Don Juan's posse had to hunt them for over a month and a half before they finally arrested Mixcoatl. Only when they heard that Mixcoatl was arrested did the Franciscans send Marmolejo to the sierra to begin an investigation.

Like the tlahtoqueh in Texcoco and Chiautla, Don Juan's motivations seem to have been political rather than religious. As Xicotepec did not yet have a parish, friar, or priest, Don Juan could not have been deeply indoctrinated in the Christian faith. However, he was well connected to the tlahtoqueh in Tulancingo and other highland leaders who were more familiar with the friars. It was also possible that Don Juan had a collaborative political relationship with the corregidor assigned to him, who, as a crown official, may have felt compelled to enforce church doctrine in the area he governed. Native leaders like Don Juan needed to exercise prudence in protecting their communities from the unwanted attention of Spanish authorities, which these practicing nanahualtin sometimes attracted.[24] But their wariness was more than fear of the Spanish threat. In prehispanic and colonial times, the nanahualtin had the unfortunate tendency, from the perspective of autocratic native leaders, of failing "to conform to [their] place in society . . . [and might] release harmful magical forces that could contaminate one's family and neighborhood."[25] While supernatural powers were desirable, the unpredictability of those powers could also be frightening for nobles, especially if the nanahualtin used politically destabilizing rhetoric, as Mixcoatl sometimes did. As Ocelotl suggested in his supposed encounter with Motecuhzoma before the conquest, a tlahtoani might kill a nahualli for having divine dreams that created doubt about his native leadership.

While Ocelotl's trial transcript gives little information about other nanahualtin, Mixcoatl's transcript demonstrates that there was a significant community of nanahualtin in the sierra. The Franciscans in

Tulancingo were vaguely aware of them, but the local native leaders seem to have been worrying about the nanahualtin for some time. An example was Mixcoatl's companion, Tlaloc, who had been offering his services around Tulancingo and Xicotepec. Mixcoatl refers to him as his brother, and Marmolejo seems to have taken this literally, although the evidence suggests that Mixcoatl was speaking metaphorically or claiming a blood connection in order to frighten the sierra people into doing what he wanted. Another nahualli, who called himself Huitzli, was friendly and cooperative with Mixcoatl and was preaching in the area around Tutotepec. The friars also uncovered a nahualli named Mocahuque preaching in a barrio of Tulancingo, who seemed to know Mixcoatl and the others.[26] Fray Francisco de Lintorne, the guardian of Tulancingo, who supported Marmolejo in his investigation, said that there was another nahualli preaching in Tepeapulco during the absence of Fray Andrés de Olmos, another in Tulancingo named Tenancatl, and another some ten to twelve leagues from Huauchinango who was, according to Lintorne, "as bad as Mixcoatl."[27] It was clear in Marmolejo's and Lintorne's reports that the friars only needed to ask the locals and they would learn of nanahualtin throughout the sierra.

The wandering nature of these various nanahualtin was problematic for the early colonial mission. While Ocelotl and Mixcoatl do not constitute a pattern, one can imagine that several of these other nanahualtin may also have been outsiders who had moved from the more colonized valley into the countryside in the first twenty years after the conquest. One has the sense that the wandering nanahualtin's strangeness, their knowledge of sophisticated religious ideas, and even their exoticism enhanced their charisma and the perception of the potency of their magical powers, especially in comparison with the official native priests. This was the case with Mixcoatl. In the first phase of his peregrinations, Mixcoatl passed through Tepeapulco, which had suffered four desperate years of drought. He "made his chants in which he burned copal and paper, and then it rained a lot overnight and continued until the middle of the next day."[28] Satisfied, the people of Tepeapulco later murdered their own ineffectual native priest.

Other things also worked toward the easy reception of the wandering nanahualtin in the sierra. For one, as Franciscan cultural control expanded into greater concentric circles beyond the major altepemeh, their visitas policy appears to have been somewhat effective in undermining the official state cults of prehispanic religion, especially economically. The nanahualtin, on the other hand, were physically independent, economically enterprising, and always beyond the grasp of the friars. As H. B. Nicholson indicates, while the formal priesthood collapsed, the "individual magic practitioners easily survived the best efforts of the missionaries to destroy them."[29] That two of the major trials of Zumárraga's Inquisition were of itinerant nanahualtin is perhaps an indication that the friars realized early on that this particular class of spiritual specialists required extra attention. Marmolejo and Lintorne turned readily to the stringent measure of Inquisition, hoping that it would rid them of the pesky nanahualtin. They recommended to Zumárraga that Mixcoatl be tried in the city of Mexico and be returned to Tulancingo for punishment in front of the indigenous leaders around Huauchinango. The native leaders would then understand and "see the blindness that was committed here," referring to the disregard of Christianity.[30] Marmolejo argued that this exemplary punishment of Mixcoatl would be "worth eight years of proselytizing ... because when we preach in one place they [the nanahualtin] simply go to another and pervert it."[31]

A SPIRITUAL *TLAHTOANI*
"The friars tell us lies and falsehoods"

As Mixcoatl wandered farther into the mountains, away from the Franciscan convento and the tlahtocayotl of Tulancingo, his inventiveness with the "núcleo duro" of religious belief seemed also to evolve, if occasionally in bizarre ways. He increasingly represented himself as a godlike presence in the sierra, and in his last few months of freedom, as a kind of spiritual tlahtoani who virtually dictated to the simple people of the remote sierra. As Gruzinski notes, in that final period when Mixcoatl became a kind of cultural dictator, the sierra community divided into two camps in their attitudes toward him. The first group contained the major tlahtoqueh, such as Don Juan of Xicotepec and the native town council of Tulancingo. While they were hardly reliable converts to Christianity, these leaders were nevertheless disdainful and dismissive of Mixcoatl as a kind of charlatan and potential disrupter of their uneasy perch between the Spanish authorities and their own people.

The second group included the macehualtin, the minor tlahtoqueh, and the achcauhtin of Huauchinango. These commoners and the lower level of native leadership, Marmolejo concluded, should be dealt with leniently because they had been motivated by the fear of losing crops and therefore were easy victims of Mixcoatl's "tricks."[32] Indeed, some of their testimony against Mixcoatl suggests a compulsion, or a very strong attraction, on the part of the second group toward Mixcoatl's guidance, if for no other reason than to reinforce the weakening "núcleo duro" of traditional religion. One witness anxiously argued that "he took Andrés for a god because the corn and cotton fields had to be looked after," as if he had no choice but to turn to the nahualli.[33] One indigenous leader who had initially rebuffed Mixcoatl changed his mind and called him back, saying, "Now we do not want to lose the cotton fields.... Send the clouds away to someplace else so we do not lose the fields."[34]

Had Mixcoatl discovered a window of opportunity, a period of wavering spiritual leadership among these simple people, that he could exploit, if for a short time? After the conquest, according to Louise Burkhart, "the Aztec state-cult no longer proclaimed Tenochtitlan the navel of the universe; each community in its own small way was able to order itself around its own sacred and moral center."[35] Because of the shortage of friars and their lack of accurate knowledge about native cultural and spiritual ways, the size and scope of the Franciscan mission were inadequate to the task of establishing and enforcing a new sacred and moral center. As Burkhart notes, "the Indians were thence forward left alone to practice their own version of Christianity, centered on community rituals and the saints as embodiments of the divine."[36] Thus, according to Burkhart, the natives "Nahuatlized" Christianity; that is, they made Christianity conform with their "núcleo duro," a process evident in the trials of the 1540s and 50s. However, the trials of Ocelotl and Mixcoatl indicate that there was another evangelical gap that was being filled. It was the period after the precipitous decline of the native state-cults in the

1520s and before the instruction of Christian sacred and moral concepts was of sufficient magnitude to be "Nahuatlized" in the 1540s and '50s. Mixcoatl's story suggests that nanahualtin like him occupied this brief void in the 1530s and early 1540s (and in some areas perhaps even later) and responded to the native people's most basic spiritual cravings with a variation of the "núcleo duro" that had little to do with Christianity except to counter the Franciscan presence.

According to a standard historical interpretation of the transition from prehispanic religion to Nahuatlized Christianity, the nanahualtin were a group that would come to represent the old ways: "Among the people, the role of these men as defenders of the ancient faith united them, because they were opposed to the European invasion and Christian indoctrination."[37] But, while the nanahualtin opposed Christianity, their own activities were not necessarily reactionary or bound by tradition. They changed rituals readily, introduced new religious ideas to the sierra, invented variations on medical preparations, and even suggested interesting new roles for themselves in the communities. Their strategic uses of native religion had the same innovative, practical, educative, and enduring characteristics as the process of "Nahuatlizing Christianity" that Burkhart describes.[38] In other words, the "núcleo duro" itself was highly flexible, so the native communities were comfortable accepting the nanahualtin's variations of it in the evangelical gap; and by the same token, these same communities later readily Nahuatlized Christianity. Those historical processes were of a piece with the native imagination and very different from the strict, doctrinaire faith of the Franciscans.

A close analysis of the activities of Mixcoatl and the other colonial nanahualtin indicates that their improvisations on the "núcleo duro" had the goal of a cult of personality. In the last few months of Mixcoatl's freedom in the summer of 1537, he was clearly attempting to transform himself into the spiritual tlahtoani of his remote hideout in the sierra. The precipitating event seemed to be when Don Juan of Xicotepec angrily confronted Mixcoatl in the market of Copila and narrowly missed arresting him.[39] After that, the friars in Tulancingo became aware of Mixcoatl and encouraged Don Juan to track down the nahualli and bring him to Tulancingo. From June through August, his last ninety days of freedom, Mixcoatl was a hunted man, and he probably suspected that he would end up banished to Spain, as Ocelotl had been just a few months before. Thus, he retreated to the more remote sierra in the triangle between Tulancingo, Huauchinango, and Xicotepec, especially to four very small mountainous altepemeh: Metepec, Zacatepec, Apipilhuaxco, and Atlixtaca. The region formed a kind of redoubt where he was able to elude Don Juan for many weeks. His own fear, yet his need to show bravado before these simple people, led him to become more defiant, angry, and anti-clerical in his rhetoric.

While Ocelotl had tried to appeal to major tlahtoqueh through their servants and with gifts and hospitality, Mixcoatl handled the people in these small altepemeh in a dictatorial and commercially exploitative manner. He demanded ever-larger amounts of ceremonial products from his followers, including copal, *amate*, and *ulli* (incense, ceremonial paper, and rubber). In Apipilhuaxco, he told the local leader that he would be back in a day or two, during which time the man was to find copal and amate. When Mixcoatl returned, he found that "he was not given as much as he wanted" and threatened the leader for more.[40] Mixcoatl demanded cotton from the same leader and then became furious when the fellow only provided a small crate of it. The leader soon came to Mixcoatl with a large load of cotton, enough to make many blankets to sell at market.[41] Apparently, when the locals brought Mixcoatl a load of pinewood or cotton, he would have them carry the goods to Texcoco, where he still maintained a house; no doubt, he was going to resell the goods in the city.[42] Metepec, Zacatepec, Apipilhuaxco, and Atlixtaca all contributed labor to build homes for him in each altepetl. Mixcoatl then demanded corn from these altepemeh and they all complied.[43] His renown was such that in his final two months of freedom, "three merchants preceded him into the town to sell the paper, copal, and ulli.... They called out, 'Buy paper for sacrifice; Mixcoatl has arrived.'"[44] While the evidence is not conclusive, it is probable that the merchants had an arrangement with Mixcoatl to sell the excess copal, amate, and ulli back to Mixcoatl's devotees.

During this post-conquest period, when, according to Burkhart, these communities were just beginning to Nahuatlize Christianity, Mixcoatl presented himself as an alternative spiritual leader around whom a cult could congregate. He and his colleagues explored the native conceptual frontier between priest, god, and god impersonator (ixiptla), much as Ocelotl had. In response to Mixcoatl's demands, leaders in the remote altepemeh gave him land and provided the workers to cultivate it. Some of the minor leaders testified that they "gave him the most charming of their daughters in order to make a race of masculine gods."[45] In Xucupan, Mixcoatl "stubbornly" demanded to be given a woman; he claimed that he "felt sorry for them and gave them to understand that he wanted to remedy" their problems by having relations with a local woman. Reluctantly, they gave him a woman, and he sat on a blanket with her, casting corn and performing "chants that are called in their language *tlapully* [*tlapalli*, spirit] in order to know the heart of the woman and what she was thinking."[46] After learning that she was married with children, Mixcoatl moved her family out of the house and bedded her.[47]

Marmolejo uncovered twelve separate episodes in which Mixcoatl made death threats, claiming that he could make people ill or cause them or their family members to die. One hapless leader handed over more and more cotton to Mixcoatl (who then had it delivered to Texcoco), because the nahualli told him "if he did not want to give more, he would die and so would his sons."[48] Marmolejo was astonished by the credulity of the people who caved in to Mixcoatl's threats. As he took the testimony of Tlylancalqui, an *achcauhtli* (barrio leader) in Huauchinango, the man refused "to stand in front of Andrés [Mixcoatl]; he did not want to give testimony because he said that this one knows if I have to die or live much longer and that those who do not obey him will have to die." Marmolejo proclaimed that the fear of the people was amazing; "I have never seen such a thing in all my life."[49]

Mixcoatl's trial provides evidence that the many nanahualtin in the sierra were working in coordination and supporting one another's activities. In the province around Tutotepec, the nahualli named Huitzli called on his local followers to greet Mixcoatl as he entered the province and to bring him not only copal, amate, and ulli, but also ten blankets, *pajas* (mats) to sit on, and *asientos* (special chairs that the nobility often used). Huitzli told them, "All come . . . that such a god was here. . . . Bring your women to offer to him."[50] When the tlahtoani of Xicotepec, Don Juan, made his initial accusation against Mixcoatl, he also implicated as a co-conspirator the nahualli whom Mixcoatl referred to as his brother, Tlaloc. Apparently, Tlaloc sometimes appeared with Mixcoatl, and sometimes Mixcoatl referred to the notoriety of Tlaloc in order to instill extra fear in the people. In Copila, Mixcoatl told the people that Tlaloc "was the lord of the wind and that he, Andrés, had the power over him" to get him to bring destructive winds. Mixcoatl continued that they had better listen to him because in another altepetl, when they did not give Tlaloc something, "he made the wind blow so that they lost the corn."[51] Don Juan argued that Tlaloc invited Mixcoatl to his altepetl because Tlaloc had had success there and wanted to spread his good fortune. Evidently, the nanahualtin in the sierra shared a corporate ethos. Perhaps they were united in their opposition to the friars, but they also established multiple new economic and social structures that blended traditions from the sierra, the valley, and their own interests.

Without question, Mixcoatl liked to contrast himself with the friars, and by association, with leaders who would not follow him or do as he wished. He advised the people in Atlixtaca, his most frequent sierra residence, that "they should not leave the things of the past and forget them, because the gods that they adored before took care of them and gave them all that they needed. The friars tell lies and falsehoods and they do not bring the needed remedies. They do not know us and we do not know them. Did our fathers and grandfathers know these friars and believe what the friars say about this God? No, it is not so, it is a lie."[52] In Mixcoatl's condemnation of the new God and the friars, he alleged that they did nothing for the peasants. He, on the other hand, would give them the needed spiritual remedies because he "felt sorry" for the people and their leaders. Later, he insisted, "I want to make the sacrifices and I do not have to stop doing them because of [the friars]."[53] But when Zumárraga asked Mixcoatl whether he made human sacrifices, he was quick to point out that he did not (a denial that Ocelotl also made).[54] Mixcoatl's remedies, like Ocelotl's, were not intended for community penance, but to magically promote the goals of tlahtoqueh and other individuals who sought cures and better weather.

To cope with the people's problems, Mixcoatl brought a blend of traditional and new ceremonial products and rituals. Central to his innovations on the "núcleo duro" was his use of hallucinogens, incense, and herbal remedies for virtually everything. Wherever Mixcoatl went, he demanded copal, a tree resin that was broadly used for incense in ceremonies across central Mexico.[55] Copal came from the *Bursera bipinnata* tree, which grew in abundance in the southeastern slopes of the Sierra Madre Oriental in the modern state of Veracruz.[56] In particular, the high-quality, lighter copal, *B. excelsa* (as opposed to the darker, "mud" copal), was frequently offered to the gods and grew in the lower elevations near the coastal plains of tropical Veracruz. Mixcoatl seemed to be referring to the difference in qualities when he kindly informed two old women who brought him copal, "This copal [probably mud copal] I do not eat, only burn. I thank you very much."[57] In any case, copal in early colonial times was highly valued because it had to be brought from a distance and had to be harvested and distributed secretly.[58] He also received offerings of amate paper, which he cut into traditional ceremonial shapes that represented the gods or certain concepts of death, fertility, illness, and more.[59] Mixcoatl also requested ulli (rubber), which was used to make balls for the Mesoamerican ceremonial ball games but also was sprinkled on amate paper and burned.[60] While amate was relatively abundant in central Mexico, ulli was a rarer product because the rubber tree grew even farther south in the tropical zone of southern Veracruz and the Yucatan.

Anthropologists have recently suggested that there was "a symbolic connection between maize and copal, most notably copal's use as food for the gods," and that copal smoke was "employed for trance induction" by nanahualtin in central Mexico.[61] The transcript of Mixcoatl's trial seems to be definitive evidence for the association. According to Marmolejo, Mixcoatl's "same custom wherever he goes" was to call together everyone in the altepetl and ask for copal and amate "to make his sacrifices and chants."[62] At night he burned the copal and amate in a "great fire, and later he made predictions to them, saying, 'Do not be afraid. Your corn will not freeze. Everything that you have under cultivation will be fine.'"[63] Often, Mixcoatl brought out what the Spanish referred to as a *"sahumeria,"* or what the natives called *"popochcomitl,"* an incense burner or black-glazed pottery bowl in which coals were placed and the copal sprinkled on top.

When given the amate paper, Mixcoatl cut it into figures "as they used to do in the old days," according to one witness.[64] Unfortunately, Mixcoatl's cut figures were not described, but a witness explained that Mixcoatl once cut the amate into the shapes of two brothers who had died some days before. He threw the paper figures into the fire and watched the smoke, "because he had the dead ones rest where he wanted them to be," which suggests that the ceremony was intended to guide restless ghosts to some point in the hereafter where they would not disturb the community or family.[65]

The use of hallucinogenic drugs was an important skill of many of these nanahualtin.[66] Mixcoatl often passed around *nanacatl* (hallucinogenic mushrooms, sometimes called *hongos*), to his devotees as they sat around the fire. According to one witness, the nanacatl "takes away the feeling, and they say it causes devilish visions in whoever eats them. They say it is the body of the devil, and you will see if you are going to die or be rich or poor or if you are going to have some misfortunes."[67] The comment about "the body of the devil" refers to *teonanacatl*, "the flesh of the gods," another name for hallucinogenic mushrooms. Nanacatl was apparently collected locally in the forest areas of the sierra and was nothing new to the sierra people, but Mixcoatl's fire ceremonies and his sharing of the nanacatl with macehualtin may have been. One or two of these mushrooms would induce a period of frenetic activity, which was why prehispanic nobles liked to eat them, with honey to take away their bitter taste, before the larger ritual ceremonies to Huitzilopochtli. The frenzy was soon accompanied by dreams and imaginings that probably encouraged many to think they were seeing the future. Mixcoatl had his devotees dance about the fire and then lie next to it, hallucinating until they fell asleep. While Mixcoatl demanded copal and amate from the people, he gave them the nanacatl, in a kind of symbolic sharing of his prophesying powers. Apparently, he asked some of his devotees to collect nanacatl so that he could redistribute it to other followers in order to create this gift exchange network.[68]

Another herb Mixcoatl used was *iztauhyatl*, or *Artemisia mexicana* (Mexican wormwood) employed nowadays by native *curanderos* for *mal de ojo* (evil eye).[69] Sahagún reports that a tea made of iztauhyatl was commonly used as medicine in the Valley of Mexico for urinary diseases and to reduce fever.[70] The little medicinal work that Mixcoatl was called upon to do consisted of providing iztauhyatl to women, who were instructed to apply the herb to the bodies of their sick children.[71] More often, Mixcoatl employed iztauhyatl as a divinatory herb. He sometimes burned iztauhyatl in the popochcomitl, and sometimes he simply waved the cut bunches of iztauhyatl along the fields. He claimed to his followers that "with the herb he could send the clouds away and that the odor of this herb goes to the clouds and makes them go away."[72] There is no reference in Sahagún's *Florentine Codex* for the divinatory use of iztauhyatl. However, an earlier work of Sahagún, *Primeros memoriales*, describes the divinatory uses of iztauhyatl in precisely the same way as Mixcoatl employed it.[73]

OCELOTL'S BROTHER
"The Christians will return to Castile"

Mixcoatl's case does not suggest that the nanahualtin had come to the point of a mutual conspiracy, a series of coordinated activities to keep the friars from entering and effectively proselytizing the sierra. At best, the nanahualtin were birds of a feather taking advantage of the opportunity to become cult leaders in remote communities that were desperate for spirituality in their lives. Nanahualtin mutually supported one another in both spiritual authority and their lucrative enterprises. But Ocelotl's notorious banishment, of which the nanahualtin were well aware, seems to have created a stronger cohesion in the wandering nanahualtin, and at the very least, angered them. They felt threatened by this new legal machinery of Inquisition. Any one of them could become the Inquisition's next victim, and they tried to stay one step ahead of the friars. But Mixcoatl and Tlaloc had the misfortune of attracting the attention of the native leader, Don Juan of Xicotepec, in the marketplace at Copila, and Mixcoatl had the greater misfortune of being caught. Marmolejo's report indicates that Mixcoatl's rhetoric had become more radical and anti-clerical as he felt the pressure of eluding Don Juan's men in the summer of 1537. During these few months of hiding, Mixcoatl began to make wild representations that included the prophesy of the return of Ocelotl, the conflation of himself with Tezcatlipoca, and allusions to cosmic warfare waged against the Christians.

When Mixcoatl was finally brought before Zumárraga in September 1537, he admitted, "It might have been four years ago that I became a god." Marmolejo's report had no dearth of witnesses who claimed that "they took [Mixcoatl] for a god" and therefore did as he said.[74] One wonders, however, if something was missing in Marmolejo's understanding or translation of the witnesses' words, especially the Nahuatl word for god, "*teotl.*" We have no way of knowing whether Marmolejo was making the translation or having the witnesses' testimony translated for him by a nahuatlahto. As Marmolejo could not have been in New Spain for more than six years, he probably needed a nahuatlahto to deal with the dialects of Nahuatl that he encountered in the highlands.[75] Possibly, the witnesses actually said "teotl" for the benefit of Marmolejo's more limited understanding of native religion. Or the witnesses may actually have said or meant "ixiptla," a close approximation of what Mixcoatl was doing and saying near the end. In any case, as seen in the earlier trial of Ocelotl, the ixiptla of Tezcatlipoca was carefully selected and trained to impersonate the presumed manners and talents of the god. Gruzinski has explained, "Where we would say that the man-god *possessed* the force *teotl*, the Nahua understood that the man-god *was teotl*, that he was the very authority that he adored."[76] Without doubt, the valley residents who encountered Ocelotl understood the subtle conflation of teotl and ixiptla, god and god-impersonator, in his representations of Tezcatlipoca. No one had accused Ocelotl of claiming to be the god Tezcatlipoca. Mixcoatl, however, intentionally conflated himself more directly with Tezcatlipoca. The question remains whether the sierra people who encountered Mixcoatl and referred to him as a "god" in Marmolejo's report were as familiar as the valley people with the subtle conflation of god and god-impersonator in the spiritual complex of Tezcatlipoca. On the whole, Marmolejo's report suggests that the sierra people may have been a bit confused.

While the valley shared some of their advanced religious ideas with the sierra in the prehispanic period, it does not necessarily follow that the education was complete. Tezcatlipoca did not fit into the class of primeval gods of the "núcleo duro" of weather and harvest.

As noted in the previous chapter, he was a complex god who reflected the anxieties and Weltanschauung of late prehispanic valley groups who were fighting for supremacy and survival in the great imperial game of central Mexico. Tezcatlipoca's ixiptla was revered and touted all over the Valley of Mexico for a year leading up to his sacrifice at his annual festival, Toxcatl, in the valley altepetl of Chalco.[77] In prehispanic times, Tezcatlipoca's ixiptla traveled only as far as Tepeapulco for feting. It was likely that people in the more remote parts of the sierra had heard about him but had never seen him or participated in his ceremonies.[78] There seems to have been a slight difference between the valley and sierra interpretations of Mixcoatl: the former seeing ixiptla and the latter seeing teotl. According to Marmolejo, Mixcoatl created "a great turmoil" one day in July 1537 when he entered the market of Huauchinango, at perhaps the high point of his notoriety. Many people came over from the market stalls to see him and offer him copal and amate.[79] But on that day there were also "many people in the market that had come from Texcoco and Cuautitlan [a large altepetl near Texcoco] and Mexico and other towns," who created a great fuss over Mixcoatl. "They went to see Andrés, as if he were a person known everywhere, and they brought him food and copal and paper."[80] This was precisely the kind of ritual behavior that was done in honor of an ixiptla in prehispanic times, and most particularly, the ixiptla of Tezcatlipoca, as he went from market to market in the valley and received the accolades of his devotees.

Yet the sierra people seemed confused about the subtleties of the ixiptla concept, at least as Mixcoatl, Tlaloc, and other nanahualtin were presenting it. In order to structure a devoted and powerful cult of Tezcatlipoca, the nanahualtin rhetorically floated alternative roles for themselves as Tezcatlipoca or his ixiptla or his priests. For example, Mixcoatl sometimes acted as a priest and threatened many of the barrio leaders of Huauchinango, the achcauhtin, "If you do not give me blankets, I will know what to do; I will speak to the god of fire and make him angry."[81] But when they brought the blankets, he also had them create for him a *ramada*, or woven canopy of flowers and pine boughs, and had them bring young women to sing for him "as if he were a god," writes Marmolejo. It was very similar to what was done for Tezcatlipoca's ixiptla when he visited various altepemeh.[82] Mixcoatl then instructed the achcauhtin on how to conduct a complex ceremony of reverence for the ixiptla: "Two *principales* [leaders] who have charge of the town held the papers [that Mixcoatl had prepared] in their hands," and "later he gave the paper to the principales, so that they could raise the paper with the proper reverence."[83]

Sometimes Mixcoatl refrained from eating in front of his devotees to give the impression that he was an actual god. He claimed, "I do not eat anything except copal and I want you to give it to me."[84] A resident of Apipilhuaxco seemed to learn the lesson well when he said that "since he did not see [Mixcoatl] eat anything, only ask for copal, and indeed he did not want to eat, he thought that [Mixcoatl] was a god and for that he honored him."[85] At one of Mixcoatl's meetings, his colleague Tlaloc told the congregation and its leaders, "the poor have suffered a great deal from too much rain, and Telpochtli [Tezcatlipoca] says that there is going to be no more rain and that he will send the clouds elsewhere."[86] This seemed to be in reference to Mixcoatl as Tezcatlipoca, for, in the next sentence, Tlaloc pointed to Mixcoatl and said, "Look and listen to what Tezcatlipoca wants to say."[87]

On the other hand, in Zacatepec, after Mixcoatl had performed his chants and ceremonies, he turned to the people and said, "Be happy, everyone, because Telpochtli says that it will rain and that you will harvest much corn. No hail will fall and you will lose nothing."[88] Here he seems to be the mediator or priest for Tezcatlipoca. We can imagine that there was considerable temporary advantage for the nanahualtin in having all of these interchangeable roles to play in the sierra. However, there was also a drawback to the inconsistency of this kind of preaching. Toward the end, when Mixcoatl found himself hotly pursued by Don Juan's men, he quickly left a town where he had boasted of his supernatural powers. One formerly devoted follower became extremely agitated when he saw that Mixcoatl had run away: "Why do you flee? This is not like a god. Who are you afraid of, if you are a god?"[89]

We can imagine that if Mixcoatl and the nanahualtin had had time to work out some of these complex and seemingly contradictory spiritual concepts in the sierra, time to successfully conflate the "núcleo duro" as understood in the sierra with new valley ideas, and also time to consolidate their commercial interests, they might have been able to form a cult. But the mission frontier was not far enough away. Though the friars did not understand the concepts that Mixcoatl was exploiting, they definitely understood the potential problems inherent in large crowds congregating around a spiritual man. As Fray Francisco de Lintorne warned, "In secret there are a lot of these prophets around the area."[90]

What was most alarming to the friars was testimony they received from a man named Cristóbal Papalotl, a new devotee of Mixcoatl and former loyal servant of Martín Ocelotl. When Ocelotl was banished, Papalotl had returned home to Tulancingo and lived quietly for a few months until he heard about Mixcoatl from two old women there. They said, "In Xucupan, the Telpochtli fellow, who is called Tezcatlipoca, said that he is not afraid of anybody." Papalotl went to Xucupan and heard Mixcoatl make some provocative comments that were typical of his last days before capture: "The oidores and the justices say what they want and stir things up against me as they want, but I did not go to Castile. Instead I went to the mountains with the rabbits and deer. It is true that my messenger went to Castile. We will see what the emperor orders. After my messenger returns, I will teach the people once more."[91] Papalotl immediately recognized that Mixcoatl was talking about Ocelotl, though Mixcoatl did not use the name, because the name of the old nahualli of Texcoco did not mean anything to the remote communities in the sierra. As noted in the previous chapter, the residual anger in Texcoco about the Ocelotl case was not about his persecution but that so many people and their estates had been caught up in the Inquisition's heavy-handed confiscation of Ocelotl's many properties. Nevertheless, Ocelotl's persecution was very much on the minds of the nanahualtin. His banishment was a direct threat to them as a group, and Papalotl was at least a sympathizer with them.

Two complex rhetorical associations are buried in Mixcoatl's comment. One was for the people in the sierra, and it was at once a call to a higher authority and a rejection of authority altogether. In Mixcoatl's interpretation of Spanish law, local Spanish authorities—the friars and justices—did not matter because he could appeal to the greater justice of a distant authority in Spain called the emperor, an esoteric but useful millennial concept for the indigenous people in the 1530s. The interesting reference about going to "the mountains with the rabbits and deer" has three possible anti-authoritarian symbolic associations for people in the sierra. According to Burkhart, the rabbit and deer are references to the Chichimec hunting ancestry and the Chichimec god Mixcoatl-Camaxtli. The rabbit and the deer were symbols for drunkenness and sexual proclivity, which suggested the edge of moral behavior, unsuitable for men but acceptable in the gods because they were gods. They denoted rebellion against norms, not only Spanish and Franciscan norms but also the rules of native leaders.[92]

The other message was for Papalotl and perhaps for all sympathizers of the beleaguered nanahualtin: that Mixcoatl represented the return of Ocelotl. The unhappy Papalotl, who missed his master and knew the imagery of Ocelotl was now considered subversive, immediately understood the millennial undercurrent in the message, as did the friars when they heard this testimony. Having met Papalotl in Xucupan and learning of his connection to Ocelotl, Mixcoatl had a private conversation with him in which he continued the millennial narrative: "A judge [apparently in Castile] told Martín Ocelotl, 'Look, do not return as a lizard or anything else; the emperor will only let you return as a man and he will let you leave Castile and return here [to New Spain]. The people can raise you up and place boughs and sacrifices before you in your honor and the common people will believe in you and we the Christians will return to Castile.'"[93] So, how would Mixcoatl know what the judge in Castile told Ocelotl? Because, as Papalotl dramatically testified, "He is Martín Ocelotl, whom Your Excellency sent to Castile."[94]

What do we make of Papalotl's equation of Mixcoatl and Ocelotl? It is very possible that Papalotl desired the return of his master so much that he conceived of Mixcoatl as the returned Ocelotl. Or perhaps Mixcoatl realized that the easiest way to make a devotee of Papalotl was to impersonate Ocelotl. In any case, Papalotl was the only witness who heard Mixcoatl's claim to be Ocelotl. The story, however, reflects the strategic thinking of Mixcoatl and the nanahualtin. By reasoning that the Spanish would leave if the nahualli refrained from turning into "a lizard or anything else," Mixcoatl seems to have believed that Ocelotl's problem was his power to turn himself into an animal. Perhaps nanahualtin who refrained from this personal power of supernaturalism (as well as human sacrifice) would be protected from Spanish wrath. This would allow Ocelotl to return —or Tezcatlipoca to return, because teotl, ixiptla, Mixcoatl, and Ocelotl were all becoming conflated at this point—and then pre-hispanic religion would not only reign, but "the Christians will return to Castile"—a strong millennial statement. The notion that Ocelotl's concession of his ability to turn into an animal would lead to his return, which would then lead to the departure of the Christians, was not a particularly coherent set of ideas, but then millennial ideas rarely are.

The consequence of this message was that Papalotl transferred his loyalty from Ocelotl to Mixcoatl, which was probably what Mixcoatl intended. Subsequently, perhaps on Mixcoatl's own initiative or encouraged by Papalotl, Mixcoatl told the people in the remote altepemeh where he lived in the high sierra, "Telpochtli asked that we give five arrowheads to make arrows with which to fight the Christians." Others testified that Mixcoatl requested "1,600 arrowheads in order to make arrows . . . and told them that this Telpochtli wants this in order to make arrows quickly, because Martín Ocelotl, who is in Texcoco, sent to me to make the said arrows in order to fight the Christians." Another witness remembered the same event but said the number of arrows was 3,600.[95] One of the witnesses who testified to this information opined that the arrows "were for defensive arms," which suggests that Mixcoatl wanted to defend himself in case Don Juan of Xicotepec finally arrested him.[96] However, when Zumárraga had Mixcoatl before him in the city of Mexico two months later, the cowering and frightened Mixcoatl would admit to almost all of his other sins except this one. He insisted that he had only asked for "arrowheads made of wood and that they gave him five,"[97] emphasizing that these were symbolic objects. True, they were prohibited, but they were not indicative of insurrection. Obviously, Mixcoatl knew well enough that collecting a real arsenal of weapons would have been sufficient for the Spanish to execute him.

Whether Mixcoatl had made a request for symbolic or real weapons remains inconclusive. Yet it almost does not matter in terms of the millennial outcome that Mixcoatl was proffering. The request for arrowheads tapped into strong local religious concepts of the sierra people, and in some ways, reflected Mixcoatl's maturity as a millennial and spiritual leader in the sierra. The arrowheads came from the myth-history of Mixcoatl-Camaxtli, the ancient god revered among the Otomi and Chichimecas of the sierra and the adjacent province of Tlaxcala. The Otomi had worshipped the god Mixcoatl-Camaxtli as the Red Tezcatlipoca, and valley myth had it that Tezcatlipoca had transformed himself into Mixcoatl-Camaxtli in order to bring fire to humans. (Therefore, Mixcoatl's previous statement that he would "speak to the god of fire and make him angry" probably referred to Mixcoatl-Camaxtli, or the Red Tezcatlipoca.) Mixcoatl-Camaxtli was the stellar hunting deity of the Chichimecas and his festival was Quecholli in the veintena of October–November, just before the military season and the great festivals in honor of the Mexica war god, Huitzilopochtli.[98] One of the signature acts during Quecholli was to make arrows and darts for five days, which were collected into bundles "to offer at the graves of the dead," specifically, the deceased tlahtoqueh.[99]

The major festival of Quecholli was celebrated most fervently in the Sierra de Puebla near Tlaxcala, which was not far from Mixcoatl's safe redoubt of altepemeh.[100] The Quecholli rites took the Chichimecas back to their hunting origins, and more importantly, to the "origins of cosmic warfare" of the gods. The ceremonies of arrow-making assured the Chichimecas that Mixcoatl-Camaxtli would look kindly on their military campaigns over the dry winter season beginning in November.[101] When Mixcoatl told the natives that Ocelotl "sent to [him] to make the said arrows in order to fight the Christians," he cleverly linked the call for cosmic warfare—associated with Mixcoatl-Camaxtli and Quecholli—to Ocelotl's return.[102] The friars were alarmed by the suggestion of real armed rebellion, but what they were actually facing, unbeknownst to them, was a spiritual struggle for the indigenous cosmology. Thus, in a move typical of millennial rationalization, Mixcoatl's message in the summer of 1537 blended together the religious fervor in the sierra for the ancient god Mixcoatl-Camaxtli with the recent history of Ocelotl's banishment.

Why did Mixcoatl, who had already had one close call with Don Juan's men in the early summer, push back so hard? The evidence in the transcript indicates that he had premonitions of his own arrest and fall from godlike status and seemed to waver between defiance and fear. Ten or twelve days before his capture, Mixcoatl sat near a fire with Papalotl and another devotee and pointed out to them an insect that "they call *pinauiztli*" and then a spider "called *texuantocatl*," which pursued it. He turned to his colleagues and said, "You see these insects; the people of the church will grab me very soon."[103] According to Sahagún, the word "pinauiztli" "comes from 'I am ashamed' or 'I shame someone' . . . something shameful, afflicting will befall me.'"[104] The "people of the church," the friars, were not necessarily the spider; but the sighting of the spider in prehispanic lore spelled doom, and the specter of doom would soon result in his shameful imprisonment.[105] Mixcoatl was arrested just two weeks later in early September 1537.

CONCLUSION

The public arrest of Mixcoatl, his subsequent transport down the mountain to the city of Mexico for a quick trial, and his return to Tulancingo for exemplary punishment were intended for one audience—the ineffectively Christianized leaders in the hinterland who needed to learn what to do with a wandering nahualli the next time. Thus, Marmolejo recommended to Zumárraga that "it would be well that the most principal towns where Andrés has done the most damage, at the very least the ones that did not bring Andrés here [to Tulancingo], have to come together to see how he is punished and be preached to about this."[106] The tlahtoqueh of the major altepemeh, such as Don Juan of Xicotepec and Don Julián, the tlahtoani of Tulancingo, who helped Marmolejo orchestrate the investigation of Mixcoatl in the sierra, were exonerated. In fact, Don Julián further profited, as he sold to his own wife at a very reasonable price the confiscated properties of Papalotl in Tulancingo.[107] The trial transcript is not specific about the lessons the less exalted leaders learned, though it is likely they were cowed by the friars and the greater tlahtoqueh. Nevertheless, while Don Juan's men carried Mixcoatl down the mountain in chains, the sierra experienced a particularly devastating rainstorm that swelled the rivers and destroyed crops and altepemeh everywhere, which the locals attributed to the jailing of Mixcoatl. Even Mixcoatl's guards were on the verge of bolting for most of the trip.[108]

The lesson the friars learned was that it had been unwise to banish Ocelotl, because they believed his absence had provided an opportunity for the remaining nanahualtin to inspire a millenarian backlash. Still, as we have seen, there was not much real evidence of the sierra people revolting at Mixcoatl's instigation. The Franciscans had missed a far more important lesson. That was how the natives clung to the "núcleo duro" of their religion, how they quickly sought out new spiritual leadership after their own official cults crumbled, how the new spiritual leadership could be quite creative and imaginative in adapting the "núcleo duro" in colonial times, and how the minor leaders who were closest to the people in the altepemeh were under considerable pressure to respond to the spiritual needs of their people when not directly threatened by the Spanish. All of these social facts would bode ill for the certainty of Christianization in any community that was beyond the immediate circle of Spanish control and beyond the archipelago of Franciscan conventos.

CHAPTER FOUR

THE KEEPERS OF THE HUITZILOPOCHTLIS
THE TRIAL OF MIGUEL POCHTECATL TLAYLOTLA

In the last few pages of his *History of the Indians of New Spain*, Fray Toribio de Benavente, known as Motolinía, discusses the Inquisition's hunt for "idols" in Mexico:

> In each town they had an idol or demon whom they considered and called their principal patron; this one they honored and adorned with many jewels and robes. . . . These principal idols that I speak of, the Indians concealed in the most secret place they could as soon as the great city of Mexico was taken by the Spaniards. . . . When they were questioned about the principal idols and their dress, they would dig one up, all rotten—of which I am a good witness, for I saw it happen many times. . . . In the years '39 and '40 some Spaniards—some of them with authority and some of them without it—to show that they were zealous in the Faith, and thinking that they were doing something worthwhile, began to stir things up and disinter the dead and put pressure upon the Indians to make them give up their idols. . . . Mingled with the righteous zeal that they displayed in hunting for the idols, there was no small amount of covetousness.[1]

The "principal patron" gods that Motolinía writes about, which in Inquisition trials the Spanish called "Huitzilobos" (a corruption of "Huitzilopochtlis"), and Zumárraga's intensive hunt for them from June 1539 to May 1540 are the subject of this chapter.[2] Though the Spanish were still woefully ignorant of native religion, their investigations—particularly while hunting for the Huitzilopochtlis—augmented their knowledge of native religion and piqued the interest of a small group of Franciscans around Zumárraga. On the other hand, authorities in Spain and local Spaniards such as Motolinía were troubled by the way Zumárraga's Inquisition would "stir things up" in the fledgling colony.

Zumárraga's investigative turn away from native nanahualtin such as Ocelotl and Mixcoatl and toward native leadership networks that were hiding idols or protecting those who did, represented an active new phase in his Inquisition. Testimony suggests that Zumárraga gave sermons throughout the Valley of Mexico in 1538–39, in which he demanded that natives hand over votive objects and denounce the secretive native lords. His fervent appeals finally inspired two young native men to come forward.

On June 20, 1539, Mateo, a native painter and illustrator for the friars, the noble son of a prehispanic lord and priest of Tenochtitlan, formally accused a network of nobles in the city of Mexico of hiding Huitzilopochtlis. However, what Mateo attempted to convey and what the Spanish actually understood about these objects were two different things. The Huitzilopochtlis were not statues, as the Spanish at first thought, but bundles containing relics associated with the Mexica war god, Huitzilopochtli, and several other gods in the Mesoamerican pantheon. The principal noble accused of keeping them was Miguel Pochtecatl Tlaylotla, a Mexica priest or nobleman. A half-dozen other nobles from Azcapotzalco, Culhuacan, and the city of Mexico were implicated in a conspiracy to hide the Huitzilopochtlis.

In a second case two days later, on June 22, 1539, Francisco, the brother of the tlahtoani of Chiconautla and a student at the Colegio de Santa Cruz de Tlatelolco, testified against the tlahtoani of Texcoco, Don Carlos Ometochtli, who was formally accused of bigamy, hiding sacred objects, and dogmatizing against Christianity. The Don Carlos trial is the subject of the next chapter. In many respects, however, the trials of Pochtecatl Tlaylotla and Don Carlos were interrelated, because the hunt for the Huitzilopochtlis motivated both trials. The two young neophytes' information gave Zumárraga ammunition for a series of showcase trials that confronted uncooperative native lords throughout the years 1539–40.

Three questions arise about this broad hunt for the Huitzilopochtlis. First, what exactly did these bundles represent to the native leaders who were protecting them? Second, who were the keepers of the bundles and what do their activities tell us about the strategies and adaptations that the early colonial native leaders undertook? Finally, what did the Franciscans know about the bundles, and what did Zumárraga hope to accomplish in tracking down these particular representations of native religiosity, even at the expense of agitating the native community and alarming the Spanish authorities?

THE HUITZILOPOCHTLIS
"Nobody who was not very important unwrapped it"

In order to explain the chain of custody and nature of the Huitzilopochtlis, we need to examine closely an illustration in native pictographic writing, glossed in Spanish, that accompanied Mateo's testimony and which he may well have drawn for Bishop Zumárraga (figure 1).[3] The illustration explains the custody of five bundles that are seen in the center of the picture. The left side of the picture shows the custody arrangement of the bundles from 1521 to 1526; the right side shows the transfer of custody in 1526. Mateo and later his brother, Pedro, testified that their father, Tlatolatl, seen at the lower left of figure 1, some time during or shortly after the conquest came into possession of a bundle he called a "Huitzilopochtli"—the black bundle on the left. It represented the Mexica tutelary god, or "principal patron." According to Mateo, "the idol was covered up and weighed a lot. . . . Nobody who was not very important unwrapped it. . . . They said that, if they did, they would die."[4] Thus, the brothers could not vouch for the exact contents of the Huitzilopochtli, but their father worshipped the bundle and also may have opened it periodically.

Later, Tlatolatl seems to have taken the Huitzilopochtli bundle to a group of nobles in Azcapotzalco, seen at the upper left of figure 1, who were in possession of four other bundles identified in the drawing as Cihuacoatl (a pre-Mexica earth goddess who is either the mother or wife of Mixcoatl-Camaxtli), Telpochtli (Tezcatlipoca), Titlauque Tezcatlipoca (Red Tezcatlipoca, another name for Mixcoatl-Camaxtli), and a fifth and mysterious god named Tepehua. Karttunen

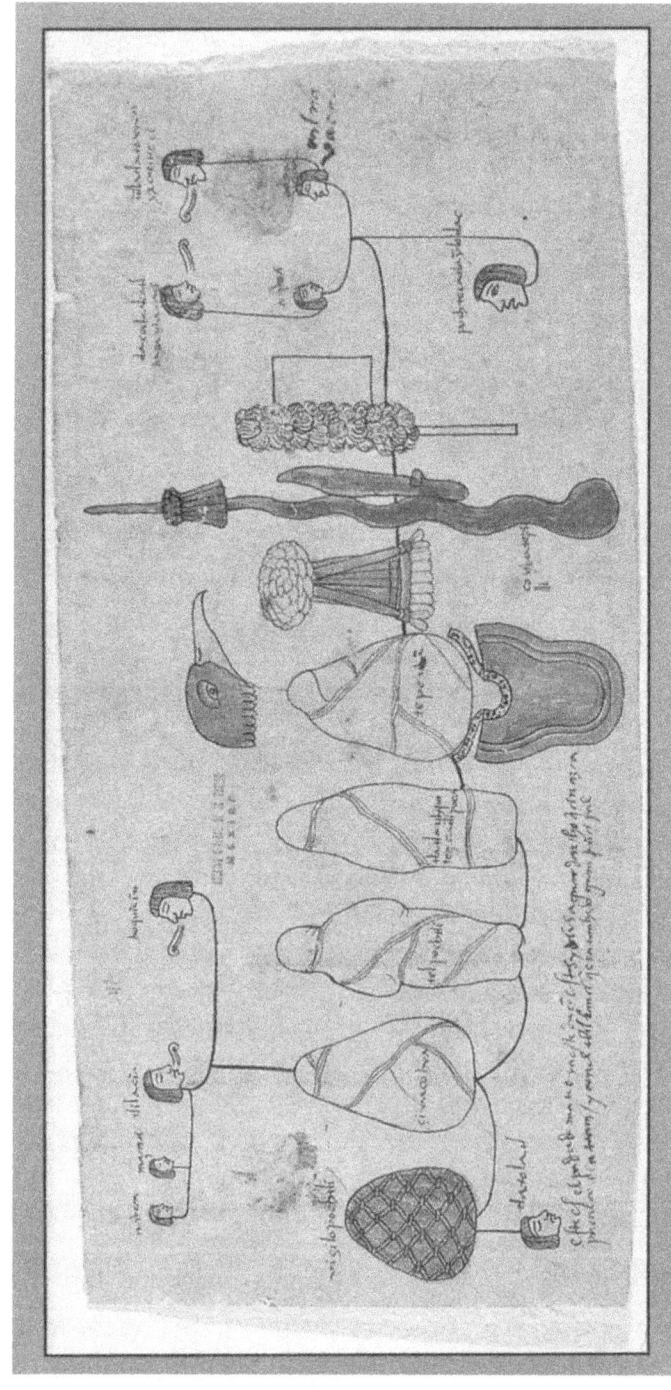

Figure 1. Native painting, probably made by Mateo in 1539, describing the dispersion of the Huitzilopochtlis. Adapted from Richard Greenleaf, *Zumárraga and the Mexican Inquisition*, 1961. Courtesy of Academy of American Franciscan History.

notes that *tepehuah* means "resident of a town."⁵ *Pehua* means "to go forth . . . or to drive forth something ahead of oneself, to vanquish one's enemies." She notes that it often occurs with the non-specific human prefix "*te-*," which may suggest someone who vanquishes his enemies. In general, the words "tepehua" and "pehua" were often used to denote a lord or various gods.⁶

Above the fifth bundle is a bird's head with a long beak. The feathers in the original colored manuscript are green with little red tufts of feathers around the eye. It lacks the characteristics of birds considered sacred in the Mexica pantheon, such as the quetzal or the hummingbird, or even the parrot, and it is not certain that the bird's head is intended to identify the fifth bundle.⁷ Below the bundle is an upside-down hill sign, or more exactly, a cave, with a strip of possible jaguar spots. The strip seems to closely associate this bundle or perhaps all the bundles with hiding in a cave, and the trial transcript indicates that the bundles were indeed located in caves for most of the years 1521–26. To the right of the bundles are a feathered panache; a *coatopilli* (serpent staff) with what is probably a decorative bunch of feathers hanging from its top; a knife or ax; and a sacrificial banner, probably of paper hanging from a narrow stick with eagle down (paper and eagle down are both associated with sacrifice).⁸ Central Mexican origin stories tell us that these ceremonial objects accompanied sacred bundles of the gods as they were carried from location to location, and they were used during important ceremonies.

According to Mateo and Pedro, the caretakers of the other four bundles were "Boquicin" (Oquitzin), who was a tlahtoani of Azcapotzalco at the time of the conquest,⁹ and "Tlilacin" (Tlilantzin), a "principal" who was possibly either Oquitzin's brother or the cihuacoatl (domestic ruler and second in command) of Azcapotzalco.¹⁰ The two men are indicated by the larger heads at the upper left with speech scrolls, a symbol of their status as leaders. Mateo's testimony indicates that Oquitzin received the bundles during or shortly after the fall of Tenochtitlan and kept them until about 1524. That year, Cortés forced Oquitzin and Tlilantzin to accompany him on his ill-fated journey to Honduras, along with Ixtlilxochitl, Cuauhtemoc, Cohuanacoch, and most of the rulers of the Valley of Mexico. During the nearly two years that the native leaders were in Honduras, Tlatolatl, father of Mateo and Pedro, apparently died, and the direction and care of the bundles fell to "the eldest principal" remaining in Azcapotzalco, a noble named Nahueca. His smaller head is shown at the far upper-left of the painting (the other leader, Mamol, is not explained in the transcript). Nahueca told Mateo and Pedro, "You know that we have to take care of these idols and keep them until the time that the lords demand them of us."[11] Thus, Mateo and Pedro apparently stayed on duty guarding all the bundles in Azcapotzalco until they learned in 1526 that Oquitzin and Tlilantzin had died in Honduras along with nearly a generation of prehispanic leaders.

Shortly afterward, according to Mateo's testimony, Yxcuecueci, the toltectlahtoani (tlahtoani of the Toltecas, which probably meant the Aztec empire or the empire of Motecuhzoma), and Nanahuanci, the tlacuxcalcatl (military leader), demanded the bundles. One night in 1526, Nahueca, Mateo, and Pedro took the idols "to Mexico to the house of Puxtecatl [Pochtecatl] Tlaylotla, who is now called Miguel, and they left them there."[12] They obviously moved the bundles at the behest of Yxcuecueci and Nanahuanci, whose heads (with two unknown subordinates) are shown with speech scrolls at the upper right of figure 1. Possession and transfer lines indicate that the two leaders gave the bundles to Miguel Pochtecatl Tlaylotla, the last known recipient of the bundles, whose head appears at the lower right.

Ten days later, Yxcuecueci and Nanahuanci called Mateo and Pedro to their presence. Nanahuanci told Mateo "in loving words, 'Oh poor ones, your father is dead, here I am if there is something you need, because your father was father to us all.'"[13] The two brothers were taken to Pochtecatl Tlaylotla's house, where they made offerings of ash and tortillas to the bundles. A Spanish gloss at the bottom of the illustration explains the transactions: "*Este es el padre de Mateo y a este dieron estos y dichos a guardar . . .* [illegible] *y dan al tlahtoanhi que era tambeyn un gran principal* (This is the father of Mateo and to him they gave these and the said [objects] to keep . . . [illegible] and they gave them to a tlahtoani who was also a great leader)." The tlahtoani referred to in the gloss is probably Yxcuecueci but could also be Nanahuanci.

Mateo and Pedro made it clear in their testimony before Zumárraga that this was the last they had seen of the idols. However, they admitted to hearing of them again. Yxcuecueci and Nanahuanci sent their man Coyoci to them, demanding, "These idols that you brought are not there [in Pochtecatl Tlaylotla's home]; where have you taken them?" Mateo and Pedro protested to Coyoci that they did not have the sacred bundles.[14] R. C. Padden has suggested that Coyoci's meeting with Mateo and Pedro was nothing more than a ruse. He believes that Nanahuanci was actually an obscure character in postconquest history named Anahuacaca. Anahuacaca was a "prince of the house" (possibly a tlazopilli, esteemed son) who had a legitimate claim to be tlahtoani of Mexico, as he was Cuauhtemoc's nephew and a direct descendant of Motecuhzoma; thus he had a vital interest in keeping the sacred bundles safely out of the hands of the Spanish. He sent Coyoci to throw the brothers off the scent of the idols or perhaps even to intimidate them.[15]

Mateo's and Pedro's lives after that incident probably gave the lords who were hiding the idols in the city of Mexico good cause to distrust them. Their father, Tlatolatl, had obviously been esteemed as a high priest and probably a *tlacuilo* (scribe). He had very likely taught this skill to Mateo, who took up the painting trade as a young man.[16] After their father's death, like most young nobles of Mexico, Mateo and Pedro eventually came into the orbit of the friars. Although the trial transcript uncharacteristically omits details of his baptism and Christian education, Mateo seems to have been on familiar terms with the friars and had found employment as a tlacuilo with them, possibly at the Colegio de Santa Cruz de Tlatelolco. Mateo's illustration, in its clean and neat regularity, is reminiscent of the figure drawings in the early colonial *Codex Mendoza*, a compendium of drawings about Mexica trade and economy. The *Codex Mendoza* was produced in the pictographic Nahuatl style by a group of native illustrators in the city of Mexico in 1540–41, about the time of this Inquisition trial.[17]

In 1538, while the Inquisition proceeded apace, Mateo's brother, Pedro, suggested that they tell the Franciscans about their long-ago, direct experience of guarding the bundles. The transcript tells us that in June 1538, Pedro was in Toluca, a major altepetl west of the city of Mexico, when he heard one of Zumárraga's sermons exhorting the natives to turn in anyone who knew of hidden idols. In the city of

Mexico, Pedro argued with his brother to "go to Father Alonso de Santiago so that he can fix this and save your soul."[18] Exactly when the brothers went to Fray Alonso, who may have been their local friar, can not be pinpointed, but it seems that the brothers went back and forth about the possibility of revealing the existence of the Huitzilopochtlis for much of the year. They may have felt pressured by a trial that Zumárraga convened in November 1538 against a group of lords hiding religious objects in Azcapotzalco. The objects there were not the same Huitzilopochtlis that the brothers had guarded; nevertheless, it was logical for Mateo and Pedro to fear that their participation in hiding the bundles so many years before might eventually be revealed. In any case, they probably told their story to Fray Alonso in early to middle June of 1539.[19]

This brings us back to the question of the nature of the Huitzilopochtlis that were so carefully hidden by a network of high-placed nobles in the years 1520–26. It is evident from Zumárraga's initial questions to the witnesses and the Inquisition text that the interrogators at first thought the bundles were "wood or stone" statues of Huitzilopochtli. Mateo had said they were "the idols that had been in the pyramid of Huitzilopochtli with many other demons that they adored,"[20] and the conquerors had told the friars that those idols were statues of Huitzilopochtli. But Bishop Zumárraga also asked for an illustrated rendering, which indicates that he began to suspect at the time of Mateo's testimony in June 1539 that these bundles were different from the statues and hidden votive objects that Zumárraga, the friars, and the conquerors were accustomed to seeing.

And indeed they were different. The bundles represented a very complex linkage of gods, festivals, and relics. Representations of the Mexica gods came in three varieties. One was the actual statuary, large and small, of clay, wood, or stone, the kind that Motecuhzoma had shown to Cortés in the Templo Mayor and that the conqueror claimed to have destroyed. The second was temporary, but in most cases more precious: a figure made of the dough of amaranth seeds held together with a honey substance and sacrificial blood and shaped into humanlike figures for festivals; the dried dough was intended for communal consumption. Motolinía's description, at the beginning of this chapter, of "rotten" votive objects that natives dug up to appease the Spanish refers to this type of representation. Sahagún included the Huitzilopochtli dough god in his description of the Toxcatl festival of May 1520 in book 12 of his *Florentine Codex*.[21]

The third and most secret and sacred representation, called tlaquimilloli (sacred bundle), contained actual relics associated with the gods. From all the testimony and Mateo's painting, the Huitzilopochtlis were evidently this third type of representation, about which the Spanish knew very little in 1539. These bundles contained what Christians would have associated with saint's relics—the bones or other precious physical remains of the saints while they lived on the earth. Philip II, the future king of Spain, was known to possess one of the largest collections of saints' relics in Europe, so the general sentiments expressed by the native worship of the relics would not have been foreign to the Spanish. Moreover, the Inquisition transcribers would probably have readily described them in Spanish as "reliquias" instead of "Huitzilopochtlis" if the Inquisition secretary, Zumárraga, or Fray Alonso de Santiago (the friar to whom Mateo initially turned) had understood what they were.

The concept of tlaquimilloli was central to complex ideas about native spiritual representation, which Zumárraga confessed that he found "difficult to understand." For the Mesoamericans, teotl (god) was not the physical statue. "Its actual meaning is something close to the Polynesian idea of mana, a sacred and impersonal force or a concentration of power.... Sacred power, mana, or teotl is called forth by the creation of *teixiptla*" (ixiptla), or statues, or most important, the tlaquimilloli.[22] When Ocelotl and Mixcoatl presented themselves as the ixiptla, or impersonator, of Tezcatlipoca, they were in effect invoking teotl, and as his physical representatives, they *became* the god for the time they were engaged in ceremonial performance. A tlaquimilloli, however, was even more revered because it was believed to contain the actual relics of the gods. The natives believed, according to Alfredo López Austin, that "the patron gods strengthened their co-essence [oneness] with their charges [believers] by means of a relic, a bequest that each patron god left to its people."[23] Central to Mesoamerican spirituality was the belief that humans owed the gods everything because the gods had sacrificed themselves to a "death they had to undergo in Teotihuacan so that the sun could follow its path through the sky." Before death, the gods left behind with their worshippers things they wore or parts of their bodies. The believers wrapped these relics around "certain poles" made of wood, and then wrapped them a second time with high-quality cotton wraps.[24] The relics included loincloths, femurs, snakeskins, jaguar skins, and precious green stones that represented the heart of the god. Only the high priests of the cults, such as Tlatolatl and possibly Miguel Pochtecatl Tlaylotla, could unwrap these sacred bundles, a ceremony that was witnessed by the highest members of the nobility and priest cults.

The tlaquimilloli is prominent in Mesoamerican pilgrimage stories.[25] For the Mexica, the tlaquimilloli and staffs, panaches, and headdresses of Huitzilopochtli were carried by four priests on their journey from their mythical place of origin in Aztlan through various impermanent temples throughout the Valley of Mexico and finally to the island on the lake that became their great city of Tenochtitlan. At each location along this long pilgrimage in search of their permanent home, the Mexica built a temple in which their highest priests would periodically unwrap the tlaquimilloli and use the loincloth in ceremonies for their most important monthly festivals and rites. They eventually wrapped up the relics and hid them in the most secret places of the Templo Mayor; only the high priest and the tlahtoani knew their whereabouts. "The people regarded these sacred and protective bundles as their legacies, their trusts (*intlapial*); and they were obliged to worship them as a heritage."[26] The *Codex Borgia* provides an excellent illustration of the sacred power of the tlaquimilloli, showing the moment that the high priest unwraps the bundle and releases a host of "essences" to all corners of the universe.[27]

The tlaquimilloli also had an important political dimension that was represented in the sacred precincts. All communities had a tlaquimilloli for each of their principal patrons, their tutelary gods. The altepemeh subject to Tenochtitlan were obliged to hand over their tlaquimilloli when they were conquered by the victorious Mexica. The Mexica, in turn, kept these sacred bundles in a building in the sacred precinct called the *coacalco* (pantheon), a "kind of prison for foreign gods."[28] As the tipped-over and burning temple in Mexica manuscripts "signifies that the structure, symbols, gods, energy and essences of a community have been destroyed,"[29] so the imprisonment of the tlaquimilloli—the essences of the conquered altepetl—had the effect of discouraging revolt against the Mexica. The Mexica themselves had suffered under this coldhearted reasoning. When they were subject to the Culhua of Culhuacan, about 150 years before, "they gave their divine relics to the Culhua as a sign of their submission."[30]

The tlaquimilloli was also essential to the celebration of the veintena of Toxcatl. This ancient festival was held in late April to early May to honor Tezcatlipoca, the closest thing to an overarching god in the Mesoamerican pantheon shared by all communities. As has been noted in the two previous chapters, the ixiptla who impersonated Tezcatlipoca journeyed to many places around the valley before he was ritually sacrificed in Chalco, giving Toxcatl a broad ceremonial base in the Valley of Mexico. Gods revered in the month of Toxcatl also included Huitzilopochtli, Cihuacoatl, and Quetzalcoatl, shown in Mateo's illustration and perhaps linking it to the Toxcatl ceremony.[31]

In Tenochtitlan, the Mexica attempted to meld the power of Tezcatlipoca with that of their patron god, Huitzilopochtli. As part of the festivities for Toxcatl, they built their giant dough statue of Huitzilopochtli at the top of the Templo Mayor, unwrapped the tlaquimilloli of Huitzilopochtli, and reverently carried his loincloth up the steps of the pyramid to the dough figure as one of the high points of the festival.[32] Moreover, as *hueytlahtoani* (great leader) of the Valley of Mexico, Motecuhzoma was personally responsible for the selection and care of the ixiptla who played the part of Tezcatlipoca. He also selected an ixiptla for the god Tlacapehua, companion of Tezcatlipoca, who likewise participated in the yearlong ritual performance. The Mexica, however, gradually came to rename this companion "Huitzilopochtli," a late-prehispanic theological move to elevate their own tutelary god in the Mesoamerican pantheon.[33] The ixiptla imitating Huitzilopochtli led a serpentine dance of young men and women in another high point of the Toxcatl festival. Shortly after Tezcatlipoca was ritually sacrificed in Chalco, his companion, the ixiptla of Huitzilopochtli, was sacrificed in Tenochtitlan.

Politics and cosmology were closely intertwined in most ceremonies, and particularly in the festival of Toxcatl. The two god impersonators, Tezcatlipoca and Huitzilopochtli, were the sacrificial representatives of Motecuhzoma. The Mexica king, as hueytlahtoani, the closest representation of the gods on earth, was obligated to reenact the sacrifice of the gods during Toxcatl. Naturally, he could not sacrifice himself, so he selected the ixiptla to be sacrificed on his behalf. Motecuhzoma was the official greeter of the two god impersonators and their official dresser, often calling them "his beloved gods."[34]

Besides the ceremonies of the god impersonators, another ceremony involved the tlaquimilloli. Guilhem Olivier says that the loincloth of the Huitzilopochtli bundle was unwrapped at Motecuhzoma's observance of Toxcatl, but it was also unwrapped and used ceremonially for the enthronement and funerary rites of each tlahtoani.[35] Thus, the Toxcatl festival not only conflated traditional requests for a rainy season and good harvest and honor for the great sacrifice of the gods, but when properly performed, it reinforced the rulership of Motecuhzoma and the Mexica. Given the political and religious importance of the tlaquimilloli, it is understandable that the colonial Mexica leaders in the midst of the conquest were obliged to preserve and hide each tlaquimilloli. It was a desperate and heroic effort to facilitate the possible revival of Mexica kingship, even as the Spanish threatened to overrun and finally overran their civilization.

THE KEEPERS
"Well-known prophets in their heathenness"

The Inquisition officers knew little of the political and religious complexity of the objects they sought, but they understood that the Valley of Mexico leaders considered them important to the preservation of native religion. Still, Zumárraga faced something of a problem in Mateo's and Pedro's testimony—they could only trace the path of the Huitzilopochtlis up to 1526, twelve years earlier. The logical place to pick up the trail was at the residence of Miguel Pochtecatl Tlaylotla in the city of Mexico. Pochtecatl Tlaylotla at first denied having the sacred bundles and then admitted that he had kept them for ten days. He testified, according to the trial scribe, that two men, who were apparently no longer living, "carried the five idols from there, the same ones who had brought them, and he does not know where they took them."[36]

As the related trial of Don Carlos of Texcoco was reaching a climax in the fall of 1539, Zumárraga hit a plateau in his case against Pochtecatl Tlaylotla. Unable to locate other keepers of idols, he turned in October to a young native nobleman, Francisco, who had been the principal accuser of Don Carlos of Texcoco in his trial (see chapter 5). Francisco helped get the case of the Huitzilopochtlis rolling again by implicating a list of men he claimed were "well-known prophets in their heathenness," meaning that they were among the high priests of Tenochtitlan in the time of Motecuhzoma.[37] Two men on the list were brought before Zumárraga. The first, Culoa Tlapisque, identified himself as a "prophet who kept track of the demons and was responsible for taking care of them."[38] Culoa Tlapisque was therefore a high priest, or quetzalcoatl; he was fifty-seven years old and had never been baptized. The second, Don Pedro Achacatl, was a prominent Mexica nobleman; he was fifty-five years old and had been baptized only the year before in 1538.[39] Late baptism or no baptism at all was a pretty good indication of obduracy on the part of these men.

A frightened Culoa Tlapisque nevertheless testified against his fellow accused. He said that in 1530–31; that is, four or five years after the bundles had been brought to Miguel Pochtecatl Tlaylotla's home, Don Pedro Achacatl and other prominent nobles of the city of Mexico had talked to him as if they knew where the idols were, and that Don Pedro had told him in 1532, "I have seen my god with my own eyes and he is in Tepuchcalco and in Temascaltitlan, because they keep them there."[40] Tepuchcalco was a sacred cave used in prehispanic religious rites near Coatlinchan, in the Acolhua area of the valley, just south of Texcoco (see map 4). When Zumárraga asked Don Pedro Achacatl about the hiding place, he angrily denied everything Culoa Tlapisque had said. Zumárraga decided to give Don Pedro a second chance to "search his memory well and tell the truth and that he could confess in eight days."[41] But Zumárraga did not interrogate Don Pedro again, and the nobleman may well have disappeared after his first close brush with the Inquisition. We also have no testimony to indicate that the cave near Coatlinchan was found and searched, but it seems likely that Zumárraga attempted it and probably failed.

Zumárraga kept pulling at the threads of these testimonies, following leads in Culoa Tlapisque's story to Culhuacan and in December

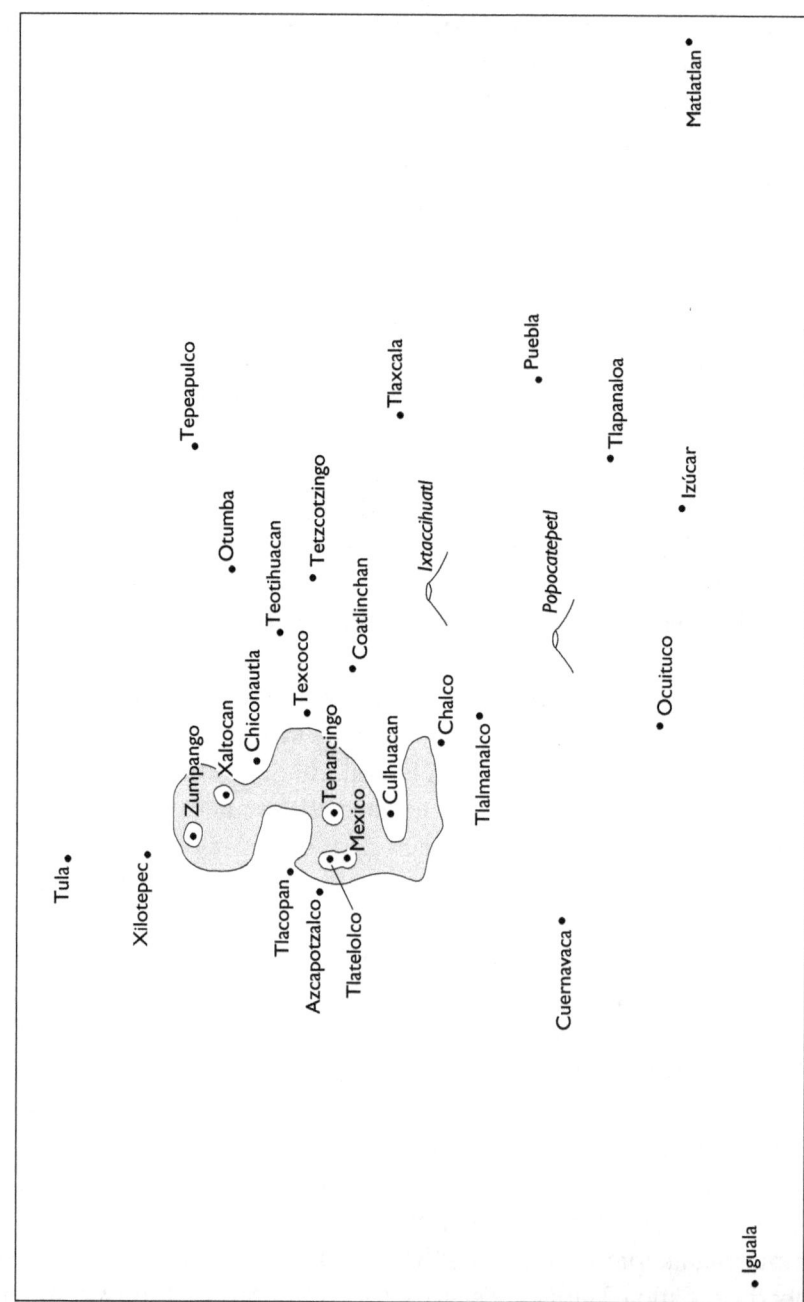

Map 4. Mexico, Texcoco, and Surrounding Area

1539 bringing in its tlahtoani, Don Baltasar, for questioning. Don Baltasar desperately tried to distract the interrogators with several complicated stories about the journeys of the sacred bundles between 1520 and 1526.[42] But he could not add the next chapter after 1526. A Culhuacan nobleman, Don Andrés, testified more fulsomely but could not say what had become of the bundles since 1526. Zumárraga released the two nobles.

His inquisitors tried cases in Ocuituco in August and Izúcar in September, looking for the sacred bundles, but it was evident that these other cases had nothing to do with the bundles. The investigative path led back to Pochtecatl Tlaylotla and Culoa Tlapisque, so the bishop brought them in again for further interrogation.[43] From June 1539 to May 1540, Zumárraga kept Pochtecatl Tlaylotla locked up, and the Mexica priest's health began to deteriorate. He was brought before Zumárraga in March 1540 and told that he would soon be tortured unless he revealed what had become of the sacred bundles after 1526. Pochtecatl Tlaylotla's attorney managed to delay the torture until May 1540, when Zumárraga finally ordered for him to be put on the *burro* (rack) and given the *toca* (water torture). Before the torture, Pochtecatl Tlaylotla defiantly said through his interpreter, he "knows nothing and if [the torture] kills him, so be it."[44] Pochtecatl Tlaylotla withstood the rack but lost consciousness with the second jar of water in the water torture. Perhaps fearing that he might kill Pochtecatl Tlaylotla, the torturer suspended the procedure, saying, "the man is old and skinny," and referred the matter back to Zumárraga.[45] The bishop abruptly suspended the case against Pochtecatl Tlaylotla and ordered him to the custody of Fray Pedro de Gante of the monastery of San Francisco, who was supposed to instruct him and try to get more information out of the unreformed victim about "where he is keeping the idols."[46] We hear nothing more about Pochtecatl Tlaylotla or the Huitzilopochtlis after May 1540. But Zumárraga's concern about killing the man and his willingness to give up his yearlong investigation so abruptly suggests that the bishop was already beginning to feel the general disapproval for his Inquisition activities by the early summer of 1540, the reasons for which are discussed in the following chapters.[47] While the historian can become as frustrated as

Zumárraga in sorting out the complicated and contradictory stories of these many witnesses, nevertheless, a reasonable chronology about the journeys of the sacred bundles in the colonial period can be discerned from the testimony and our current knowledge of native religion. The path of the sacred bundles from the conquest to the early 1530s tells us a great deal about the intentions of the keepers and Mexica resistance in the early colonial years. In Cortés's second letter to Charles V, he describes the "idols" that Motecuhzoma showed him in the Templo Mayor in the winter of 1519–20. "The most important of these idols, and the ones in whom they have most faith, I had taken from their places and thrown down the steps, and I had those chapels where they were, cleaned, for they were full of the blood of sacrifices; and I had the images of Our Lady and of other saints put there, which caused Mutezuma and the other natives some sorrow."[48] As has been noted, these statues were "of wood and stone," not tlaquimilloli, and we can establish that it was unlikely that Motecuhzoma would have given Cortés access to the bundles, the most sacred and necessary ritual objects of Mexica kingship and religion. Nevertheless, Cortés believed that he had overturned their most important idols, and he and the conquerors proceeded to loot the Templo Mayor of all the gold, silver, and precious stones contained there.

Given the Spanish looting and overturning of the statuary in the Templo Mayor, Motecuhzoma, according to three witnesses, became concerned about the safety of the tlaquimilloli in the spring of 1520 and signaled to his confidants that he wanted the sacred bundles removed from the Templo Mayor and even Tenochtitlan.[49] But the testimony is not consistent about if and when this happened. As best as can be determined, the Mexica leaders may have taken some of the sacred bundles out of Tenochtitlan in May 1520.

About that time, Cortés had to go to Veracruz to quash the expedition of Pánfilo Narváez, who had come to Mexico on the order of the governor of Cuba to arrest Cortés. Cortés left Motecuhzoma and the situation in Tenochtitlan in the hands of his most trusted lieutenant, Pedro de Alvarado. In Cortés's absence, Alvarado gave the Mexica nobility permission to hold the festival of Toxcatl in the sacred precinct, which would have been about May 1520. Having built the giant dough figure of Huitzilopochtli, the native priests performed the ceremony of unwrapping the tlaquimilloli and carrying Huitzilopochtli's loincloth up the steps to the dough figure. They followed this ceremony with the famous serpentine dance of the young noblemen and women. In the midst of the dance, according to the native writers of the *Florentine Codex*, Alvarado and his men attacked the Mexica nobility, killing many. The Spaniards captured the two ixiptla of Tezcatlipoca and Huitzilopochtli and tortured them, trying to determine if Motecuhzoma had used the festival as a pretext to rally the Mexica to slaughter the Spaniards and their allies.[50]

The preemptive Spanish massacre of the nobility and torture of the god impersonators sparked a general riot in the city, and soon the Spanish were isolated in the sacred precinct along with Motecuhzoma and the highest members of the Mexica elite. Hearing of the desperate situation, Cortés rushed back to Tenochtitlan in early June with a large army of Spanish and indigenous soldiers. Because not only the tlaquimilloli of Huitzilopochtli, but also of Cihuacoatl, Tezcatlipoca, Mixcoatl-Camaxtli, and Quetzalcoatl were worshipped in the festival of Toxcatl, it is probable that Motecuhzoma tried to arrange for the removal of the bundles shortly after the disastrous massacre. The fact that he wanted to take the most potent symbols of Mexica kingship out of Tenochtitlan suggests that he feared his life was at an end but wished to preserve the possibility of the revival of Mexica kingship should he die and the city fall. Notwithstanding his air of defeat, which both Spanish and natives at the time commented on, Motecuhzoma was not prepared to hand over the "essence" of Mexica civilization to Cortés and make his people subject to the Spanish in the way they had once been subject to the Culhua.[51]

Removal of the bundles to safe redoubts was the aim of the next actions of the nobility. Recounting these events in the trial almost two decades later, Don Baltasar and Don Andrés of Culhuacan said that Motecuhzoma gave the responsibility of removing the tlaquimilloli to his son Axayaca, and that the intended destination seemed to be Culhuacan. They had heard this from their cousin (possibly Pitzotzin, the tlahtoani of Culhuacan at the time of the conquest).[52] Here the testimony about what happened in May 1520 is contradictory. The cousin of Don Baltasar and Don Andrés said that some bundles had not arrived (perhaps the Huitzilopochtli bundle). But two bundles—Tezcatlipoca and Topilci—were supposed to have been hidden in a cave called "Tencuyoc" (Tenayuca) near Culhuacan. Tenayuca or any of the other caves where these bundles were later taken could be the upside-down cave in Mateo's illustration. The bundle called "Tepehua" in the illustration may be the one referred to as "Topilci" in the trial transcript (since we know the names of all the other bundles). "Topilci" literally means "our lords," which could mean almost any god bundle. Many Spanish accounts of the time refer to the Toltec god Quetzalcoatl interchangeably as Topiltzin. However, while these comparisons between illustration and text are interesting, we can not say definitively that the fifth bundle was Quetzalcoatl.

Don Baltasar and Don Andrés of Culhuacan testified that the Tezcatlipoca bundle was taken to the island altepetl of Xaltocan, north of Lake Texcoco. Next, it was thought to have been taken to a sacred spring called El Peñol on the sacred island called Tenancingo, just east of Tenochtitlan in Lake Texcoco.[53] Culhuacan and Tenancingo are two sites that the ixiptla who represented Tezcatlipoca is supposed to have visited during the veintena of Toxcatl, so these would be logical, safe, and sacred places to put the tlaquimilloli of Tezcatlipoca if it was in fact spirited out of Tenochtitlan in May 1520.[54] The two Culhua nobles claimed that the Cihuacoatl and Tepehua (Topilci) bundles were also carried to Xaltocan and then to Xilotepec, an altepetl north of the lakes, in the Mexica tributary territory.[55] These locations had caves that were destinations for prehispanic ceremonies and pilgrimages. Culoa Tlapisque testified that the sacred bundles were taken to Tula, north of Xilotepec, a hint that the intended final home for the sacred bundles may have been the ancestral home of the Toltecas.[56] Thus, Mateo's illustration and trial testimony suggest that the sacred bundles of these important gods were separated in May 1520, sent to various secret and sacred locations, and then brought together and taken to Azcapotzalco at a later date. The tlaquimilloli of Huitzilopochtli, however, may have stayed in Tenochtitlan or perhaps was removed briefly and returned. Historical accounts of the fall of Tenochtitlan correspond with that scenario.

In late June, the Mexica uprising became so intense that Cortés and his army were forced to leave Tenochtitlan. In the last days before the

Spanish left, Motecuhzoma died under circumstances disputed to this day. On June 30, 1520, according to Cortés's record, the Spanish made a costly retreat they called the "noche triste" (sad night), because, as they marched by night over the causeways and out of the city, they were attacked and lost half of their army as well as the great treasures looted from the Templo Mayor. Eventually, Cortés was able to bring a small part of his army to the safe harbor of the neighboring kingdom of Tlaxcala. The native accounts of the *Florentine Codex* indicate that the triumphant Mexica believed the Spanish were too defeated to return, and throughout the year from June 1520 to June 1521, the Mexica went back to their normal ceremonial life.[57] They cleaned the Templo Mayor, fished the gold and treasure out of the lake where the desperate Spanish soldiers had abandoned it, and celebrated each of the festivals, including Toxcatl in May 1521. For that, they would have needed the tlaquimilloli of Huitzilopochtli. Moreover, Motecuhzoma's successor in the kingship of Tenochtitlan, Cuitlahuac, who reigned from June to November 1520, would have needed the tlaquimilloli of Huitzilopochtli for his enthronement rites, as would Cuauhtemoc later that year when he was enthroned after the untimely death of Cuitlahuac.[58] But Cortés had not gone away; he stayed in Tlaxcala and meticulously organized a second assault on Tenochtitlan and by June 1521 had brought the bulk of his Spanish and indigenous army to the western lakeshore nearest the city.

The Mexica leadership over the next sixty days was again forced to pursue the same goal as Motecuhzoma—to keep the "essence" of Huitzilopochtli, his sacred bundle, out of Spanish hands in order to preserve Mexica kingship in case of defeat. From June to August 1521, Cortés laid siege to the island and sent three armies from the north, south, and west into Tenochtitlan. Taking the tlaquimilloli out would have been most disheartening, so it was probably not done until it appeared that the Mexica could no longer repel the Spanish and indigenous army. That moment, in a sense, is chronicled in the Inquisition testimony of Don Baltasar and Don Andrés of Culhuacan, whose cousin claimed to have been witness to the events.

> As the war was going on in the plaza of Mexico between the natives and the Christians, [the cousin] climbed to the top of the pyramid of

Ochilopuztl [Huitzilopochtli] with the lord of Tacuba, who was called Tepanquetzal and the Christians called Don Pedro, who had a mirror the Indians called naualtezcatl that could foretell the future. . . . Don Pedro took out the mirror in the presence of Cohuanocotzin [Cohuanacoch], lord of Texcoco, and of Ocuici [Oquitzin], lord of Azcapotzalco . . . and Cuauhtemoctzin was also supposed to see it but he was too discouraged to go there. . . . [Having looked into the mirror,] Don Pedro told them: "Tell the señor, Cuauhtemoctzin, that he is defeated because Mexico is lost and everything must fall."[59]

The details of many native stories of the conquest must be judged carefully, as the nature of Mesoamerican history required such omens of great transforming events for the historical world to make sense. Whether the foretelling of the end happened in this way or not, the story suggests many logical probabilities that the cousin may indeed have witnessed and that Don Baltasar and Don Andrés retold as a way of explaining the fate of the tlaquimilloli. First, the removal of the tlaquimilloli was a decision of all of the high leadership of the alliance, and, second, those decisions were not made until it was obvious that the Spanish would take over Tenochtitlan. Cortés's letters affirm that when the Spanish took over the marketplace next to the sacred precinct, the plaza of Mexico, he learned from a couple of Mexica refugees that the Mexica in their shrinking redoubt of the sacred precinct were starving and that "we already knew that the Indians in the city were very scared."[60]

The taking of the plaza was, according to Cortés, just days before the Christian feast of Santiago, July 25, 1521, and therefore, the consultation of the native leaders on the pyramid was either in the last days of July or the first few days of August. That the lord of Azcapotzalco, Oquitzin, was there at the meeting suggests that he helped coordinate the removal of the sacred bundles to their eventual temporary home in Azcapotzalco. It was probably also at this time that the attempted escape of Cuauhtemoc was planned. About a week later the defenses of the Mexica collapsed in Tenochtitlan. On August 13, 1521, as thousands got into canoes and even swam into the lake in order to escape the Spanish and indigenous armies that were pillaging the city, Cuauhtemoc attempted to leave in a canoe from the north side of the island near Tlatelolco, perhaps not coincidentally heading for the lakeshore near Azcapotzalco.[61]

If Cuauhtemoc had been successful in his escape, he might have been able to hide with the tlaquimilloli in Azcapotzalco and head west toward Toluca or perhaps north to Tula. From there he might have been able to stage a serious resistance. But the Spanish captured him on the lake in August. A living, though captive, Cuauhtemoc was still a powerful symbol of the viability of Mexica rule, especially with the sacred bundles in hiding and out of Spanish hands. But this hope was severely disrupted in 1524 when Cortés took the native nobility to Honduras, including Oquitzin, Cuauhtemoc, Cohuanacoch, and the tlahtoani of Culhuacan, and executed them, eliminating a generation of valley rulers. If Cortés had been aware of the existence of the tlaquimilloli of Huitzilopochtli, he probably would have ransacked the various altepemeh of the valley looking not only for it, but also the gold and silver that he assumed accompanied all important representations of Huitzilopochtli. As it was, Cortés tortured and executed numerous Mexica high priests and leaders in fall 1521 in a futile effort to locate the gold and precious goods his men had lost on the causeway on the night of the "noche triste."[62]

In sum, the story of the journey of the sacred bundles and the effort to shape a Mexica resistance to Spanish rule after the conquest went hand in hand. Tlatolatl, the father of Mateo and Pedro, was enlisted to take the tlaquimilloli of Huitzilopochtli from Tenochtitlan, possibly to Azcapotzalco, in August 1521, to await the instructions of an escaped Cuauhtemoc and the other great tlahtoqueh of the alliance. The other sacred bundles were apparently in other locations, possibly outside of Tenochtitlan, but managed to find their way to Oquitzin and Tlilantzin in Azcapotzalco. Oquitzin, Tlilantzin, Tlatolatl, and later Nahueca protected them and kept them so secret that the Spanish were unaware of them. The Honduras expedition of 1524–26 dealt the hopes of Mexica kingship a heavy but not fatal blow. Anahuacaca, a nephew and presumed successor to Cuauhtemoc, seems to have wanted to resist Spanish colonization and ordered the tlaquimilloli brought back to the city of Mexico in 1526, probably to keep alive the possibility of a Mexica reemergence. But Cortés did not allow the young prince any form of rule. Instead, he put more compliant and less prestigious indigenous leaders in charge of the native barrios of the city of Mexico—Don Pablo Xochiquentzin, who called Ocelotl to his deathbed for medical help, was one—and Anahuacaca died in 1539 never having managed to rally other leaders to his cause.

The plight of the sacred bundles suggests that some of these other prehispanic leaders who wanted to resist Spanish rule lost heart in the years after the execution or death of their leaders in Honduras in 1524–26. One of the last keepers of the Huitzilopochtlis, Culoa Tlapisque, the high priest of Culhuacan, testified about a conversation he had in 1530–31 with nobles in the city of Mexico that indicated this gradual change of heart:

> In Azcapotzalco, Don Diego [Huanitzin], the lord of Mexico now, and [Don Pedro] Achacatl and three other nobles discussed among themselves what to do about the friars preaching to them about giving up the Huitzilobos [Huitzilopochtlis]. Don Diego said that they ought to give the Huitzilobos to the friars. Achacatl said that they should not give them up or say anything about them to the friars, and so they did not.[63]

Don Diego Huanitzin was a very important colonial noble, the nephew of Motecuhzoma. Motecuhzoma had appointed Don Diego tlahtoani of Ecatepec, a northern lake stronghold of the Mexica.[64] In fall 1521, Don Diego was held prisoner with Cuauhtemoc and Oquitzin and, like them, was tortured in order to get information about the lost treasure of the Templo Mayor. He also was forced to go on the journey to Honduras with Cortés, though he was spared execution and also managed to survive the arduous journey back. Perhaps any desire he had to defy the Spanish was diminished by his terrible experiences in Honduras. In any case, he returned to Ecatepec, where he remained tlahtoani until 1538. That year, Viceroy Mendoza decided to choose a more prestigious native governor for the city of Mexico than the one Cortés had selected and chose Don Diego from among the surviving relatives of Motecuhzoma's family.[65]

Two conclusions can be derived from this information. First, if Culoa Tlapisque's testimony about Don Diego Huanitzin and Don Pedro Achacatl was true (Don Pedro denied it), it suggests that in the early 1530s, many leaders such as Don Diego had decided that the days of viable resistance were over. Instead, like Ixtlilxochitl and Don Pedro Tetlahuehuetzquititzin, tlahtoani of Texcoco, they were inclined to follow a path of arbitration of avoidance—deflecting or avoiding confrontations with the Spanish but also keeping the reins on reluctant nobles such as Don Pedro Achacatl who wanted to continue with their prehispanic religious fervor. If Don Diego had come over to the Christian camp, as the Spanish assumed (since the viceroy would not knowingly have appointed a hostile royal family member to the important post of native governor), he had four long months from June to October 1539 to come forward and tell Zumárraga what he knew about the existence of the tlaquimilloli. After all, in the summer of 1539, the bishop was going from altepetl to altepetl digging up idols, interrogating nobles, and looking for the Huitzilopochtlis; the hunt was then at its high point. But Don Diego did not come forward. It was instead a compliant Christian neophyte, Francisco, who had to step in and revive the investigation by fingering Culoa Tlapisque and other prominent native nobles and priests in October 1539.

Second, from October 1539, Don Diego Huanitzin was clearly implicated as a keeper of the sacred bundles, yet Zumárraga did not bring him in for questioning. Perhaps Zumárraga was satisfied that Don Diego had wanted to do the right thing in 1531 and turn over the sacred bundles. Or perhaps the bishop did not want to disrupt Don Diego's relations with the viceroy. In any case, Don Diego's lack of voluntary cooperation was definitive evidence, if the bishop had any doubts, that even the most cooperative of native nobles was perfectly willing to make choices and follow strategies at odds with the Christian message.

THE HUNT
"To learn more about them and about their idolatry"

Though Zumárraga had decided not to interrogate Don Diego Huanitzin, in the fall of 1539 he proceeded rapidly toward the execution of Don Carlos of Texcoco and zeroed in on Miguel Pochtecatl Tlaylotla for harsher treatment and torture. By these tougher actions, he hoped to send a signal to the other nobles of his determination to obtain their powerful sacred objects. Each day during the summer and fall of 1539, he was alarmed by more and more details about the importance of these sacred bundles. The Inquisition interrogations and new information from the early "ethnographic" studies of a small group of Franciscans were beginning to spell out the extent of the problem of native religiosity. They added to Zumarraga's concern that he was dealing with an apostate class of native leaders that had to be taught a lesson.

Some historians have suggested that the Franciscan "ethnographic" studies of native culture, particularly Sahagún's *Florentine Codex* and the grammars and dictionaries of Fray Alonso de Molina, represented a turn away from the failed punitive measures toward a more intensive educational mission in the 1540s.[66] Zumárraga's efforts to publish catechisms and religious tracts in the 1540s have been cited as a reversal of policy from litigation to education. However, the activities in Zumárraga's Inquisition, particularly the trial of Miguel Pochtecatl Tlaylotla, demonstrate that it was less a reversal of Franciscan policy than a general turn toward more systematic and centralized proselytizing, including punitive measures, ethnographic studies, and educational efforts, that began in the mid-1530s and continued thereafter.[67]

One can see the genesis of the combination of punishment, information gathering, and education most clearly in the Inquisition of Pochtecatl Tlaylotla, though in his case the effort was suspended. Sahagún and Molina both assisted Zumárraga as interpreters and witnesses in his various Inquisition trials, particularly those of 1539–40, but neither actually began his formal studies of native culture and language until after 1540. The friar most knowledgeable about native culture and religion in the late 1530s was their older colleague, Fray Andrés de Olmos, the good friend of Zumárraga who had accompanied him to New Spain in 1528. It was through Olmos and particularly his residency at the Colegio de Santa Cruz de Tlatelolco in 1536–39 that education, Inquisition, and ethnographic studies came together.

Olmos's studies about native culture began just before the Inquisition. Throughout the late 1520s and early 1530s, the crown requested from its First and Second Audiencias a detailed description of people, places, and conditions of the new colony of New Spain. In 1532 the president of the Second Audiencia, Bishop Sebastián Ramírez de Fuenleal, decided to give this job to the Franciscans, as the order best educated and most knowledgeable about the natives, geography, and flora and fauna of the land. Bishop Ramírez de Fuenleal intended to add to this report a study of native culture and religion, and he gave that task to Olmos, the friar with the best linguistic skills and the most varied experience dealing directly with native communities.[68] Apparently, Olmos was relieved of fixed missionary postings for a few years and was given the latitude to interview elderly native priests and nobles in the eastern communities of the valley: Texcoco, Tlaxcala, and Tepeapulco, an ancient prehispanic pilgrimage site. Apparently, while he was in Tepeapulco interviewing the elders around 1533–34, Olmos founded a Franciscan mission, and as noted in the previous chapter, it was after Olmos left Tepeapulco that Mixcoatl successfully moved in and acquired a following for his version of native religion.

Olmos was back in the city of Mexico, composing his treatise on native culture, by the April 1536 chapter meeting of the Franciscan Order. Perhaps encouraged by his colleague's accumulation of information, Fray Antonio de Ciudad Rodrigo, the Franciscan provincial who was soon to be deeply involved in the Ocelotl trial, asked another friar, Motolinía, to compose a treatise on native culture and religion as well. Motolinía reluctantly agreed and by late 1540, the end of Zumárraga's native Inquisition, had substantially completed the manuscript that would become his *History of the Indians of New Spain*, the last passage of which is quoted at the beginning of this chapter.[69]

These early efforts were furthered in 1536 when Zumárraga and Ramírez de Fuenleal decided to expand the functions of a small school for native children at the convento in Santiago de Tlatelolco. The small colegio there had been in operation since August 8, 1533, and on January 6, 1536, the two men officially founded the Colegio de Santa Cruz de Tlatelolco on the same site, as a larger, more centralized educational institution to which the Franciscans would send all of the most prominent sons of the indigenous nobility of the valley. The goal was to train the next generation of native leaders of the valley away from the influence of their families and cultures. The colegio also provided a central place where the most knowledgeable friars could share their studies and provide translation skills, including those applied to Zumárraga's Inquisition trials. Olmos, Sahagún, Fray Alonso de Molina, and several other noted and erudite friars joined the faculty of the colegio, and Motolinía's book suggests at many points that he was in touch with his colleagues in the colegio about their mutual studies. On the whole, however, the only one of these men who had studied native culture well enough by the late 1530s to be aware of the very secret tlaquimilloli was Olmos. From what remains of his work, one may gauge how much information he could have provided to this small, well-informed community of friars.

Unfortunately, unlike Sahagún and Motolinía's writings, most of Olmos's ethnographic writings have been lost. The extent of his knowledge of the sacred bundles and other key evidence in the Pochtecatl Tlaylotla trial must therefore be pieced together from a few sparse sources. The original and three copies of Olmos's early ethnographic manuscript of the mid-1530s, which his colleague Gerónimo de Mendieta described as "a very full book," were distributed to people in Spain in 1540, but Olmos believed they had all been lost within a few years.[70] In 1546, at the request of Fray Bartolomé de Las Casas, Olmos completed a *Suma*, or summary of the manuscript, mostly from memory and from a few notes from his mid-1530s research that he still had in his possession. Olmos made copies of the *Suma* and distributed them as well, but this time he kept the original. Years later he gave this original to the younger Franciscan friar Gerónimo de Mendieta, who used it to document accounts of native religion in book 2 of his *Historia eclesiástica indiana*.[71] No copies or originals are extant today of the lost manuscript of 1540 or the *Suma* of 1546. Thus, historians interested in Olmos's early knowledge about native religion have been obliged to piece the information together from Mendieta and a variety of other subsequent colonial manuscripts that seem to have relied on information derived from Olmos's 1540 manuscript or his 1546 *Suma*.

According to Jeffrey Wilkerson, "the *Codex Tudela*, in conjunction with the *Historia de los mexicanos por sus pinturas* [hereinafter *Pinturas*], represents a major portion of the missing 'very full book' of Fray Andrés de Olmos."[72] He argues that "most if not all of the material for the *Codex Tudela* and *Pinturas* dates to the second decade of the Spanish presence in Mexico," that is, the mid- to late 1530s, the time of the Inquisition.[73] Wilkerson also suggests that Olmos's collection of *huehuetlahtolli* (formal Nahuatl speech), entitled *Arte de la lengua mexicana*, and a Nahuatl translation of a Spanish book on witchcraft, which Olmos called the *Tratado de hechicerías y sortilegios*, published in 1552, appear "to relate, topically if not structurally, to the *Tudela-Pinturas* ethnography and the lost larger work."[74]

Georges Baudot further argues that *Pinturas*, though produced in 1547, was not derived from the *Suma*; rather, it was based on the original 1540 manuscript, which was once located in Ramírez de Fuenleal's library in Cuenca, Spain.[75] Ramírez de Fuenleal was one of several high-level Spanish officials to whom Olmos sent his early work in 1540. Baudot believes that *Pinturas* is actually the rather "poor summary" of the 1540 book that a Spanish copyist and editor produced. Apparently, Bartolomé de Las Casas found the "lost" 1540 copy of Olmos's early work in Ramírez de Fuenleal's library and arranged for a Spanish copyist to extract a short version, which Las Casas used in his various legal battles defending the New World natives before royal councils in the 1540s.

In short, both Wilkerson and Baudot agree that *Historia de los mexicanos por sus pinturas*, despite its shortcomings, provides us with the most authentic representation of Olmos's knowledge of native religion in the late 1530s and that it is the earliest documented knowledge of any Franciscan about the rhyme and reason of native culture and religion. As it happens, *Pinturas* deals primarily with the origin myths of the Mesoamericans and the long odyssey of the Mexica from their ancient land of Aztlan to Tenochtitlan, both topics pertinent to the subject of the sacred bundles or Huitzilopochtlis, as the Spanish called them. In fact, the congruence between the information Olmos records in *Pinturas* about the tlaquimilloli and the testimony about Huitzilopochtlis in the Inquisition transcript is very good.

There is also congruence between the origin histories in *Pinturas* and the trial transcripts. For example, in the first chapter of *Pinturas*, Olmos describes the "principal gods" and the "creation of the world." He relates that there were four principal gods who were brothers; in birth order, they were "Tlaclauque Teztzatlipuca, Yayanque Tezcatlipuca, Quizalcóatl, Uchilobi."[76] The first god in

Pinturas, Tlaclauque Teztzatlipuca, who is called "eldest brother," corresponds with the fourth bundle in Mateo's illustration (figure 1). Olmos describes him as "the god of those in Huexocingo and Tlaxcala who took him for their god and called him Camastle; he was totally Red"; in other words, the Red Tezcatlipoca, or Mixcoatl-Camaxtli.[77] Yayanque Tezcatlipuca in *Pinturas* is identified as the "greatest and worst; he has more command and power than the other three" and corresponds with Mateo's third bundle. This god, according to *Pinturas*, "knows all thoughts and is everywhere and knows the hearts . . . he is all-powerful."[78] Quetzalcoatl in *Pinturas* is described as a younger brother god and may or may not be the fifth mysterious bundle. Uchilobi in *Pinturas* corresponds with Mateo's first bundle, Huitzilopochtli, and is identified specifically as the god of the Mexica.

The birth order Olmos gives for the four brother gods is more or less an historical chronology of the communities that settled in central Mexico. The Red Tezcatlipoca or Mixcoatl-Camaxtli, the principal god of the older Chichimec communities, is the eldest, as these communities date back to the Classic period when Teotihuacan reigned in central Mexico. Tezcatlipoca and Quetzalcoatl were gods of later Chichimec communities in the valley and the remaining communities of the Toltec dynasty, with capitals in Tula and Culhuacan. Huitzilopochtli, the youngest brother, was the principal god of the Mexica, the last group dominant in the valley at the arrival of the Spanish.[79] The bundle labeled "Ciguacoatl" in the illustration corresponds with Cihuacoatl, the earth-mother goddess, whom Olmos identifies in *Pinturas* as the wife of Mixcoatl-Camaxtli. Thus, Olmos's 1540 work was knowledgeable enough about the origin myths and gods of central Mexico to explain much of the information in Mateo's illustration.

Olmos also had figured out some of the characteristics of the tlaquimilloli by the late 1530s. In *Pinturas*, writing of the journey of the Mexica to their final destination of Tenochtitlan, he explains that they carried the "mástel y manta de Uchilogos," by which he means the clothing of the gods, particularly their loincloths, which they left behind as relics that their devotees kept in sacred bundles. Olmos also explains that the Mexica "reverently carried" the "mástel y manta," or sacred bundle, to each of their destinations in and around the valley, and in each location "they built a temple where they put the mástel of Uchilogos."[80] These locations included Tula, Zumpango, Cuautitlan, Tenayuca, and El Peñol, among others. Several of the sites along the journey where they stopped to house the sacred bundles were the same as those Don Baltasar, Don Andrés, and Culoa Tlapisque of Culhuacan had identified in Inquisition testimony as sacred sites for the Huitzilopochtlis that were hidden in 1521–26.[81]

Olmos demonstrates in *Pinturas* some understanding of the Huitzilopochtli bundle's political importance; he explains that the Mexica, while they were subject to Culhuacan, "gave the loincloth and cotton wrapping of Huitzilopochtli to the Culhua."[82] He also notes that at this time the Mexica began to revere "Ciguacoalt, wife of the god of fire [the Red Tezcatlipoca, or Mixcoatl-Camaxtli], whom the Culhua had for their god."[83] Thus, he provides some background that explains why the sacred bundle of Cihuacoatl appears in Mateo's illustration. Missing from Olmos's *Pinturas* is the the sacred bundles' specific importance to a tlahtoani and his identity and to the altepetl's political sense of itself.

A second, later source through which to trace Olmos's interpretation of the tlaquimilloli is in Gerónomo de Mendieta, who, as noted above, employed Olmos's lost *Suma* of 1546 in his own *Historia eclesiástica indiana*. In the text about tlaquimilloli in book 2, chapter 2, "Of how the sun was created and of the death of the gods," Mendieta makes it clear that he is citing Olmos's *Suma*. Mendieta's origin myth is similar to that of *Pinturas* except in a few important details about the contents of the tlaquimilloli that Olmos may not have known in 1540 but may have come to understand better by 1546, when he completed his *Suma*. While *Pinturas* contains Olmos's explanation of the sacrifices each of the four brother gods performed, Mendieta, based on Olmos's increased knowledge, adds richer detail and better clarity to the concept of the tlaquimilloli:

> Each left the clothes he was wearing to the devotees that he had, in memory of his devotion and love. And the sun indeed continued on its course. And the devotees and servants of the dead gods wrapped these clothes around certain sticks and made a muesca [notch] or agujero [hole] in the

stick, and they put in it a heart of some green stones and the skin of a snake and a jaguar, and this bundle they called a tlaquimilloli, and each one had the name of the demon who had given the clothes and this was the principal idol to which they gave much reverence. And this they revered more than the figures of wood or stone that they had. Fray Andrés de Olmos found one of these idols wrapped in much cotton cloth in Tlalmanalco, though they had tried to hide it.[84]

This incident in Tlalmanalco happened in 1543.[85] In 1540, Olmos did not know the Nahuatl name for the bundles or much about them, but he had learned a good deal more by 1546. The bundle found in Tlalmanalco clearly filled in some blanks, but it is also likely that the data and Mateo's illustration, produced in the summer of 1539, from the Inquisition trial of Pochtecatl Tlaylotla contributed to Olmos's more sophisticated understanding of this persistent aspect of native spirituality.

Yet to be explained, however, is how Olmos shared his knowledge of origin myths with the small band of Franciscan ethnographers around Zumárraga who had in their possession the illustration and testimony by Mateo. Olmos was not in the city of Mexico in June 1539 when Pochtecatl Tlaylotla's Inquisition trial began. Having finished his "very full book," Olmos had left to return to missionary work in Hueytlalpan in the province of Puebla in April 1539, shortly after an ecclesiastical junta of all the bishops and orders in March–April of 1539. Though Olmos completed the composition of his manuscript in the spring of 1539, young native scribes in the colegio still had to produce the three copies. Therefore, we can surmise that the original was in the hands of Zumárraga's close associates in the summer and fall of 1539 and probably guided them as they worked their way through the trials of that year.[86] Thus, while Olmos was not available for direct consultation in Pochtecatl Tlaylotla's trial, which began in June 1539 and continued to May of the following year, his complete work thus far on the subject of native religion was.

Which of the friars was familiar with Olmos's manuscript and also assisted Zumárraga in Pochtecatl Tlaylotla's trial? Comparisons between the trial transcript and Mateo's illustration provide hints. While the transcript (written by an Inquisition secretary) consistently refers to "Huitzilobo" or "Uichilobo," the Spanish caption on the Huitzilopochtli bundle in Mateo's illustration says "Uiçilipochtli." The correct suffix "pochtli" suggests that the writer was someone with a more acute ear for the Nahuatl language than either the Inquisition secretary or Fray Alonso de Santiago, who was the interpreter for Mateo's initial testimony on June 20, 1539. A second hint is provided in the transcript, which identifies "Fray Bernardino" as someone working on the interrogations at least by September 1539 and possibly before; this was certainly Sahagún, who was probably the one working with Mateo to gloss his illustration. Thus, it is probable that after receiving Fray Alonso de Santiago's translation of Mateo's verbal testimony, Zumárraga asked one of the friars at the colegio, most likely Sahagún, to assist in taking Mateo's illustrated testimony (the illustration probably dates from about June–July 1539). It is also possible that Zumárraga asked for this further pictorial testimony on the advice of Sahagún precisely because this friar was becoming more aware (through Olmos's work) of other representations of the gods besides wood and stone statues.

Again, the ethnographic work of the friars can not be separated from the perceived need to apply penalties for religious transgressions; learning about the culture and punishing sin went together. The critical information obtained in Pochtecatl Tlaylotla's trial was soon combined with the ongoing collection of information in the trial of Don Carlos of Texcoco, which began on June 22, 1539, just two days after Mateo's testimony in the Pochtecatl Tlaylotla case. Two weeks later, Bishop Zumárraga arrested Don Carlos for speaking against the Christian mission and completed an inspection of his properties. The bishop was quite disturbed to find stone statues of various prehispanic gods built into the walls of one of Don Carlos's homes, a common technique the natives used for preserving native religion in the home in the years after the conquest. Though there was some question whether Don Carlos or an elder relative had hidden the objects,[87] Zumárraga was furious to find a member of the Texcocan royal family in possession of these items in a community he had believed to be reliably proselytized years before. The next day, he summoned the native cabildo (town council) of Texcoco. All the council members were Don Carlos's half brothers or cousins. They included Don

Lorenzo de Luna, a council elder who had hastily been appointed native governor after the arrest of Don Carlos; Don Hernando de Chávez, a future native governor; and Don Antonio Pimentel Tlahuitoltzin, a future tlahtoani.[88] Zumárraga told them, according to the transcript, that

> He had found the idols for anyone to see in the house of Don Carlos in the center of the town. It seems that everybody knew about it and saw it and there was much more than this. He admonished them that, if they had an idol or a house of idolatry in or outside their homes or if they knew of anyone who had one, they are to come and say so before the bishop and denounce the persons. By doing so, they would receive mercy if they promised to observe Christianity and not do a single thing against it.[89]

Piecing together the bits of information that were coming together from studies by the friars and Inquisition interrogations, Zumárraga began to take direct action with the supposedly Christian nobles. He brought each member of Texcoco's native council in for interrogation, separately and secretly. Several of the nobles, apparently wanting to distract the bishop from his focus on Texcoco, stated that they thought the cult of Tlaloc, the rain god, was being revived in the sierra above Texcoco. Don Lorenzo explained that in prehispanic times, their neighbors, those of Huexocingo, "for hatred of the Mexicans, had broken the idol [Tlaloc] on the mountain."[90] Ahuitzotl, Motecuhzoma's immediate predecessor as hueytlahtoani, had dug up the statue and repaired it with "gold and copper wire," and they had embedded a great stone, a symbol of the heart of the god, in the statue.[91]

Don Lorenzo claimed that about two months before, in May 1539, he had sent men to Tlalocatepetl (Mount Tlaloc) to prevent people from worshipping at the prehispanic sanctuary of the rain god. The men found sacrificial objects—amate, copal, and small dead birds—at the site. And later they found oil and seed from chia and corn attached to the Tlaloc statue. The native guards finally took the statue away in order to discourage the revival.[92] The bishop requested anything valuable taken from the statue, but the nobles claimed to have "seen nothing of that."[93] Dissatisfied with the responses of the Texcocan nobles, the bishop on July 7 went into the sierra of Tetzcotzingo, where the prehispanic baths and gardens of Nezahualcoyotl lay and where a fountainhead irrigated many of the communities in the valley. Nezahualcoyotl and Nezahualpilli had filled the gardens in Tetzcotzingo with the statuary of Tlaloc. Zumárraga ordered all of the statues to be destroyed "in a manner such that they would no longer be remembered."[94]

In a few days, however, Zumárraga's attention was brought back to Texcoco when a macehualli (commoner), Gerónimo de Pomar, came to the bishop to confess an incident that had happened nearly four months before, in February 1539, when the tlahtoani Don Pedro of Texcoco was still alive. Pomar had exhorted Don Pedro to tear down a "house of the devil," meaning a temple, and "if he did not, Gerónimo would tell the bishop. . . . Don Pedro did not respond except to shut the doors of the house."[95] Don Pedro told Pomar "not to say anything to the bishop and to forget about it."[96] Pomar, however, "began to think it was a bad idea after a while and went to the bishop when he [Zumárraga] came to Texcoco [in the wake of Don Carlos's arrest] and told him" the story.[97]

Having found themselves once again under the scrutiny of the bishop, the nobles tried to appease him. The very next day, Don Lorenzo de Luna returned to Zumárraga with a good quantity of "stone and wood idols" and a considerable load of gold, silver, and precious stones that he said he had found with the idols. The bailiffs took possession of the gold, melted it down, and put it in deposit to the Inquisition.[98] Whatever Zumárraga's motivations in pressuring Don Lorenzo, it seems that the native governor's actions were classic examples of the arbitration of avoidance. From Don Lorenzo's perspective, the offering of gold that was supposedly found with idols was obviously an inducement to turn the bishop away from further investigation into the activities or non-activities of Texcoco's council members. And indeed, Zumárraga seemed after that to be relatively satisfied with what the council had done.

Neverthless, this transaction had unwanted consequences. While the pressure on Don Lorenzo abated, Motolinía's account suggests that Zumárraga's hunt for idols and his acquisition of the cache of gold only encouraged local Spaniards to harass other native leaders, drag up bodies from their graves, and hunt through caves and homes looking for "idols" and whatever gold they could find. There were even cases of conspiracy to implicate native leaders. The most notable case involved the tlahtoani of Ocuituco, Don Cristóbal, and his wife, Catalina, and brother, Martín. The local parish priest of Ocuituco, Diego Díaz, had worked with a slave in Don Cristóbal's household to implicate the leader in hiding Huitzilopochtlis.[99] In August 1539, Zumárraga sent his good friend Juan González, a priest, as a commissary of the Inquisition to Ocuituco to investigate the charges. None of the notorious sacred bundles was actually in Ocuituco. In fact, a year later, the bishop learned that the priest, Diego Díaz, was a scoundrel, blackmailing Don Cristóbal with testimony he had trumped up and demanding bribes to get the accusations to go away. Don Cristóbal had refused but was convicted of keeping other types of idols. Moreover, Don Cristóbal confessed to performing a large number of prehispanic rituals and made the matter-of-fact claim that everyone in that area kept idols, and that there were in fact "witches," meaning nanahualtin, roaming all around his region.[100] He apparently felt no obligation to stop any of these practices, as they were so widespread. In August 1539, Zumárraga confiscated his large estate; the properties that made up Don Cristobal's estate took up three pages of the transcript.[101]

CONCLUSION

If ever there was hysteria in Zumárraga's Inquisition, a high-pitched moment where fear and avarice drove both Spaniards and natives to testify against one another willy-nilly, then the closest thing was the summer of 1539. Ironically, the objects that created this alarm were highly perishable bundles that may well have been rotting away in some cave, as Motolinía suggested, while Zumárraga rushed about the valley looking for them. The sacred bundles that Mateo had brought to Zumárraga's attention were never found, but the reasons have less to do with the objects and their symbolic power than with their keepers and how they saw themselves in the new colonial reality. Ultimately, indigenous leaders in the late 1530s were less interested in some long-ago dream of resistance than they were in maintaining the hierarchy of the native social system and their own relevance to it. That required that they look the other way or help hide the ubiquitous and persistent prehispanic worship in New Spain in the 1530s. Thus, the otherwise compliant Don Diego Huanitzin, whom the Spanish had appointed to lead the native community in the city of Mexico, did not rush to Zumárraga to implicate his fellow noble, Don Pedro Achacatl (for withholding information about the location of the idols) the moment Miguel Pochtecatl Tlaylotla was arrested. And Pochtecatl Tlaylotla nearly died in water torture rather than say which noble had ordered the removal of the sacred bundles. Even Culoa Tlapisque, who initially was intimidated into testifying against Don Pedro Achacatl, refused to give more evidence when he was called back a month later, saying, "Perhaps His Excellency would kill him, because it was an important thing that he kept."[102] The older nobles banded together to protect themselves from this latest onslaught of Spanish interference and disruption in their political lives. Instead, it was the slaves, ambitious commoners, and young nobles kept for years in conventos away from the influence of their native families—men who did not have as much of a stake in preserving the prehispanic native hierarchy—who made the case against the keepers of the Huitzilopochtlis.

The friars were driven to learn more and more about the native religion, but each new revelation about its persistence alarmed and discouraged them. When they saw how these violations of Christian teaching were carefully abetted and sustained—for a variety of religious and political reasons—by the actions and inaction of native leaders, the friars developed an increasingly hostile attitude toward the native leaders as a group. The resulting ill-will eventually came to a head in the most notorious trial of the era, the Inquisition trial of Don Carlos of Texcoco.

CHAPTER FIVE

THE TLAHTOANI
THE TRIAL OF DON CARLOS OF TEXCOCO

The Inquisition, trial, and burning of the indigenous leader Don Carlos Ometochtli of Texcoco was the most famous trial of Zumárraga's Inquisition. It has been cited dozens of times in Latin American historiography, especially after Richard Greenleaf wrote about the case in 1962.[1] Don Carlos was a grandson of Nezahualcoyotl, a son of Nezahualpilli, and a younger half brother of Ixtlilxochitl. Unlike his legendary ancestors, Don Carlos was more famous in death than in life, as he was the most notorious native victim of an Inquisition in the sixteenth century and the only indigenous leader in Zumárraga's Inquisition to pay with his life at the stake. Although Don Carlos was also accused of bigamy and idolatry, he received his death sentence for the crime of heretical dogmatism. The accusation and trial against him exposed internal disputes among native leaders about how accommodating they should be of the Franciscan intrusions in their communities.

For a variety of personal reasons, Don Carlos resisted European taboos against bigamy and marriage consanguinity; in fact, he conflated the authenticity of his leadership with the exercise of these male prerogatives. His insistence on male prerogatives not only invited conflict with the Franciscans, it also defied the Texcocan leaders' pattern of arbitration of avoidance. His defiance flew in the face of indigenous values and discourses that expected a leader to put his community's need to deflect Spanish intrusion before his own desires. Unfortunately, Don Carlos also had a troubled ascension to the leadership of Texcoco because of longstanding irregularities in the Texcocan royal line. Thus, even before Don Carlos was brought before Zumárraga for violating the Christian doctrine, he was a wounded leader. After Don Carlos's arrest, in a pattern of avoidance reminiscent of previous trials, the Texcocan nobility readily abandoned him to the Spanish stake.

THE SUCCESSION
"He was always trying to take the señoridad *by force"*

After Don Carlos was denounced on June 22, 1539, he was arrested, and Zumárraga completed an inquiry in the next two weeks that involved more than thirty witnesses, including Don Carlos himself. By the time the tlahtoani was allowed to submit a formal denial of the charges against him through his attorney, it was August. In the next two months, he was tried, finally sentenced in an auto de fé on November 30, 1539, and executed the next day, December 1. His formal denial of the charges contains one particularly interesting assertion that opens up the whole question of who Don Carlos was and how he became vulnerable to charges of heresy. According to the record, he protested that he had been accused "because he is the *señor* of the village, which he is legitimately and by the wish of his brother, and he had to punish people, and they accused him for this reason."[2] Elsewhere in the transcript, the testimony of Don Carlos's half sister María seems to corroborate his sense that the succession dispute was at the core of his problems in Texcoco. Clearly angry at Don Carlos's elevation to power, she testified that their mutual sibling Don Pedro, who chose Don Carlos to succeed him, had to "manage things for Don Carlos because he wanted him as leader after his death." Don Carlos, she complained, "was always trying to take control of the *señoridad* [rule of a leader] by force and be señor of Texcoco."[3]

The statements of Don Carlos and his half sister reveal that at the time of Don Carlos's arrest, Texcocans felt considerable animosity toward Don Carlos and a good deal of anxiety about the legitimacy of his rule. They also reveal that during his trial and perhaps all the way to his death, Don Carlos assumed that his denunciation had come from Texcoco and that he had been betrayed by his own people. However, we know with near certainty from the trial testimony that his accuser was not a Texcocan but a young Christian neophyte named Francisco from Chiconautla, an altepetl some ten kilometers away (see map 4). The testimony was kept secret from Don Carlos, as was the case in all Inquisition trials. Zumárraga was careful in his questioning of Don Carlos not to reveal Francisco's identity. But Don Carlos's belief that it was a Texcocan who denounced him indicates that his leadership had a legitimacy problem. Some historians have suggested a possible native conspiracy in the trial of Don Carlos, but there is little evidence to support the contention. Don Carlos's inheritance of the leadership did not lead directly to the accusations against him, but the climate of dispute and the air of illegitimacy that attended his elevation to the leadership did affect his decision making in the months before his arrest and led indirectly to his being denounced in Chiconautla. These disputes over his succession had begun long before 1539. In fact, disputed succession in Texcoco preceded the conquest, simmered in the difficult first two decades of the colonial period, and finally boiled over in Don Carlos's unhappy and brief reign in 1539.

Texcoco was the most powerful altepetl of the Acolhua, the Nahuatlized Chichimecas who had settled in the Valley of Mexico on the east side of Lake Texcoco in the thirteenth century. In 1427, the leader of the Texcocans, Nezahualcoyotl, formed the Triple Alliance with the Mexica of Tenochtitlan to the southwest and the Tepaneca of Tlacopan even further west. Tenochtitlan employed a modified form of fratrilineal succession, though Texcoco was more inclined toward father-to-son succession.[4] Texcoco's new alliance, however, complicated the rules of succession. All three monarchs of the alliance had numerous wives and concubines, but they also ranked marriages by the principle of hypogamous marriage—the wife's status determined the status of the children. This tied the elite families of the valley together politically in a complex hierarchical network.[5] In the new environment of the Triple Alliance, the Texcocan royal children of high-status marriages, especially with Mexica wives, had the advantage over the king's brothers in terms of succession. Consequently, Nezahualcoyotl, himself the son of a Mexica marriage alliance, named his young son,

Nezahualpilli, also the son of a Mexica princess, as his heir. There were some objections, but father-to-son succession in Texcoco survived and continued.[6]

Nezahualpilli ruled from approximately 1471 to 1515. Historians have suggested that throughout his reign, the Triple Alliance was drifting steadily toward complete Mexica dominance. In the sixteenth century, Motecuhzoma increasingly ignored treaties with Texcoco, kept a good number of Nezahualpilli's sons under his control in his palace in Tenochtitlan, and even suggested that the Triple Alliance was over.[7] In his last years, Nezahualpilli retreated from public life and declined to proclaim a successor from among his sons.[8] Upon his death in 1515, however, two groups of his sons had the upper hand under the father-to-son inheritance system of the alliance. All were the sons of Mexica sisters of Motecuhzoma; one unnamed wife had a son named Cacama, while another, Tenancaxhuantzin, had a multitude of children, including eleven sons (see figure 2).[9] All were potential legitimate heirs if Nezahualpilli had chosen, but he did not.

Exercising Mexica dominance, Motecuhzoma interceded in the Texcocan succession and chose his favorite nephew, Cacama (1), as the new king (numbers in parentheses refer to the order of royal succession in Texcoco). Several of Cacama's eleven half brothers, who similarly had his Mexica bloodline, immediately accepted the decision. As noted in chapter 1, however, the middle brother, Ixtlilxochitl, disagreed, and between 1515 and 1519, the eve of the Spanish conquest, he wrested from Cacama most of the important northeastern tributary lands near Otumba and Teotihuacan. Cacama eventually negotiated a truce with the rebellious Ixtlilxochitl that allowed Cacama to remain the official king and live in Tenochtitlan, while Ixtlilxochitl ruled the northern tributary lands he already held. Cacama's loyal half brother, Cohuanacoch, ruled the homeland around Texcoco, though prehispanic histories are unclear whether his role was governor for Cacama or leader in his own right.[10] In any case, the second most powerful ally of the Triple Alliance, Texcoco, was in disarray and vulnerable on the eve of the conquest.

When Cortés made his assault on Tenochtitlan in 1519, Cacama sided with the Mexica and made war against the Spanish conqueror.[11] In solidarity with Cacama, Cohuanacoch and three of his full brothers

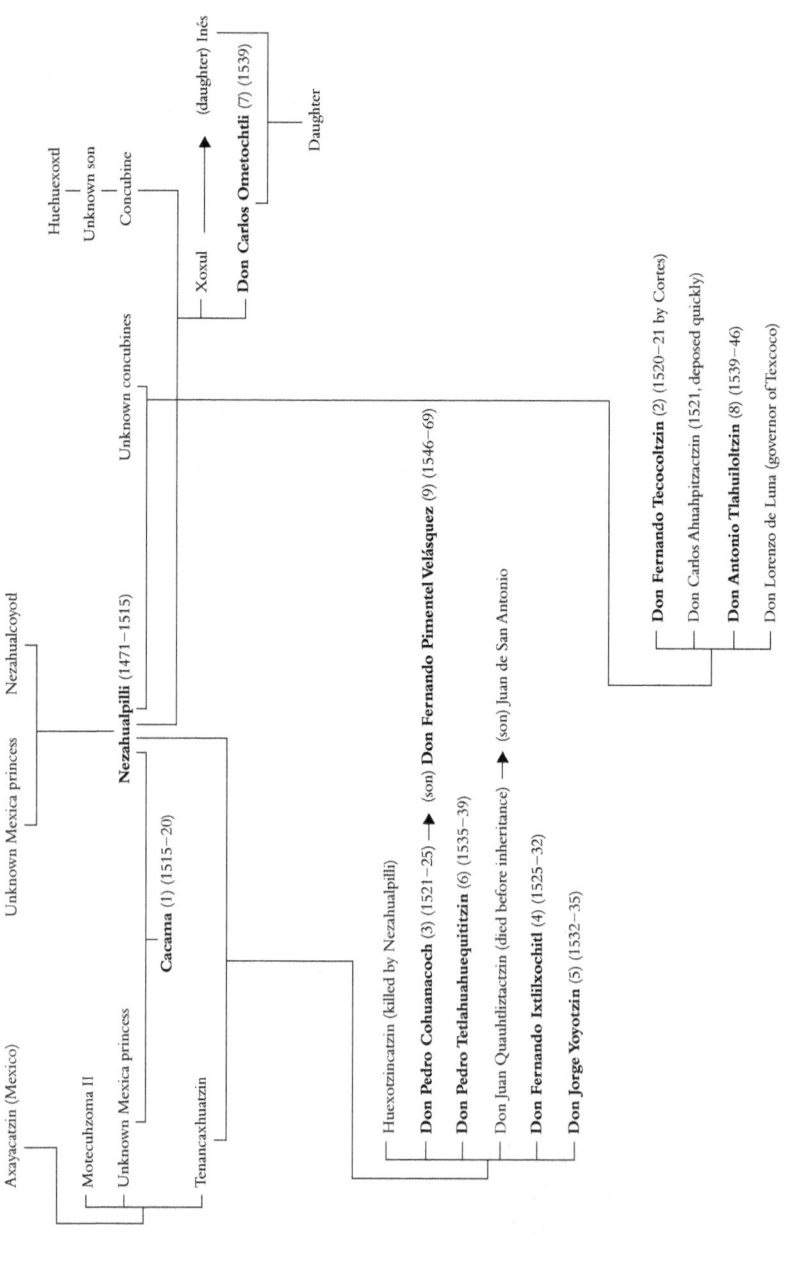

Figure 2. Selective genealogy of the Texcocan royal family in the sixteenth century. (Numbers in parentheses refer to order of succession.) From Patricia Lopes Don, "The 1539 Inquisition and Trial of Don Carlos of Texcoco: Religion and Politics in Early Mexico," *Hispanic American Historical Review* 88, no. 4 (November 2008), 579.

led an army in alliance with the Mexica against Cortés in the final stand in Tenochtitlan.[12] The wily Ixtlilxochitl, however, threw in his lot with Cortés, in effect declaring war against his brothers.[13] Cacama died while in the hands of the conquerors in Tenochtitlan, but many of the remaining rebelling and non-rebelling brothers survived. The victorious Cortés now tried to play the role that Motecuhzoma had attempted unsuccessfully six years before—to impose a ruler on the Texcocans. At that moment, however, the relative youth of the royal family and the deaths of many royal males by war and plague forced Cortés to choose from among brothers, inadvertently returning succession back to fratrilineal inheritance.

For four years Cortés selected different brothers from inside and outside the Mexica line, studiously avoiding his ally Ixtlilxochitl for reasons he never articulated; it is possible that Cortés preferred to elevate weaker, more malleable princes. On Cortés's ill-fated expedition to Honduras in 1524–26, he executed Cohuanacoch (3), the eldest brother, and Cortés finally accepted Ixtlilxochitl as lord of Texcoco, baptizing him "Don Fernando" after the former Spanish king, Ferdinand.[14] As noted in chapter 1, however, even with Cortés's assent, Don Fernando Ixtlilxochitl still had to wrest control of Texcoco from the many interlopers who had taken over during his own absence in the Honduras expedition. From 1526 forward, Don Fernando Ixtlilxochitl reluctantly arbitrated and managed an alliance with the Franciscans and established Texcoco as a bastion of the Catholic church in the late 1520s.[15]

Don Fernando Ixtlilxochitl's (4) reign, while stable, was also short-lived; he died in 1532. In Don Fernando's final year, the Franciscans had begun their morals campaign in Texcoco, forcing marriages on the Texcocans and punishing reluctant men, with the grudging agreement of Don Fernando's successors. In addition to creating anger and anxiety in the Texcocan male nobility, the morals campaign of the 1530s also complicated inheritance principles by introducing the European concept of child legitimacy through church-sanctioned monogamous marriage. While Texcocan male nobles and princes continued to hang on to concubines, the Franciscans, with the help of Spanish civil authorities, were able to direct the royal line toward sons of church-sanctioned marriages, that is, legitimate heirs in the European sense.

Thus, since Don Fernando's reign, the Texcocan leaders attempted to blend Spanish and native principles in the selection of royal heirs.

Don Fernando had only daughters by his chosen wife, Doña Beatriz, but exercised the traditional prerogative to choose his heir from among his full brothers of the old Mexica line.[16] It was an uncomfortable choice, as his elder brothers, Don Pedro Tetlahuehuetzquititzin and Don Juan Quauhtliztactzin, and his younger brother, Don Jorge Yoyotzin, had been among those who had allied with Cohuanacoch and the Mexica against him and Cortés in 1520. Apparently, Don Fernando also decided to irritate his eldest surviving brother, Don Pedro, by preferring the other brothers, Don Juan and Don Jorge, for the crown. Don Juan died before the transfer could be made; thus, Don Jorge Yoyotzin (5) became the Texcocan monarch upon Don Fernando's death in 1532.[17] In a few years, Don Jorge, in turn, died without an appropriate male heir. Thus, the embittered Don Pedro Tetlahuehuetzquititzin (6), the last of the preferred Mexica line among the sons of Nezahualpilli, who was overlooked by his father, his uncle Motecuhzoma, Cortés, and even his own full brothers, finally came to rule Texcoco in the year 1535.[18]

Since the rise of Nezahualcoyotl in 1427, the same branch of the royal family, related to the Mexica, had ruled for a total of 108 years with only one slight break in 1521. It is a testament to the importance and endurance of this royal line and its principles of inheritance that it survived for two decades into the colonial period, despite many obstacles. Don Pedro was the dead end of this inheritance strategy, however. He had no sons by his church-sanctioned marriage and no full brothers left. He could either select one of his Mexica nephews—Don Fernando Pimentel Velásquez, the son of Cohuanacoch, or Juan de San Antonio, the son of Don Juan Quauhtliztactzin—or break the long-ruling Mexica line by selecting a non-Mexica half brother for the crown. Don Pedro chose to go outside the Mexica line and invest rule in his half brother, Don Carlos Ometochtli (2 Rabbit, his calendrical name) Chichimecateuctli (Chichimec lord; also Chichimec military leader, a position immediately subordinate to the tlahtoani), which put the succession onto a new, contentious path.[19]

Don Carlos's (7) early life is fairly obscure and has been gleaned mostly from his trial transcript. It appears he was born around 1505, just a little later than his string of Mexica half brothers, who, like him, were sons of Nezahualpilli.[20] Unlike his half brothers' prestigious royal Mexica mother, however, Don Carlos's mother was a concubine. His maternal great-grandfather, Huehuexoxtl, was a noble of the Tepaneca and his grandfather was unremarkable. This made Don Carlos a *calpanpilli* ("house son"), placing him below *tlazopilli* ("esteemed son"), which had more prominent maternal bloodlines and included the Mexica half brothers who had preceded him in the succession.[21] The trial transcript, our best contemporaneous evidence, makes it clear that he was called Ometochtli by his brothers and sisters and that he and Don Pedro added "Chichimecateuctli" to indicate his position as successor.

Don Carlos was probably fourteen to sixteen years old at the time of the conquest, an age when he was required to learn arms, but we do not know if he actually used them to fight on one side or the other in the conquest wars.[22] After the conquest, he lived in Cortés's house in Coyoacan, where Cortés kept many sons of the royal houses of the Valley of Mexico, under a kind of forced Hispanicization program. The young noble seemed to learn a great deal about Spanish ways. At his Inquisition trial, he said he had been baptized "about fifteen years before [by] Fray Juan, who is now dead," meaning about 1524–25.[23] He was back in Texcoco by 1528, because he had fathered a son out of wedlock there, a minor indiscretion.[24] Historians have repeated the error in the preface by Luis González Obregón of the 1910 publication of the trial transcript, which states that Don Carlos was schooled in the Colegio de Santa Cruz de Tlatelolco. This was unlikely, given that Don Carlos was already nearing thirty when the colegio was initially opened, and the Franciscans preferred to recruit children ten to twelve years old for instruction at the colegio because of their intellectual malleability at that age. Nevertheless, Don Carlos seems to have been aware of the school and the activities of the Franciscans there.[25]

In fact, Don Carlos readily interacted with the Franciscan friars and Spaniards in Texcoco. Texcocans testified that in 1531, Don Carlos had asked his half brother Don Fernando Ixtlilxochitl for the use of the palace at Oztoticpac on behalf of a Franciscan friar who lived in Texcoco at the time.[26] Given the date, the friar was very likely Fray

Antonio de Ciudad Rodrigo, the guardian at Texcoco, who later would become instrumental in advising Zumárraga in the trial of Martín Ocelotl. In 1532, Don Carlos was either advocating for the Franciscans or, more likely, playing a middle game between the Franciscans and his half brother as a means to get possession of the valuable property. As has been seen in chapter 1, Don Fernando Ixtlilxochitl turned down Don Carlos's request. By then, Don Fernando had become more wary of his alliance with the Franciscans and instead gave the palace to his intended heir, Don Jorge Yoyotzin. By 1536, Don Carlos was doing business with a Spaniard, Pedro de Vergara, in a large-scale enterprise to plant European fruit trees on one of Don Carlos's properties, the two of them splitting the profits.[27] In short, Don Carlos was at the time behaving in a manner that was probably typical of a good number of unbeliever nobles. He engaged the Spanish and Franciscan world when he could gain some economic or political benefit; however, most of the time, he intentionally and habitually distanced himself from the friars and their circle of neophytes.

Don Pedro Tetlahuehuetzquititzin, who had designated Don Carlos as his sucessor as ruler of Texcoco, seems to have preferred Don Carlos to his nephews for two reasons. First, there was the problem of the nephews' age. By 1539, they were probably still in their teens, not ready for marriage or rule, as Texcocans regarded bachelors as unsuitable for office.[28] Second, Don Pedro did not seem to trust his nephews. According to one of the nephews, Juan de San Antonio, members of Texcoco's native town council told him that his uncle was angry at him and had complained of his nephew's ambitions: "It is said, because my nephew is male, when I die he will come in here and take the little house I have arranged for myself and the little walled enclosure."[29]

Since there was bound to be unhappiness over Don Pedro's choice of Don Carlos, Don Pedro took measures during his four years of rule to improve Don Carlos's wealth, stature, and prestige in the town, primarily at the expense of the nephews. His nephew Juan de San Antonio recalled what Don Pedro had said at a meeting of nobles prior to his death: "Perhaps you noblemen feel uneasy . . . for I say that my younger brother Don Carlos Ometochtzin Chichimecatecutzintli is poor. Therefore, I give him, I assign him, the cultivated property of Yahualiuhcan that my nephew Juan de San Antonio is working."[30] As heir apparent, Don Carlos also needed a residence. Don Pedro gave the Oztoticpac palace to Don Carlos, just as Don Fernando Ixtlilxochitl had given it to his heir, Don Jorge Yoyotzin. Apparently, the gift of the Oztoticpac palace, the largest and most luxurious residence left in colonial Texcoco, had become the signal of succession in Texcoco.[31] It seems that many family members felt thrust aside in these decisions, as Juan de San Antonio clearly did when he complained, "We knew Nezahualpiltzintli loved his elder brothers and sisters, because he kept their property for them; he was the representative of their father."[32] The implication was that Nezahualpilli's son, Don Pedro, had not protected his relatives' material interests and that Don Pedro's half brother, Don Carlos, certainly would not.

The lamentations and concerns of Juan de San Antonio and other relatives were probably attributable to two elements: anguish over their dwindling share of tribute and the disputed succession of Don Carlos. Tribute was the basis of power in the so-called "empires" that made up the Triple Alliance, and altepemeh such as Texcoco and Tenochtitlan were not so much territorial empires as tribute empires. When Cortés defeated the Mexica, he completely undercut the tribute network and probably did so even before the completion of the conquest, which explains the rapid downward spiral of Mexica power.[33] Losing even more control over tribute to the Spanish in the first decade of the colonial period, it was impossible for Texcocan royal heads of households in the 1530s to support their large extended families as old leaders like Nezahualpilli had when vast amounts of tribute and war booty were available. There was only enough wealth left to keep the highest members of indigenous royalty in the style to which they had become accustomed.

Decisions about colonial inheritance, therefore, not only determined the right to rule, but who among the royal family would become economic winners. Available real estate was limited, so Don Pedro made the decision to concentrate the wealth and endow his lone successor with it. But the supreme leader's inability to provide economic support and protection to a wide circle, as in prehispanic times, left the leader highly vulnerable to intrigue. In the first two decades after the conquest, this scramble to endow one's immediate relatives in the extended royal family with the remaining altepetl wealth and create a dynasty was a contentious dynamic in the larger noble households. Don Carlos's unpopularity, therefore, was fueled by the sense that he was about to deprive large segments of the extended family of their livelihoods.[34]

The second element contributing to the Texcocan royal family's uneasiness about Don Carlos was the heightened rhetoric about the legitimacy of succession. The succession of tlahtoqueh in central Mexico was now accompanied by unusually high levels of regicide and usurpation. Central Mexico was a highly urban environment, and rulership was still heavily invested in chiefly structures.[35] As Kay Read has noted, though the world was controlled by the gods, great men could shape the future. The period of their ascension was a "dark and dangerous" time when rulers were judged by which one "effectively shaped change." An unlucky ruler brought about terrible calamities, causing "the universe to be thrown out of balance, drought to descend, and the cosmos with all its inhabitants to starve."[36] Rival members of the extended royal family pointed out that Don Carlos's rule was illegitimate because of his lack of Mexica connections, which portended ill for Texcoco. The power of the Mexica was long gone, but the Mexica heirs clung tenaciously to their prehispanic privileges by manipulating the family tradition. In a rhetorical environment somewhat controlled by the Mexica line of the royal family, Don Carlos had achieved "señoridad" only "by force"; in other words, his rule was portrayed as tyrannous. The late Don Pedro's methods of rule, and by association Don Carlos's ascension to the throne, challenged not only the honor of the Mexica line but also the non-Mexica half brothers, who felt just as entitled as Don Carlos to the shrinking privileges and land. Each constituency used the emblem of family honor and legitimacy to build itself up and tear down its competitors.

THE DISCONTENTED MAN
"He began to treat her badly"

The tension over succession created an environment in mid-1530s Texcoco where discourses of leadership, masculinity, and authenticity flourished. Don Carlos began to change from a practitioner of the arbitration of avoidance to a hostile agitator against the Franciscans in the late 1530s. In part, he may have become exasperated with the opposition to his pending succession. For the second cause, however, we must "look for the woman." In the early 1530s, when Don Carlos was approaching thirty, the age of mature reflection, marriage, and leadership responsibilities, he became enamored of his niece Inés, the daughter of his full sister Xoxul; he had two daughters by Inés, one of whom survived.[37] There was no prohibition on consanguineal marriage in prehispanic Texcoco; however, the tlahtoani always had the power to overrule or approve marriages within the royal family. At trial, Don Carlos claimed that his brothers were angry about the affair, and that Don Pedro had compelled him to marry another woman, Doña María, in a Christian ceremony in 1535. Little is known about Doña María except that she was suitable by church standards, a very distant relative, and acceptable by Texcocan standards, as she was from a noble family in Huexotla, a former Texcocan tributary altepetl.[38]

The decision to force Don Carlos into this marriage is indicative of the policy of arbitration of avoidance. As was demonstrated in the Ocelotl trial, Don Pedro was hardly sympathetic to the friars or the moral restrictions of the Christian church. Nevertheless, the colonial tlahtoqueh generally oversaw family matters so as not to invite Spanish and Franciscan interference in Texcoco's affairs. According to Louise Burkhart, "Moral temptation was not an indigenous concept. . . . To be moral is only to behave within common sense, to do what is obviously the desirable thing to do."[39] The sensible and desirable thing for nobles to do in the colonial indigenous communities was to avoid excessive desires and problems that might bring outside scrutiny to the community, as Don Pedro had recommended when he ended Don Carlos's affair with Inés. In the environment of arbitration of avoidance, Don Carlos and other nobles were susceptible to being labeled as "bad," not in the Christian moral sense, but according to prehispanic standards of the responsible and proper conduct of leaders. In the *Florentine Codex*, the bad leader is "impetuous . . . disrespectful of others . . . acts without consideration," as opposed to a good leader, who "unites [his people] . . . brings them together . . . is discreet."[40] As the intended next tlahtoani of Texcoco, Don Carlos's marriage and the legitimacy of his children would come to the attention of the Spanish authorities and cause difficulties for the community if the friars judged him to be unchristian.[41] By compelling Don Carlos to establish a family with another woman, Don Pedro and the other Texcocan nobles discreetly deflected Spanish attention from Texcoco and avoided further inviting the colonial authorities' interference in their towns and cities.

Within evolving priorities of leadership in the colonial period, the indigenous value of discretion was elevated above prehispanic male prerogatives of consanguinity and bigamy. No leader wanted to do this, but they obviously perceived that their colonial communities would judge them according to the former rather than the latter value. Of course, some leaders were more astute, careful, and discreet than others. They learned the arbitration of avoidance leadership strategy readily, exercised wisdom in gauging the Spanish threat, and demonstrated the patience to endure the interference of the friars. But not all nobles were capable of keeping their own counsel; circumstances could push them away from the middle ground of these accommodations to the colonial situation.[42]

Initially, it seems that Don Carlos Ometochtli was willing to exercise patience and do what was required of him because it fit the successful arbitration of avoidance pattern of his brothers from Don Fernando Ixtlilxochitl on down. But as he neared his ascension to the throne, certain events suggested that the worm had turned. In testimony, his wife, Doña María, claimed that, though their marriage had no children, it was amiable for the first two years. Around 1537, however, the marriage deteriorated and Don Carlos "began to treat her badly."[43] Though we do not have sufficient testimony on this matter to pinpoint events and bad acts that happened in the next eighteen months or more, testimony indicates that by February 1539, Don Carlos moved his old mistress, his niece Inés, into his home, and she nursed him through a serious illness. (Apparently, it was the same illness that had carried away Don Pedro at about that time and left Don Carlos in charge of Texcoco.) According to Doña María and other witnesses, Don Carlos openly insulted his wife by allowing Inés to run his house and treat his wife like a servant. Inés even told Doña María "what she was supposed to do for Don Carlos and what she was supposed to make for dinner."[44] There were even earlier indications, however, that Don Carlos had abandoned the arbitration of avoidance pattern in the conduct of his personal affairs. His eleven-year-old illegitimate son, Antonio, revealed at trial that he had not been baptized at the usual age, between six and ten, because "his father did not wish it."[45] Witnesses also indicated that Don Carlos had not been to church for some time.[46]

Why did Don Carlos ignore his brothers' counsel? Certainly, he was angry that he had been deprived of his personal and sexual liberties. He may have been reconsidering the wisdom of his brothers' efforts to adapt their behavior to avoid the ill effects of Spanish power and had become inclined to a more open opposition to the Franciscans. Don Carlos's personal rebellion, however, has to be seen in the larger context of the Texcocan nobles' reaction to the Franciscan morals campaigns of the early 1530s—the forced marriages, the determinations of child legitimacy, and the empowerment of some noble women and commoner men. The Franciscans expected the indigenous leaders to follow up mass baptism with rigorous enforcement of Christian standards. But other than the future tlahtoani's marriage, which was a matter of state, the indigenous leaders did little to remedy or discourage early and easy recidivism in sexual matters.

Why was giving up women proving such an obstacle? For one, women were the source of considerable wealth. Commodities such as precious metals and corn were valuable, but cloth was the most important product traded in the Valley of Mexico in both prehispanic and colonial times.[47] Texcoco was the virtual center of the weaving trades, and women were the primary laborers; noble wives who brought considerable households of servants contributed to income.[48] Without this income, a patriarchal family could lose its position within a generation. Additionally, in the system of hypogamous marriage, wives and daughters were the means by which the political alliance network was built.[49] A powerful man needed many of these political matches to maintain his influence. Yet the real problem was a sense of futility about the loss of female companionship and perplexity at the friars' moral prohibitions, which were so alien to native values. Texcocans regarded marriage as a civil rather than a moral matter.[50] The Franciscan sermons against temptation and for moral superiority fell on uncomprehending male ears.

Thus, the friars' insistence on enforcing Christian morality, particularly in sophisticated hierarchical communities like Texcoco, presented a social as well as a political challenge to native nobles. The prohibitions disrupted well-established social patterns, and the Franciscan grab for moral authority in the community surely caused the native nobles to lose face among their people. Trial evidence indicates that there was a backlash of rhetoric in the altepemeh asserting masculine prerogatives. In addition to Don Carlos, three other high-status indigenous leaders were tried before the Inquisition: Don Diego of Tlapanaloa, Don Juan of Matlatlan, and Don Juan of Iguala. These leaders were making claims individually and as a class for the right to consanguine marriage and sexual license with all the women of their choice in the altepemeh where they ruled. Testimony against Don Diego of Tlapanaloa alleged that he had six wives (four were his sisters), that he compelled a woman slave to abort several of his children, and that he had imprisoned the husband of one woman he tried to take. Fray Andrés de Olmos reported that Don Juan of Matlatlan had seventeen wives, one of whom was his former sister-in-law. Don Juan of Iguala's wife was a virtual servant in his home, where he kept several mistresses, and he allegedly raped a girl of ten in his town.[51]

Nevertheless, while some leaders ignored the Franciscans and exercised their perceived privileges, a close reading of the transcript testimony suggests that their overt sexual aggression was not always well received in their native communities. It seems that countervailing prehispanic values held by women and commoner men pushed back against elite male prerogatives as the colonial situation evolved. When Don Diego of Tlapanaloa tried to take the wife of another noble, the man openly defied Don Diego by uprooting his family and moving to another town. Several other villagers also left because they would not pay the tribute Don Diego wanted, and they also wished to protect the women. While Don Juan of Matlatlan was generally supported, his villagers were clearly nervous about his pattern of open polygamy. Don Juan of Iguala's wife and sister-in-law overtly questioned his claims of full control over the women in Iguala, and they regularly disputed with him in the streets.[52] The consistency of objections by lesser-status men and elite women, the vehemence of their condemnations, as well as evidence that even before the trials, complaints were widely circulated, indicates that the nobles' assertion of male prerogatives was competing with other indigenous discourses that would restrict the range of elite male sexual prerogatives. The Franciscan morals campaign seemed to provide the cultural context in which alternative native views could be expressed more forcefully.

In fact, the whole question of what the prehispanic elite male prerogatives were seems to have been an evolving moral gray zone both before and after the conquest. Prehispanic law harshly punished a man who took another's wife. Nevertheless, like powerful men everywhere, prehispanic elite males often intruded in lesser-status marriages, took liberties with unattached women, and pressed sexual license in their own households, and they were largely tolerated. However, the initial movement of Spanish authority into places like Texcoco seems to have adjusted the moral environment in favor of lesser-status men and elite women who wanted stricter observance of marital constraints on the part of the elite nobles. Don Pedro of Texcoco's wife criticized Don Carlos Ometochtli for sexual licentiousness. When Don Carlos allowed his mistress to give orders to his wife, Doña María, he not only upset her, but many other women in Texcoco, and they were happy to share their discontent with Zumárraga. As we have seen in Don Juan of Iguala's case when his wife and sister-in-law abused him in the street, principal wives in the leader's household might choose to express their objections vociferously when their husband defied the colonial decree requiring the nobles to limit themselves to one wife.

The evidence of women's conduct in these trials supports anthropologist and historian Susan Kellogg's assertion that in the first fifty years of the colonial period, as the elite male warrior society crumbled, women may have exercised greater control and agency in the household and over property.[53] In these trials of elite native males, two factors seemed to be giving the women such authority. First, the women were testing their elite status, which the Spanish legal authorities respected, against the elite male prerogatives, which the Spanish law did not. Second, and more important, in prehispanic times, both elite men and rich commoner men were allowed to marry several women, suggesting that polygamy was as much an economic as a status privilege. In the colonial period, the crumbling of the tribute system prevented the financial support of large polygamous households, undercutting the prerogative. Therefore, the wives' insistence on the new monogamy had a great deal to do with protecting their children as undisputed heirs to the diminished pools of authority positions and property.

Moreover, there was real potential hardship for nuclear family legacies in this diminished tribute environment. In the pre-conquest period, Nezahualpilli is estimated to have had 6,000 relatives and retainers in the royal household.[54] Receiving tribute from approximately 70,000 people living in the city proper of Texcoco, another 250,000 living in several dozen altepemeh in the Acolhua territory, and vast tracts of property outside Texcoco, as well as land acquired from expanding military borders, he could afford these multiple households.[55] But by Don Carlos's time, there were barely more than 60,000 residents of Texcoco and its nearby hinterland, and the former tribute altepemeh supported Spanish conquistadors and Spanish crown activities rather than the Texcocan royal family. In fact, the crown reassigned the labor tribute in various wealthy altepemeh in the Acolhua region to the friars for church construction.

Thus, the elite women's fears for their offspring were related to the general fear of their families in many places that some family members would have to be relegated to poverty and obscurity. The Spanish monogamy rules were important assets to principal wives in such an environment. Thus, at the time of their trials, Don Carlos and these three other leaders were morally constrained from within and without; in other words, their personal behavior was under scrutiny from every quarter. The native values that macehualtin and elite women clung to were not Christian but partly attributable to the prehispanic sensibility that male sexual prerogatives should only be exercised when the noble had the economic foundation to support many wives.

The question remains, however, why did these leaders press their male prerogatives over these other considerations? Clearly, an alternative rhetoric was present in the indigenous communities and popular among some elite males. It argued against concessions to Franciscans, commoners, or elite women, and it conflated effective leadership with the open and defiant exercise of male prerogatives. Franciscan constraints on polygamy, consanguinity, and male authority had already created a disharmonious environment in the altepemeh, and some nobles could easily argue that fighting back by elevating masculine values was a better way of restoring harmony than following the path of arbitration of avoidance. This alternative rhetoric was obvious not only in Don Carlos's trial and those of the other nobles, but also in the trial of Martín Ocelotl in 1536–37. In fact, Ocelotl had given the assertion of male prerogatives a philosophical justification when he urged nobles to live for today because there was no hereafter and suggested that the friars were really man-eating female demons portending the possible end of the (male) world as they knew it.[56] Don Carlos's year of turning in 1537 was the same agitated year of Ocelotl's and Mixcoatl's trials. The Ocelotl trial was particularly disturbing to the Texcocan nobles because of Zumárraga's property confiscations in and near Texcoco.

In light of these possible influences on Don Carlos's changing demeanor, what should we make of his provocative actions in the spring of 1539? The simplest interpretation of Don Carlos's behavior would be to agree with his enemies and label him a bad noble, more worried about his women than the welfare of his people. But he could just as easily be viewed as a rational actor questioning the Franciscan demands, weighing the alternatives, and changing his mind as befit his experiences and his changing circumstances. Don Carlos could not hope to assuage the many powerful enemies he had in Texcoco in the early spring of 1539, after Don Pedro had died and left him a disputed crown.[57] The logical path for Don Carlos was to take greater risk, abandon the more discreet path of arbitration of avoidance, and appeal to nobles like himself who were sick of the officiousness of the Franciscans and their interference in village and family matters. In order to secure his future, Don Carlos had to reach back to his past, to the rights, responsibilities, and privileges of a true tlahtoani.

THE ACCUSATION
"What are the things of God? They are nothing."

As noted before, the denunciation of Don Carlos came from outside Texcoco, from a group of indigenous men in the town of Chiconautla with whom he had had little previous contact. Some time in the third week of June 1539, Francisco, a younger brother of the tlahtoani of Chiconautla, Don Alonso, traveled to the city of Mexico to inform Fray Antonio de Ciudad Rodrigo about speeches Don Carlos had made in his village. On June 22, Francisco gave testimony before Zumárraga, and the Inquisition of Don Carlos of Texcoco began. Francisco testified that Don Carlos harbored a deep hostility to the church and the Franciscans, which the Texcocan leader had revealed at a meeting of indigenous nobles in Chiconautla on or about June 1, 1539. Several nobles in Chiconautla who had attended the meeting corroborated most of Francisco's accusations and expanded on his basic testimony with numerous extra details. The totality of the evidence and corroboration from various sources suggests that Don Carlos had indeed made most of the statements attributed to him.[58]

Why did Don Carlos choose to express strong anti-Christian ideas in Chiconautla, and what was he doing there in the critical early months of his rule? Francisco and others told the inquisitors that Don Carlos had come to Chiconautla to visit his half sister, María, who was married to the leader of the village, Don Alonso. María, however, later testified that she was surprised by the unexpected visit from her sibling. She claimed she had only seen her half brother twice before in her life, and he had not visited Chiconautla in her memory.[59] More likely, Don Carlos was visiting Don Alonso, for any number of mundane reasons that colonial leaders would need to consult about. While the Triple Alliance had fallen, the network of relations and mutual politics that bound the Acolhua nobles together survived for many years after the conquest. Chiconautla had been one of dozens of Acolhua towns and cities subject to Texcoco. It had not been a wealthy altepetl, but it had been a very important military partner to Texcoco, due to its strategic location between Lake Xaltocan and Lake Texcoco. In fact, when Cortés arrived in Mexico, Motecuhzoma was in the process of courting Chiconautla in order to weaken the Texcocans.[60] Though Chiconautla's military currency might have fallen in colonial times, its prosperity had increased. It was a center of the production of pulque, the indigenous alcoholic beverage, the consumption of which skyrocketed after the conquest.[61] It was also an important center of artisans for the building trades, services much needed in the early colonial period.⁶² While colonial Chiconautla was no longer subject to the Texcocan tribute system, it was under Texcoco's jurisdiction for labor drafts to rebuild the capital, Tenochtitlan, in the first two decades after the conquest.⁶³ Moreover, to bind the Acolhua elites together, the Texcocan kings required Acolhua nobles to own land in each other's altepemeh; many such property connections continued into the colonial period.⁶⁴

In short, when Don Carlos went to Chiconautla, probably to do business with its tlahtoani—perhaps to shore up support for his rule within the extended royal family—challenging Franciscan authority was probably not on his mind. Upon his arrival, however, the Chiconautlans were in the middle of holding *rogativas* (Christian religious processions) to pray for the end of drought. In Mexico, the rainy season began in June, but, for the previous two years, the rain had been sporadic and sometimes nonexistent, leaving the villages dying from famine and periodic waves of immigration. Like other villagers, the Chiconautlans had wanted to ensure the coming of rain with pagan offerings, but the ubiquitous Fray Antonio de Ciudad Rodrigo had encouraged them to use the Spanish ceremony in place of their usual pagan ones. Francisco, Don Alonso's younger brother, had been a student at the Colegio de Santa Cruz de Tlatelolco, and as a mandón, he was about the business of teaching and compelling the villagers to participate in the rogativas. Several witnesses' testified that Don Carlos was extremely angry at seeing the rogativas in progress when he arrived, and he refused to attend them. He avoided his relatives for over a day before he finally called them to assemble and hear his thoughts about the Franciscans and their religious teachings.⁶⁵

Though he did not address the troubles he was having in Texcoco, one can sense in Don Carlos's speeches to the Chiconautlans his rage against the way Franciscan restrictions had deprived his long-awaited rule of its prestige, privileges, and honor. Several nobles were in Don Alonso's home, where Don Carlos was staying, including Don Alonso, Francisco, two Chiconautla nobles named Melchior and Cristóbal, and several Texcocan men who had accompanied Don Carlos. In addressing this group, Don Carlos's strongest card was his descent from his grandfather, the great Nezahualcoyotl, and father, Nezahualpilli, who together represented a kind of Golden Age of the tlahtoqueh. The sixteenth-century histories of the pre-conquest tlahtoqueh, written by the grandsons and sons of native nobles, attest to the pair's powerful hold on the conquered nobility's imagination.[66] The Nahuatl term "tlahtoani" literally meant "speaker," and a tlahtoani's whole manner of conduct in speech and demeanor was exalted and carefully prescribed. Don Carlos's audience would have remembered this etiquette, which he made every effort to emulate. In the past, tlahtoqueh were rarely seen with anyone other than nobles, no one was allowed to look them in the face, and the pathway in front of them was always swept clean. Colonial indigenous leaders could hardly compel that level of ceremony, but Don Carlos made a point of demanding that all non-nobles leave the room, and indeed, two men were sent away. He told his remaining audience that they must "agree to be silent" about what he had to say.[67]

One of the witnesses said that Don Carlos began his *"plática"* (talk), "as in the old custom, about his ancestors."[68] He was referring to the form of speech called huehuetlahtolli. At the time, Fray Andrés de Olmos was thoroughly impressed with the tradition and collected examples of it in his book *Huehuehtlahtolli*, a good indication that colonial nobles in the 1530s were still accustomed to addressing their communities and families in this form of speech.[69] Olmos describes the speech pattern as *tenonotzaliztli*, which he glosses as "plática," or *qualli tlahtolli*, fine language reserved for use among the higher classes. Years later, Sahagún clarified that huehuetlahtolli were usually specific to the tlahtoani, especially in their references to subordinates and their strong admonitions. He devoted book 6 of the *Florentine Codex* to its study and called it "the rhetoric and moral philosophy of the Aztecs." In it, he notes the use of rhetorical questions that the speaker would answer with flourishes that tended to repeat themselves in parallel phrasing. The style was also characterized by the speaker's references to himself and his emotional state in making the speech. Frances Karttunen and James Lockhart have studied a series of published huehuetlahtolli from Texcoco and note that the speaker never uses the listeners' personal names but refers to them as "brothers," "cousins," or "uncles," depending on their age. The speeches are filled with references to Texcocan tradition and contain a strong flavor of "nostalgia for the old days of the Golden Age" before the Spanish arrived.⁷⁰ Don Carlos's patterns of speech, as related by the testimonies of others, were in this same vein, indicating that he, Don Alonso, Francisco, and the other nobles in the room were accustomed to keeping the prehispanic tradition of formal speaking on occasions when only nobles were present.⁷¹

Don Carlos's high imperial manner of argument was designed to enjoin the traditional sentiments of the elite, but the arguments he now employed were also made to appeal to their self-interest and anger over the way the Franciscans had turned women, children, and macehualtin away from their obligations to elite men. Perhaps his most strident attack on the friars, according to witnesses, was his insistence that the celibate friars' objective was nothing more than "denying us women." He complained, "All the friars talk about is sin. What is it that they name except sin?"⁷² At one point, Don Carlos called his sister, María, the wife of Don Alonso, into the room and told her,

> You have to do whatever your husband wants and needs. I think that you do not follow what our ancestors used to do. If your husband wants to take other women, do not impede him or scold the women that he takes or pay attention to the matrimonial laws of the Christians. I am also married, but, in spite of this, I do not refrain from taking your niece as my concubine. If I want to lie with her and if my wife is angry, so what, it is nothing to me.⁷³

Don Carlos was equally angry about the rogativas. In a sense, the rogativas were a metaphor for the way young people were encouraged to take over religious roles from their elders. Before the conquest, the tlahtoani had been the "representative of the deities and the purity of the noble class; he upheld the moral well-being of the state."⁷⁴ Yet, here was Francisco, "just a boy," as Don Carlos said at one point during the meeting of the nobles, teaching the Spanish and Christian way, leading the village procession, sermonizing to the community, compelling villagers to participate, and punishing those who did not. With the support and encouragement of these Franciscans, Francisco had the temerity to usurp moral authority in front of Don Carlos and Don Alonso. His actions were an affront, a challenge to their leadership over the Acolhua community and Chiconautla. In the meeting, Don Carlos warned Francisco, "Do you think what you are doing is important?" He chastised him for following the instructions he had learned in the colegio.[75] Indeed, Francisco was a junior ally to the friars, a young enforcer, a mandón.[76] In the late 1530s, some of these young people were known to have been murdered by their parents for their divided allegiances.[77] Francisco humiliated his elders and betters at the behest of the Franciscans; to Don Carlos, it was proof that the friars had turned the world upside down.

Don Carlos tried to persuade his listeners from the stage with elegant huehuetlahtolli rhetoric: "What are the things of God?" he asked, and emphatically answered, "They are nothing."[78] Then he returned to the past for the definitive proof of his statement. "You well know that my father and grandfather were great prophets and they said many things that passed and were to come and nothing did they say about these things [the rogativas]." He went on to declare the primacy of his ancestors in spiritual matters, saying, "If something were true in what you and the others say in this [Christian] doctrine, they [his ancestors] would have said so." He appealed directly to his relations:

> Understand me, brother, that I have lived and been everywhere and have kept the words of my father and my grandfather. Listen, brother, to what our fathers and our grandfathers said when they died, of the truth that was revealed about the gods that they had and that they loved, who were made in the heavens and in the earth. For that reason, brother, we must only follow what our grandfathers and our fathers held and said when they died.[79]

As if to emphasize the greater wisdom of the old ways and the prehispanic ordering of Texcocan society, he appealed to the tradition of Texcocan law. Pre-conquest Texcoco had the most sophisticated legal codes and court system in central Mexico. As Jerome Offner has noted, Texcocan law was centered on the ruling of the tlahtoani, but it was applied in a "legalistic" manner. "Only the matters pertaining to the particular points in a certain law" could be used in court, and the laws were applied without exception."[80] While the nobles obviously had privileges greater than the macehualtin, within the class of nobles, the law tended to be consistent. Interestingly, when Don Carlos argued that "the Christians have many women and get drunk,"[81] while indigenous nobles were restrained from these legitimate privileges, he seemed to be equating the conquerors with the indigenous elite and implying that the friars were legally inconsistent in their prohibition to equivalent groups. By Texcocan standards, it was a considerable breach of justice. Moreover, the friars had proved inept at enforcing the laws, he said, because the poor drank more than they ever did under the tlahtoqueh, even though the friars told them not to. Even worse, the macehualtin did not pay the food tribute to the nobles as they were obligated to do under Spanish and native law. As Don Carlos plaintively complained to Don Alonso, the real problem was that the people did not "fear and obey" anyone.[82]

Don Carlos carefully recommended some actions to his fellows, or perhaps they should be described as non-actions. He argued that the only reason that the villagers did any of the new ceremonies, the rogativas, was because the indigenous nobles, like Francisco, "encouraged, authorized, and augmented [the practice of Christianity] with their words."[83] Without the indigenous leaders' allowances for participation in Christian activities, the mendicants would make no headway in their evangelizing. He ordered Francisco, "Stop these things that are vanities, and this I tell you as an uncle and a brother-in-law, do not take care of these things and encourage the other people to believe what the friars say. . . . Just look to your house and take care of your household."[84]

Significantly, Don Carlos did not recommend violence against the Franciscans. Rather, he was counseling non-accommodation. However, he soon became his own worst enemy as he tried to persuade the nobles in Chiconautla to his point of view. The friars, and therefore, the historical record, might never have learned of Don Carlos's speeches had he not made a serious rhetorical miscalculation. Having heard Don Carlos's arguments, Don Alonso and Francisco responded in the friars' defense. Heated exchanges followed, in which Don Carlos admitted to being very "emotional." Finally, he pulled aside his brother-in-law, Don Alonso, and his sister, María, and recommended to them that they "watch themselves around" Francisco. Suddenly, in a pique of frustration, he urged them to murder Francisco and their own two young sons, Tomás and Diego, "because they are very advanced in the things of God."[85]

We have no way of knowing what crossed Francisco's mind when he learned from his brother and sister-in-law of Don Carlos's threat, except that he had good reason to take it seriously, given the stories of child assassination in the Valley of Mexico. Francisco, however, did not denounce Don Carlos right away. He needed further inducement. On June 18, 1539, two weeks after Don Carlos's visit to Chiconautla and his return to Texcoco, the viceroy ordered the reading of new ordinances that announced severe penalties for idolatry or even "speaking against the holy faith." His royal order also contained an exhortation to all native subjects to come forward and tell the religious authorities what they knew about such "crimes." The announcement was made in Nahuatl in the city of Mexico and "surrounding communities," presumably including Tlatelolco, where Francisco was at the colegio.[86] Two days later, on June 20, Mateo and Pedro revealed the existence of the Huitzilopochtlis and sparked the Inquisition of Pochtecatl Tlaylotla. Another two days later, on June 22, Francisco went before the bishop in the church of Santiago de Tlatelolco and denounced Don Carlos.

The train of events indicates that Francisco was not motivated by religious piety or loyalty to the friars alone but also considerable fear of Don Carlos and his men. Denouncing a leader of Don Carlos's rank and the in-law of his own brother was a serious step for the young man and a break from his prehispanic heritage. The fact that he waited two weeks after the meeting in Chiconautla suggests that he took plenty of time to think about it and perhaps felt some pressure from being in the cultural environment of the colegio at Tlatelolco, away from Chiconautla and near the friars. In any case, Francisco's remoteness from Texcoco completely contradicts any idea that Don Carlos was betrayed by the Texcocans. Instead, betrayal and denunciation came from a rather remote corner of the indigenous community—a young man raised for part of his childhood by the Franciscans, given intensive instruction in Christianity, sheltered by the Spanish at a remove from native ties, and physically threatened with death first by Don Carlos and then by the viceroy in his royal order of June 18, 1539.

Between June 22, when Don Carlos was first accused, and July 15, when he was at last interrogated, the Inquisition managed to take the testimony of nearly thirty indigenous people from Chiconautla and Texcoco. Witnesses included most of the important nobles in and around Texcoco and from the town council; several male and female members of Don Carlos's family, including his wife, his sister-in-law, his lover Inés, his adolescent son, and numerous retainers of his household; as well as a few native men who simply stepped forward and offered testimony of their own volition. Inside of two weeks, the city of Texcoco was turned upside down with searches for prehispanic votive objects. The surrounding hills were combed for evidence of secret religious sacrifices, idols, and altars. The Texcocan town council and its governor, Don Lorenzo de Luna, who months before had ordered his servants to keep information about clandestine sacrifices and paganism from the bishop and the mendicants, now were compelled under the watchful eye of Zumárraga to seek out the remains of secret sacrifices and pagan idols, drag them down from the hills, and dig them up along the roadsides.

The nobles who had counseled Don Carlos to look after the interests of Texcoco by accommodating the Franciscans in religious matters certainly must have felt the chagrin of being right. With regard to Don Carlos, however, the testimonies taken in Texcoco demonstrated that, of the three charges made against him of bigamy, pagan worship, and heretical dogmatism, the Texcocans had plenty to say about the first charge, very little about the second, and nothing about any statements Don Carlos might have made against the Franciscans or Catholicism. Even Don Carlos's beleaguered wife, Doña María, noted that she had never seen him worshipping or making offerings to the pagan gods, though he was by no means a churchgoing noble.[87]

The Inquisition tribunal went to Texcoco confident of finding further evidence against Don Carlos. But there was not much to corroborate the testimonies from Chiconautla. Either the Texcocans were unwilling to testify against one of their own, or Don Carlos had been more careful in concealing his thoughts about the Franciscans in Texcoco than he was in Chiconautla. He had become ill in February, seemingly part of a broad epidemic that killed his former mentor and half brother, Don Pedro, and left Don Carlos recovering from a brush with death; in fact, he may not have actively taken charge in Texcoco until April or May.[88]

On the whole, after the investigations in Chiconautla and Texcoco, the Inquisition had little incriminating testimony. Stronger evidence was necessary to justify the removal of the leader of a major city like Texcoco. On July 11, Zumárraga came back to the city of Mexico and asked Francisco if he wished to amplify his previous testimony. Re-interrogation was a typical Inquisition procedure, but it was also the phase of the Inquisition process when the most abuses arose and false testimonies were given. In his second testimony, Francisco attributed the following statement to Don Carlos:

> Who are these people [referring to the Franciscans] who bother us and perturb us and live among us and try to rule us? Well, here I am and there is the señor of Mexico, Yoanize; and there is my nephew, Tezapilli, señor of Tacuba; and there is Tlacahuapantli, señor of Tula; we are all equal and nobody is equal to us. This is our land and our way of life and our possession; the rule of it belongs to us and will remain with us. Who comes here to subjugate us, who are these people who are not our relatives nor of our blood nor equal to us? Well, here we are and we do not have to tolerate those who make fools of us.[89]

The speech was brilliant and certainly had the same combination of huehuetlahtolli, bombast, and indignation as Don Carlos's other alleged speeches before the Chiconautlans. There was one difference, however. While the other Chiconautla nobles corroborated and added details to Francisco's June testimony, they were not prepared to support him in this later, and more extreme, representation of Don Carlos's words and actions. His brother-in-law, Don Alonso, and Melchior, another indigenous noble who had heard Don Carlos speak in Chiconautla, hesitated. Don Alonso claimed that he had been too inebriated to remember everything, and Melchior said he was too busy bringing wood and drink into the meeting room to hear all the details. Don Alonso confirmed that Don Carlos had referred to the other leaders but also claimed that he "tried not to remember it but that Francisco knew more about what happened because he was more attentive and [Don Alonso] was sure that [Francisco] was telling the truth."⁹⁰ The inability or reluctance of the other witnesses to confirm resolutely Francisco's later accusations and, more important, the fact that neither Francisco nor another young noble, Cristóbal, had testified to this far more damning evidence the first time they were interrogated two and three weeks before suggests Francisco may have been offering embellished or even false testimony.

In fact, Francisco was under considerable pressure to be the model witness for the Franciscans. As seen in the previous chapter, when the bishop ran into a problem locating the keepers of the Huitzilopochtlis in October 1539, Francisco came forward and listed the names of every "well-known prophet" in the city of Mexico, the effect of which was to pull several very important native nobles into the web of the Inquisition.⁹¹ Whether it came from Don Carlos or not, the wonderfully composed speech was precisely the kind of evidence of sedition against the Spanish state that was needed to alarm the authorities and bring Don Carlos's case into the realm of executable offenses. Greenleaf notes that "this speech was probably the most important factor in the decision of Viceroy Mendoza and the Audiencia to support Zumárraga on the relaxation, or execution, sentence."⁹² Don Carlos had his auto de fé in the Plaza Mayor of the city of Mexico on November 30, 1539, and was burned at the stake outside the walls of the city the next day.

CONCLUSION

In terms of larger questions of indigenous agency, this close analysis of indigenous motivations and cultural values in Don Carlos's trial, as with the other trials, suggests an internal indigenous world of cities and towns around Texcoco filled with native discourses guided by prehispanic leaders' values: being discreet, masculine prerogatives, sex, woman possession, brotherly love, inheritance, and family rights. The discourses were well understood in indigenous communities but not generally revealed to the Franciscans. The implementation of the Franciscans' ethnographic projects in the 1530s indicates that they were becoming more aware of this complex and nuanced world of values in the native communities. Nevertheless, as they learned more, they tended to punish more. The moral duality of their world prevented them from understanding the natives' values and moral dilemmas. They surely hoped that the Inquisition would teach the native leaders to behave in a Christian manner and enforce the mission doctrine. But what the Texcocan leadership actually learned from the trial of Don Carlos was to have more care about sex and pagan votive objects. From 1539, Texcocan men kept to one wife or kept the others out of sight, while votive objects went well underground, figuratively and literally.

EPILOGUE

The Legacy of the Inquisition in Central Mexico

When the Council of the Indies in Spain learned about the execution of Don Carlos Ometochtli and the confiscation of his large estate, it decided to reprimand Zumárraga. In a letter of November 22, 1540, Francisco de Nava, bishop of Seville and royal council member, explained that while he understood that Zumárraga had ordered the execution of Don Carlos "in the belief that burning would put fear into others and make an example of him," nevertheless, he insisted that the native people "might be more persuaded with love than with rigor. . . . [One] should not apply to them the rigor of the law . . . nor confiscate their property."[1] Shortly after receiving this letter, Zumárraga stopped bringing cases against the native leaders altogether and drastically reduced the number of cases against Spaniards. In the four and a half years from July 1536 to December 1540, the bishop judged around 158 cases, but in the years 1541 to 1543, he judged only 11, and the latter trials all involved Spaniards. Eventually, in 1543, the court sent Fray Francisco Tello de Sandoval, visitador, member of the Council of the Indies, and former member of the Inquisition in Toledo, to take over Zumárraga's Inquisition powers. Tello de Sandoval tried a few cases involving native leaders in the Mixtec area southwest of central Mexico and a few disparate cases of Spaniards. But his three years of work were clearly designed to finish up Zumárraga's Inquisition, not to open a new phase. The support for a rigorous Inquisition of the natives had waned. Its legacy was different for each of the three groups—Spaniards, Franciscans, and native leaders—who had participated in the Inquisition.

SPANISH PERSPECTIVES
"It seems to us a very harsh treatment for one so newly converted"

Even before November 1540, Zumárraga's Inquisition had stirred up so much controversy that local Spanish opinion was running hard against him, and he felt it. His abrupt abandonment of the yearlong case against Miguel Pochtecatl Tlaylotla, the keeper of the Huitzilopochtlis, in May 1540, suggested that the bishop was aware that letters from local Spaniards complaining about the case of Don Carlos were probably already circulating at the Spanish court. In fact, Nava's letter of reprimand in November hinted that Zumárraga had already sent several letters to Madrid defending his actions, meaning that criticism of his handling of the Inquisition was very strong in the previous spring. Nava summarily rejected Zumárraga's previous argument that "neither physical punishment nor dishonor warns them as well as the loss of their estates."[2] Nava's opinion about Zumárraga's handling of the Don Carlos case was also clear: "It seems to us a very harsh treatment for one so newly converted to our holy faith."[3] The complaints from New Spain about Zumárraga's confiscations of property and his unjust treatment of native neophytes not only convinced Nava, but seem to have become an accepted orthodoxy in government circles in the next two years. We can read this conventional wisdom in the instructions that the cardinal of Toledo, head of the Inquisition in Spain, gave Tello de Sandoval two years later in 1543 as the latter left for New Spain.

> *Item.* The inspector is to look into a proceso that was carried out by the Reverend Father Juan de Zumárraga, bishop of Mexico, against Don Carlos, cacique, where he was relaxed, and inform himself if it was well adjudicated. Investigate what goods are left and what has been done with them and if there are children. Tell the Council [of the Indies] of this.
>
> *Item.* After investigating the proceso of Don Carlos, communicate with the bishop of Mexico about any defects that may have resulted, especially if Don Carlos made a defense and if he was given time to make it, and

asked for more time and was not given it, and if his defenses were refused. And also, in the auto, the said Don Carlos gave a speech to the Indians, in which he demonstrated contrition and repented his sins; ... investigate if it would have been possible to reconcile him.[4]

The specific legal and factual details in these instructions suggest that the primary instigator of accusations against Bishop Zumárraga that led to a change of heart in Spain was none other than Don Carlos's lawyer, Vicente Riverol, who had spent much of the spring writing letters to the royal councils complaining about Don Carlos's case. Riverol also happened to be the attorney for Don Carlos's Spanish business partner, Pedro de Vergara. Vergara had an arrangement with Don Carlos to plant Castilian fruit trees on a property near the Oztoticpac palace, the large house that Don Pedro had given Don Carlos years before, when he chose him as successor.[5] When Zumárraga confiscated Don Carlos's estate, he took the palace and lands and also Vergara's costly investment in imported tree stock. Clearly, Vergara had much to lose in the Don Carlos case.

It is also very probable that he and Riverol counseled Don Carlos to give "a speech to the Indians" at his auto de fé confessing his sins and asking forgiveness, possibly because they believed it would lead to reconciliation with the bishop and church, save Don Carlos's life, and also preserve some of the estate. Indeed, Don Carlos was suppliant in his November 30, 1539, auto de fé (compared with his indignant attitude at trial) and made an absolutely model public confession, telling the assembled natives in Nahuatl "to throw off idolatry and convert to God and not blindly follow the devils as he had."[6] Inquisition proceedings of that time allowed Zumárraga the latitude of reconciling Don Carlos in light of the "good lesson" that he had given in favor of the faith.[7] But Zumárraga decided to take the hard line. He proceeded with the immediate execution of Don Carlos the next day and confiscated his entire, very large estate. Although we know Zumárraga had complained to a friend that the church coffers in Mexico were low in 1539 and one might think that the confiscations were the motivation for his behavior, in fact, most evidence points to a desire on his part to set a tough and timely example for native leaders who might be hiding the elusive Huitzilopochtlis.[8]

Many local Spaniards, however, including Riverol and Vergara, saw Zumárraga's motives and actions in a different light. Zumárraga had appointed Riverol to defend Don Carlos as well as Miguel Pochtecatl Tlaylotla, probably expecting the usual cooperation and flexibility that most Inquisition-appointed defense attorneys provided; that is, getting the accused to confess rather than arguing with the Inquisition tribunal. Riverol had played that compliant role in his defense of Don Carlos, calling few witnesses to rebut the testimony against him. In the fall of 1539, Riverol showed the demeanor of a man who supposed that Zumárraga would sensibly reconcile Don Carlos rather than create the problems that might come with execution and confiscation of the estate of a major tlahtoani. After Don Carlos's execution in December, Riverol did not make the same mistake of compliance in Miguel's trial the following spring. He put up a far more rigorous and even defiant defense of Miguel. The transcript from March to May records numerous days in court in which Riverol suggested that Zumárraga was "unjust" and that his actions were "contrary to the tests of proof and . . . without sufficient witnesses."[9] But Riverol's angry change of heart also reflected a strong local backlash against the bishop's perceived high-handedness in the Inquisition, which aggravated the bishop's already difficult relations with the local Spaniards.

Looking back to the formula for Inquisition as laid out in Spain, after forced conversion through mass baptism and the creation of a subversive class of native leaders, the next step for Zumárraga would have been to secure a local and crown alliance (see chapter 1). Obviously, the bishop failed in the Inquisition because of his tendency to create unnecessary enemies. Zumárraga had wanted a permanent Holy Office established in the city of Mexico precisely because he understood that his legal powers were subject to question and he was not skilled at manipulating the local elites politically.

Now, in the spring of 1540, even members of the Audiencia and the church community who had previously been in his favor had their doubts about his aggressive pursuit of local native leaders, and more important, his property confiscations that ended up in the coffers of the Inquisition. The fear of stirring up the native leaders in the Valley of Mexico was growing, as the western frontier of the colony showed signs of indigenous uprisings, leading finally to the great Mixtón War of 1541–43, the most dangerous threat to the Spanish colony in the sixteenth century. Moreover, the threatened or real confiscation of large native estates—those of Ocelotl, Don Cristóbal of Ocuituco, Don Carlos of Texcoco, Don Baltasar of Culhuacan, and Don Diego Huanitzin—worried not only native leaders but also local Spaniards who did business with them. Many of the latter were beginning to line up with other Spaniards in Mexico and Spain who had already crossed swords with Zumárraga in 1532, when the bishop was briefly recalled to Spain. And without question, Zumarraga's extensive use of Inquisition to punish members of the Spanish community of the city of Mexico also created numerous enemies. In addition, the summer's hunt for idols and the way Zumárraga's actions had inspired Spanish vigilantism in the native communities caused sympathetic Franciscan observers, such as Motolinía, to reconsider the benefits of Inquisition. In the final analysis, while the perception of severity in the Don Carlos trial was the most immediate consequential argument for the end of Zumárraga's Inquisition, the range of other provocations, from native property confiscations to the fear of Franciscan power, created a hostile environment for Zumárraga and prevented the development of the social alliance necessary for the survival of the bishop's Inquisition.

In the longer term, the Spanish government's attitude toward the necessity of native Inquisition trials looked much more like Nava's careful and measured position than Zumárraga's zeal. When Tello de Sandoval departed from New Spain in early 1547, inquisitorial authority over the natives was placed in a Provisorato del Ordinario, a local office of the bishops that dealt with religious crimes of the natives (though bishops beyond the city of Mexico were expected to handle their local cases by themselves). Bishops tended to handle these native cases very quietly, and few trials against natives were brought in the next fifteen years. In 1561, the church and crown were again alarmed when the Franciscan provincial of the southern province of Yucatan, Fray Diego de Landa, conducted an Inquisition against thousands of natives. Compared with Zumárraga's Inquisition, it was more violent and lacked any sense of judicial regularity. The Landa Inquisition finally ended when a Franciscan bishop, Fray Francisco de Toral, was sent to the Yucatan to introduce order.[10] For the next decade, Inquisition trials against natives in New Spain were again somewhat rare. Finally, in 1571, with the Tridentine reforms in hand and a very large church reform project already underway in Spain, Philip II decided to establish a separate Holy Office in the city of Mexico. However, Philip left the native peoples out of the jurisdiction of the new Holy Office; the punishment of natives and their leaders for religious crimes remained in the hands of the bishops and the Provisorato. The separate Inquisition jurisdictions remained throughout the colonial period in New Spain, though the Holy Office made occasional juridical forays into native affairs.

Historians have suggested that the Don Carlos case and the Landa Inquisition were notorious landmarks that influenced Philip II's decision to keep the natives in a separate jurisdiction.[11] Yet there is a fundamental problem with this line of argument. While it is true that Prince Philip had begun to involve himself in his father's government at the time that Tello de Sandoval was sent to New Spain in 1543 (Philip was fifteen), no record has yet been found demonstrating that Philip remembered or had the Don Carlos case in mind when he made the decision thirty years later to keep the natives out of Inquisition jurisdiction. Additionally, we must remember that Don Carlos was tried and condemned by a bishop, a condition similar to what Philip ordered for the natives in 1571—individual bishops handling local cases, sometimes with the oversight of the Provisorato or Audiencia. While the Provisorato added an extra judicial layer to protect against a single inquisitor-bishop getting out of hand, in fact, it was a continuation of the same Apostolic Inquisition that had condemned Don Carlos. The conservative Philip was evidently satisfied with the judicial treatment of his native subjects and essentially allowed this variation on the Apostolic Inquisition to continue. Recent research indicates that the Provisorato throughout the colonial period was generally about as rigorous with the natives as Zumárraga had been, though not quite as showy in its pronouncements, which seemed to be fine with Philip.[12]

Another explanation for Philip's decision to leave the status quo in place returns to the discussion in chapter 1, about Spanish history and culture in dealing with unbeliever populations. In the early sixteenth century, the court and many Spaniards were troubled about extending the Inquisition beyond Jews to other unbeliever communities.

With hesitant steps throughout the sixteenth century, the Spanish court allowed the Inquisition to make inroads into Old Christian populations, especially after the start of Reformation movements, as well as into morisco communities.

A major concern of the crown was that an unholy combination of Inquisition bureaucrats and local political interests would abuse the Inquisition's power.[13] The threat was even greater with jurisdictions far from Madrid and among unbelievers too intimidated to respond effectively and—from the Spaniards' perspective—too foolish and simple to understand the faith that was supposed to govern their lives. Such sentiments and conclusions are clear in the direct archival evidence we have of advice to Philip II in 1568. The vicar general of New Spain's archdiocese, Sancho Sánchez de Muñón, wrote a letter advising Philip that an Inquisition was appropriate in New Spain, but not for the natives, "because they are so new to the faith, weak people and of little substance."[14] With the moriscos, temporary concordias that exempted them from Inquisition jurisdiction had been necessary because they needed time to turn away from a strong Islamic culture and tradition. Though the American indigenous peoples were no longer considered blank slates, as they had been in the 1520s, nevertheless, their prehispanic culture was not accorded the same respect as Islam and was not acknowledged to be a credible lure away from Christianity. Rather, the natives were simply "weak" and "of little substance," incapable of appreciating the Christian doctrine as well as they should. Philip II, whom the Spanish came to call "El Prudente," cared too much for his reputation in religious matters to tolerate the specter of Spaniards using religion to dupe simple people out of their property. He did not need the Don Carlos case or the Landa Inquisition to decide in 1571 that, as he was conditioned to see them over thirty years of reports disparaging their intellect, his native subjects were not good candidates for the complex legal environment of the Inquisition.

FRANCISCAN PERPECTIVES
"Deluded rather than deficient"

In 1540, the Franciscans had been slow to recognize that Spaniards at court were experiencing this change of mind. In January 1540, they and the bishop seemed confident that persecuting the native leaders and hunting down the idols, if painful, was for the best. And they were not alone in this opinion, as the decision to execute Don Carlos had been confirmed in the Audiencia and by Viceroy Mendoza himself. When Fray Andrés de Olmos wrote in January 1540 that Zumárraga should continue with rigorous and severe punishment of apostates, "even if they have to be put into the fire, as Your Excellency is commencing to do,"[15] it demonstrated a foregone conclusion in the elite Franciscan circle that there probably would be many more exemplary sentences in the coming year. Yet, after May and certainly after November 1540, the Franciscans gradually came to realize that the Inquisition as a solution for the apostasy and deceitfulness of the native leaders was no longer available.

Nevertheless, the widespread apostasy and deceitfulness were still there, and the native leaders were still a subversive class undermining their mission. Another solution was needed. The complaint against the Franciscans had been that they baptized without sufficient religious education, creating this "problem" class of native leaders. Two possible policies were to stop the mass baptisms or to educate the baptized adults better. Zumárraga tried both. Already in 1539, Zumárraga had agreed with the other bishops to discourage the Franciscan policy of mass baptisms. Many Franciscans, however, continued to baptize in defiance of the bishop, and Zumárraga halfheartedly complained that he was helpless in the face of their zealotry. Still, from 1540 until his death in 1548, Zumárraga published a series of books that were intended to both guide and give support to the post-baptismal education of neophytes. He also published a catechism, "Manual de adultos" (December 1540), in the hopes of creating a uniform Christian instruction of the problematic native adults; it was used to the end of the century.[16]

Education of the natives after 1540, however, did not just mean better instruction of scripture. The Franciscans found another education tactic that they believed might help them keep native apostasy in check, and it was to demonize the native leaders by labeling them representatives of the devil. The rhetoric condemning diabolism—the practice of worshipping and advocating for the devil—had not yet been theologically linked to the practices of the nanahualtin or the native leaders.[17] Zumarraga's native victims were only occasionally referred to as "brujos," and none of the indigenous gods was consistently described as the devil. This was soon remedied. In the decade following Zumárraga's Inquisition, Fray Andrés de Olmos began to make these theological linkages and equations.

Not only was Olmos qualified for this occupation because of his superior knowledge of native religion and culture, he was also more knowledgeable about European theological developments with regard to diabolism. Olmos had been with Zumárraga in 1527 when the bishop was sent to Logroño, Spain, to adjudicate Vizcayan (Basque) witchcraft trials. In Logroño, he had met the famed Vizcayan Franciscan jurist Fray Martín de Castañega and obtained a copy of that friar's manuscript about Spanish witchcraft, "Tratado muy sotil y bien fundado de las supersticiones y hechicerias y vanos conjuros y abusiones y otras cosas tocantes al caso y de la posibilidad e remedio dellas" (later published as a book in Logroño in 1529). As Olmos learned more about native religion between 1533 and 1553, he no doubt had occasion to compare what he saw in Mexico with Castañega's observations of Basque witches and their concepts and practices. In 1553, Olmos published a Nahuatl translation of the first sixty pages of Castañega's manuscript, which he called *Tratado de hechicerías y sortilegios*. Olmos translated the book into Nahuatl so that not only would the friars know what diabolic practices to look for, but they would be able to read to the macehualtin and children in their conventos about what to look for. Through their neophytes, they could continue to expose the recalcitrant native leaders and possibly isolate them from their native communities.[18]

Viewing the Castañega and Olmos manuscripts, one can see that the first parts of the two manuscripts are almost identical except for a few passages that were clearly influenced by Olmos's experiences in Zumárraga's Inquisition, particularly in the trials of the nanahualtin Martín Ocelotl and Andrés Mixcoatl. For example, Castañega asserts what would soon become the position of the Spanish Inquisition, that followers of the devil do not actually make bodily transformations but believe they do. According to Castañega, those who claim that "a man converts himself into a fox or a goat or some such thing and then turns himself back into what he was . . . are in error; it is an illusion, a trick of the devil."¹⁹ Olmos translates this as "never under diabolical influence does a man turn himself into an animal, for example a deer, or a jaguar, . . . nor can he make himself sometimes a woman. . . . It is a great trick, a lie with which the devil makes fun of the people."²⁰ Later, Olmos clarifies that the devil has super-corporeal powers, but his "nahuales" (nanahualtin, which he often equates with "brujos") do not.²¹ Of course, the possibility of transforming into animals—especially deer or jaguars—or female specters and disappearing and reappearing someplace else were all claims of Ocelotl and other nanahualtin and were specific to native supernatural beliefs in central Mexico. In a passage he added to the Castañega text, Olmos again has Ocelotl in mind when he writes that those "who promise many riches to others who do not have it and promise a life of joy with women" are also tricking the people, as the devil tricked their ancestors for centuries.²² Fray Gerónimo Mendieta writes that Olmos actually had a discussion with an Inquisition victim, a "brujo" who was "the disciple of Ocelotl"—obviously Andrés Mixcoatl or Cristóbal Papalotl. According to Olmos, the man told him "that his maestro [Ocelotl] could free himself from prison whenever he wanted." Olmos supposedly replied that the man should do the same, but, as Mendieta triumphantly reports, "he did not, because he could not."²³

In fact, the whole tone of Olmos's *Tratado de hechicerías y sortilegios*, as Georges Baudot says, portrays the devil as a "political being. . . . All the diabolic appearances had the aspect of a struggle against the return of pre-Hispanic beliefs and practices. In other words, the devil was a pre-Hispanic character when he appeared in Mexico, . . . one who wished to revive the old cults and homages."²⁴ Mendieta describes another incident in which Olmos was dealing with a man in Cuernavaca who seemed to be possessed, and the man described the devil. Olmos translated the man's words as, "He appeared as a noble or cacique, dressed with jewels and gold."²⁵ In the *Tratado de hechicerías y sortilegios*, Olmos says that the devil appeared "like a king," similar to "nobles in ancient times when they danced."²⁶ In the 1530s, writing in *Historia de los mexicanos por sus pinturas*, Olmos merely characterizes Tezcatlipoca as "greatest and worst" of the gods, because he was so admired among nanahualtin such as Ocelotl and Mixcoatl. By the end of the 1540s, Sahagún asserts in book 1 of the *Florentine Codex* that Tezcatlipoca, "we know is Lucifer himself . . . who walketh upon the earth deluding and misleading people."[27]

Therefore, for friars close to the bishop, Zumarraga's Inquisition was a learning opportunity that allowed them to create the rhetoric and ideology of New World diabolism.[28] While the friars could no longer directly persecute the leaders with Inquisition, through the rhetoric of diabolism they hoped to isolate the native leaders and nanahualtin by encouraging their erstwhile followers to now fear them and report their bad deeds to the friars. Olmos believed that his *Tratado de hecicerías y sortilegios* could become the seminal text for the friars in the same way that Castañega hoped to guide the Spanish judiciary.[29] Unfortunately for them, as Fernando Cervantes has demonstrated, over the long term the rhetoric of diabolism backfired by reinforcing the native view that their earlier religious practice was a powerful force in the world. Rather than renouncing it, they feared and worshipped it even more.[30]

On the whole, in comparing the changing Spanish and Franciscan perspectives in Mexico, one observes that the crown and local colonial Spaniards came to believe that the natives were too foolish and simple to be saved readily; on the other hand, many Franciscans merely created a variation on their earlier optimistic appraisals of the natives as "deluded rather than deficient."[31] Both, of course, missed the reality that the native leaders were actually quite busy making remarkably insightful estimations of Spanish and Franciscan motives, intentions, and limitations and doing their best to adapt their altepemeh rapidly to the ever-changing economic and political colonial situation.

NATIVE LEADERS' PERSPECTIVES
"Why did Don Antonio tell us nothing?"

Ironically, as the Spanish became more disillusioned with the use of Spanish Inquisition as a tool against native apostasy, Zumárraga's Inquisition was rather effective in intimidating some communities in the Valley of Mexico. But the intimidation did not necessarily turn all the native leaders into compliant servants of the Franciscan mission. The most persecuted community, Texcoco, provides a good example of this unexpected course of events. The notoriety of Don Carlos's trial and the way it quickly led to property confiscations, threats against native leaders, and haphazard searches for the statues of native gods had given the Texcocan leadership pause. Texcoco's new tlahtoani was Antonio Pimentel Tlahuitoltzin (8), Don Carlos's half brother, a sober and older member of Texcoco's native cabildo and one of those whom Zumárraga had berated and threatened in the midst of Don Carlos's trial. In the aftermath of the trial, Texcoco's new tlahtoani could no longer follow a path of arbitration of avoidance, as his half brothers, Don Fernando, Don Jorge, and Don Pedro had, keeping the friars at arm's distance and looking the other way as the nanahualtin competed with the friars for religious authority in the Texcocan region. Don Antonio would have to demonstrate fealty to the Christian mission and stay close to the friars. Evidence suggests that he employed the friars as some of his closest counselors as he ruled Texcoco in the next five years.

Nevertheless, Don Antonio also zealously protected the royal family and asserted the tlahtoani's economic and political privileges even as he completely conceded religious leadership of Texcoco to the Franciscans. And he soon showed that he was prepared to fight for the historical legacy of the royal family and their property, even against the interests of the church and the Franciscans. Shortly after he took the throne in 1540, he joined in a lawsuit with Don Carlos's Spanish business partner, Pedro de Vergara, claiming that Zumárraga had confiscated the Oztoticpac palace and property unjustly.[32] The legal argument Don Antonio put forward was that the palace was not Don Carlos's private property; it was communal property that rightfully belonged to Texcoco and therefore, to the royal family. The Texcocan lawsuit continued to at least 1546. The lawsuit and its participants are depicted in Humboldt Fragment VI, a partial manuscript from the sixteenth century (figure 3).

Along the left lower side are seen (from top to bottom) Pedro de Vergara, the ruler Don Antonio, and Vicente Riverol, the defense attorney who had become a thorn in Zumárraga's side. Above them is Viceroy Mendoza, flanked by two members of the Audiencia. Apparently, Don Antonio had initially received a judgment in his favor in the lawsuit, but he was soon countersued by the man who

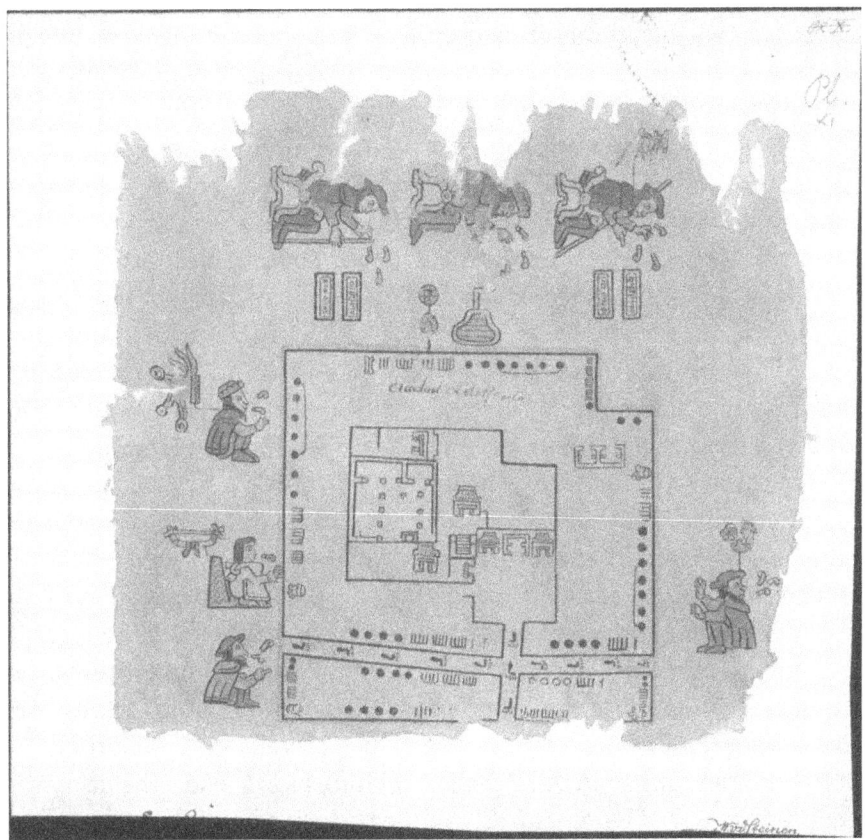

Figure 3. Humboldt Fragment VI. Manuscript 2205, Smithsonian Institution National Anthropological Archives.

had purchased the property from the Inquisition in 1540, Alonso de Contreras, who is seen on the right side of the illustration. We do not have further information on whether Don Antonio and his two Spanish companions were successful in getting back the Oztoticpac property. Don Antonio died in 1546, possibly as the lawsuit was proceeding.

The lawsuit and the effort to reclaim the Oztoticpac palace, however, sent Don Antonio and the Texcocan native cabildo onto a new path of leadership that was a variation on the pattern of arbitration of avoidance. Texcoco's claim that the Oztoticpac palace was a communal property—a claim that fit very well into Spanish legal traditions that strongly backed the *fueros* (legal privileges) of Spanish towns—had to be backed up with historical documents. Therefore, during the five years of the lawsuit, Don Antonio commissioned a host of colonial codices that explained Texcocan history and the royal family's place in it in order to further the lawsuit—possibly establishing a historical precedent for this process among native communities in the New World.[33] The codices are painted in the Texcocan native pictorial style and include the Oztoticpac Map (1540–41), which shows the division of Don Carlos's properties into private and public estates.[34] Surprisingly, although the Oztoticpac Map deals with the late Don Carlos's property, it does not refer to him as the former tlahtoani of Texcoco. Apparently, Don Antonio's new pattern of arbitration of avoidance led him to expunge unpleasant differences between natives and Spaniards in the recent past.

The elimination of Don Carlos's status as tlahtoani is also evident in several other historical-legal codices in the early 1540s, also commissioned by Don Antonio in support of the lawsuit: the Mapa Tlotzin, Mapa Quinatzin, and *Codex Xolotl*.[35] The Mapa Tlotzin lists the tlahtoqueh of Texcoco from before Nezahualcoyotl to Don Pedro Tetlahuehuetzquititzin but does not include Don Carlos, the immediate predecessor of Don Antonio. While historians have linked several codices to Don Antonio's lawsuit, a fifth, more obscure codex, the Boban Calendar Wheel, housed in the John Carter Brown Library, has not been included. Yet we can now definitively connect this codex with Don Antonio and the same lengthy lawsuit that inspired the other codices. In the final years of the lawsuit, the Boban Calendar Wheel, most likely also commissioned by Don Antonio, attempted to link Texcocan and Spanish law in support of Texcocan leadership and is an interesting interpretation of the native-Spanish relationship for the future (a detailed interpretation of the Boban Calendar Wheel and its links to the Don Carlos case is presented in the appendix).

While one appreciates the political deftness of Don Antonio and other Texcocan leaders in negotiating a space in the Spanish empire while retaining some economic and political independence, the question arises, where was the evolving strategy of arbitration of avoidance leading the indigenous communities? Could Don Carlos have been right, at least about the debilitation of Texcocan culture from all this accommodation? Was not the constant shaping of practices and history—even if according to native values and traditions—taking the indigenous leaders too far and too quickly away from the central values of indigenous cosmology that gave their lives meaning and sense?

The case of Don Carlos was specific to his time and place. In the wake of his death in 1539, the Texcocan nobles had little choice but to accommodate the Franciscans, because the Spanish completely controlled the Valley of Mexico by the threat of violence. The pace of native accommodation was balanced, on one side, by how much and how often the Spanish were willing to apply pressure and coercion, and on the other side, by how much the indigenous leaders in each community were prepared to manipulate their own culture. One imagines, in a community farther from the Spanish mechanisms of state power, colonized later in the century (when the Spanish were perhaps less enthusiastic about the mission), and possessed of a capable, experienced indigenous leadership, the pace might be slow and the change in cultural practices could take decades, even centuries.[36] In Texcoco, so close to the centers of Spanish power, and experiencing the accelerated effects of disease, immigration, and Spanish confiscations of valuable property and tribute—all within a few decades of the conquest—the pressures on the native leadership to accommodate were considerable. Zumárraga's Inquisition was an acute experience of colonial coercion. It forced leaders in Texcoco, Mexico, and the other valley communities to make decisions and negotiate understandings quickly and dramatically.

Don Antonio's effort to recast Texcoco's leadership philosophy ended with his death from *cocolitzli* (a somewhat mysterious epidemic) in 1545, and the Franciscans immediately interfered in the Texcocan succession, a practice that became more common over the sixteenth century.[37] Members of the native town council, including Lorenzo de Luna and Hernando de Chávez, complained bitterly that the Franciscans kept them away from the tlahtoani's deathbed: "Why did [Don Antonio] tell us nothing, considering that he was accustomed to making statements in our presence? But when Don Antonio Pimentel died, our Father Fray Juan de San Francisco did no more than show us the paper [on] which D. Antonio had indicated [his will]."³⁸ The will proclaimed his young nephew, Don Fernando Pimentel Velásquez (9), as his heir and simply stated that his decision was best for the community.³⁹ Don Fernando was the son of Cohuanacoch, who had been executed by Cortés, and was one of the first of a generation of young nobles who had been reliably Christianized and Hispanicized. Motolinía had personally taken the sons of Cohuanacoch under his wing while he was in Texcoco in 1526–27 and baptized them with the family name, Pimentel, of his patron, the Count of Benavente. Motolinía also spent the year 1541–42 in the constant company of the young Don Fernando and his brother, which suggests that the Franciscans had handpicked the young man for Texcoco's leadership well before Don Antonio's death.⁴⁰

Don Fernando soon did what royal family members had feared Don Carlos would do. He abandoned many of the other descendants of Nezahualpilli to poverty and obscurity and funneled the dwindling Texcocan noble wealth to his branch of the family.⁴¹ In his twenty-year reign, the one policy of his uncle that Don Fernando continued was to fight tenaciously any effort by formerly subject altepemeh to become *cabeceras* (independent principal towns) and get out from under Texcoco's tributary and political demands.⁴² Culturally, Don Fernando dressed like a Spaniard, kept his family in Spanish circles, and was quick to complain to the king and Spanish officials whenever he was deprived of some asset or privilege.⁴³ He asked at one point in the early 1550s if he could come to Spain and show his fealty to the king.⁴⁴ Probably through an arrangement made by Motolinía, the Count of Benavente in Spain asked Charles V to allow Don Fernando to carry the Pimentel family arms, and Philip granted the privilege.⁴⁵

In the end, Zumárraga's coercive efforts in the Valley of Mexico to force native nobles into marriage and to try native leaders before the Inquisition did not bring the desired submission of the native leaders. Rather, two things seemed to push and pull the native leaders along. First was the constant and ever-increasing presence of the Spanish. With the specter of Spanish violence nearby, native leaders worked individually and in small groups to arbitrate and avoid rather than confront and defy. Second, the Franciscans continued the persuasive and constant parallel policy of conventos and colegios to bring forward a new generation of colonial native leaders. In the final analysis, Zumárraga's Inquisition demonstrated that there were better alternative combinations of violence and persuasion to compel the native leaders to behave more cooperatively. Nevertheless, the Inquisition process also provided very early hints that the supple and versatile universe of native belief systems allowed its native leaders to shape the contours of Franciscan teaching in ways that showed little regard for Franciscan dreams.

Appendix

Boban Calendar Wheel

The Boban Calendar Wheel, an early colonial Mexican manuscript in the John Carter Brown Library, has received relatively little attention and has not been reliably dated until now.[1] By piecing together information accumulated from other scholars and evidence from the trial transcript of Don Carlos Ometochtli of Texcoco, it is now possible to fix a date for the Boban Calendar Wheel of about 1545–46. In addition, I argue that the document was intended to bolster the legal petition of Texcocan leader Don Antonio Pimentel Tlahuitoltzin for possession of lands that the Inquisition had confiscated from the deceased Don Carlos's estate. It is likely that Vicente Riverol, Don Carlos's lawyer, and Pedro de Vergara, his Spanish business partner, helped the Texcocans shape the documents to fit the needs of their lawsuit to recover the property and Vergara's fruit tree stock. The Boban Calendar Wheel was probably the last of a series of Texcocan historical documents, including the Mapa Tlotzin and Mapa Quinatzin, that Don Antonio, one of Don Carlos's many half brothers (see figure 2), used to support his interpretation of Texcocan royal descent in hopes of not only winning his property case but also stabilizing Texcoco in the aftermath of the unsettling Don Carlos trial.

Previous interpretations of the Boban Calendar Wheel have been hampered by a lack of information about early colonial leaders. The John Carter Brown Library catalog listing of 1530 as a possible date of production is based on the mistaken identification of two people shown in the document. It speculates that the upper left figure is

Hernán Cortés and identifies the upper right figure, Don Antonio Pimentel, as the son of Ixtlilxochitl; thus leading to an improbable early date for the document.[2] John B. Glass and Donald Robertson, in their 1975 survey of pictorial manuscripts in the *Handbook of Middle American Indians*, date the document to 1538, based on the Nahuatl notation of the year 7 Rabbit on its upper right corner.[3]

However, sixteen years earlier, Robertson had rejected 1538 as the date of production and had accepted George Kubler and Charles Gibson's argument that the document was referring retrospectively to 1538 as an important historic date.[4] Robertson argues, incorrectly, that the figure at the upper left is Don Hernando de Pimentel, whom he describes as the son and successor of Don Antonio de Pimentel, and he dates Don Antonio's reign as 1537–64. He argues that the document commemorates the beginning of Don Antonio's reign with the assistance of his "son" Don Hernando and speculates that the document was produced at Don Antonio's death in 1564. We now know that Don Antonio Pimentel Tlahuitoltzin reigned over Texcoco from 1540 to 1546, that his successor was his nephew, not his son, and that the nephew reigned until 1564. Nevertheless, Robertson's finding that the Boban Calendar Wheel makes a statement about the rule of Don Antonio and that 1538 was a critical starting date for that rule is central to the current interpretation of the document.

Charles Dibble has contributed further to the study of the document in 1990, chiefly by translating some of the Nahuatl glosses.[5] Dibble recognizes that Robertson's dates for Don Antonio's rule are wrong, and he correctly identifies the figure to the left as Don Hernando de Chávez, who was a member of the town council of Texcoco at the time of Don Carlos's trial. Dibble accepts Robertson's tentative dating of the document to 1564 as "possible," but he makes no effort to explain why it should have been drawn up almost twenty years after Don Antonio's death. He implicitly suggests an earlier date by proposing that "the contents could conceivably be construed as an abbreviated extract from such codices as the Mapa Tlotzin or Mapa Quinatzin," both of which have been dated to the early 1540s.[6] As with these more famous codices, the Boban Calendar Wheel is an attempt to make an historical statement at a point when Texcoco was vulnerable to Spanish suspicions and accusations. Native leaders

APPENDIX

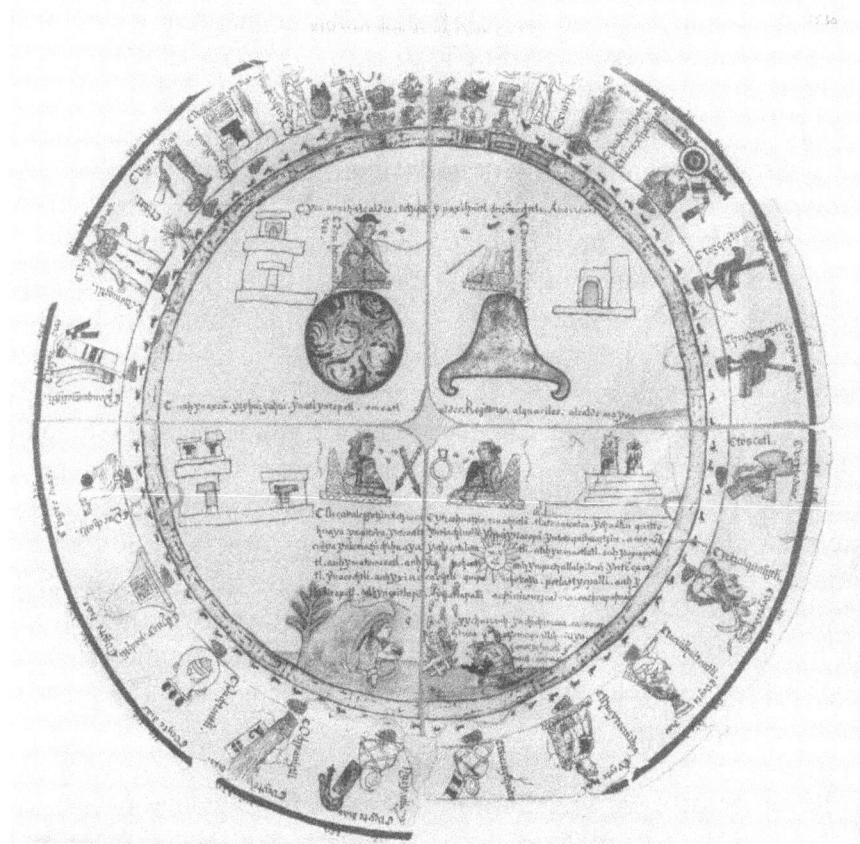

Figure 4. Boban Calendar Wheel. Courtesy of the John Carter Brown Library.

countered by exercising Spanish legal and administrative recourses, which demonstrated loyalty to the colonial Spanish government but also asserted the value and importance of their leadership and its attendant prerogatives.

The Boban Calendar Wheel (figure 4) emphasizes historical continuity in the leadership of Texcoco. Its circular periphery contains glyphs for the eighteen months of twenty days, or veintenas, employing traditional native pictographs with some European innovations.[7] The wheel of time surrounds a central, three-part history with three pairs of figures and glosses in Nahuatl and Spanish. The focus on time and the notion of three critical turning points or chapters in the rise of Texcocan civilization, according to Robertson, are typical of the Texcocan school of painting, which lends itself to historical chronology much better than other Mesoamerican schools of painting.[8] The emphasis on chronology in this and the other codices probably made Don Antonio's documents more credible to the Spanish courts of law.

Reading from bottom to top, three significant dates or turning points are illustrated in the Boban Calendar Wheel: the unknown date when the Chichimec ancestors gave up living in caves and became civilized; the year 1427, when the Triple Alliance was formed and the Texcocans became, with the Mexica and the Tepaneca, rulers of central Mexico; and the year 1538, when Don Antonio, with the help of Don Hernando, became colonial ruler of Texcoco. At the bottom of the wheel, the Chichimec ancestors, represented by female and male cave-dwellers, begin the ascent to Texcocan greatness. As Robertson notes, the artistic hand of these two small figures bears a remarkable similarity to that of the Mapa Quinatzin.[9] A little higher are pictures of two leaders of the Triple Alliance, Nezahualcoyotl and Itzcoatl, each seated on an icpalli (throne woven of reeds). The gloss reads, according to Dibble:

> Nezahualcoyotzin was ruler of Texcoco. Itzcohuatzin was ruler of Tenochtitlan. They declared the so-called water-conflagration (war). And Totoquihuatzin was ruler of Tlacopan. Not without purpose did they take that with which one was arrayed: precious capes, and breechclouts, and plaited collars and armbands, and leather bands for the calf of the leg, and head bands with sprays of quetzal feathers, labrets, ear plugs and blue sandals. They governed the city and the commoners. And in this manner were they raised, reared.[10]

The war (1427–28) was the seminal event of the Triple Alliance, when the three leaders of Tenochtitlan, Texcoco, and Tlacopan vanquished their opponents in Azcapotzalco and took over the tribute systems of the Valley of Mexico. Between the two monarchs are war symbols: arrows, an obsidian sword, and a shield. While historians generally regard Itzcoatl of the Mexica as the dominant partner of the alliance, the position of Nezahualcoyotl and Itzcoatl facing each other suggests an equality of power that the Texcocan scribe preferred to emphasize.[11] At any rate, the point is made, especially in the final line, that these leaders ruled well, received many spoils of war as a benefit of their leadership, and, most importantly, were "raised" and "reared" to rule, as were their descendants, Don Hernando de Chávez and Don Antonio Pimentel, depicted above them.

This brings us to the most pertinent figures in the document, the paired colonial indigenous leaders at the top. Don Hernando de Chávez, the Texcocan leader and half brother of both Don Carlos and Don Antonio, sits on the left. From the trial transcripts, we know that Don Hernando was an alcalde on the Texcocan town council along with Don Antonio and figured prominently in Don Carlos's trial in the summer of 1539 when Bishop Zumárraga was pressuring the Texcocan council to turn over religious objects.[12] Don Antonio Pimentel Tlahuitoltzin, who brought the lawsuit with Riverol and Vergara, sits on the right. Don Hernando and Don Antonio, along with Lorenzo de Luna, were rivals of Don Carlos and were probably opposed to his ascendancy to the Texcocan throne. More importantly, they were central to the lawsuit and the effort to get Texcoco back on its feet after the terrible chapter of Don Carlos's trial and execution.

The two rulers, who bear some of the trappings of Spanish rule and are glossed with titles of Spanish authority, sit across from each other above pictographic symbols of water and a mountain, a combined symbol of *"in atl in tepetl,"* or altepetl—a clear reference to Texcoco as a city sovereignty.[13] Above the heads of the two colonial leaders, the Spanish and Nahuatl gloss is only partly legible. After a few illegible words, it states, *"alcaldes tetzcoco ypa xihuitl chico(m) tochtli Ano* [illegible] (Texcocan council members in the year 7 Rabbit, in the year [illegible])." Below is another gloss, *"auh yn axca(n) y yhui y atl yn tepetl. Ome atl a* [illegible] . . . *aldes Regittores, alguaciles. alcalde mayor."* Dibble translates this as "and presently conditions are such in the city on the day 2 Water: alcaldes, regidores, alguaciles, alcalde mayor."[14]

The Spanish word "alcalde" is equivalent to the position of council member, and an "alcalde mayor," as it is used here, is a mayor. Regidores were crown representatives who often held the position of alcalde mayor, and alguaciles were sheriffs. From the earliest years of the colony, the crown allowed the appointment of Spaniards to the position of encomendero of native towns and some cities and also appointed them regidor. From the mid-1530s, Viceroy Mendoza also had the policy of appointing (or approving the appointment of) native former tlahtoque as mayors, sheriffs, and town council members, mostly because they were necessary to assist the Spaniards in governing native towns. Thus, the native council and the local encomendero often jostled for leadership in the native towns. Add to them the Franciscans, who had a strong interest in native government, and many triangular struggles for regional and local power arose.

Don Antonio seems to be trying to make the case that he was a town council member with Don Hernando in 1538, but then he, with the help of Don Hernando, came into control of the official native government of Texcoco, holding all of the government positions: responsible for talking to crown authorities as regidor, legislating as alcalde, deciding justice as alcalde mayor, and enforcing the law as alguacil. In effect, Don Antonio makes the case that he is still an all-powerful ruler, but now with the sanction of the Spanish government and under the guise of its official titles. Don Hernando de Chávez may have been Don Antonio's intended heir in the early 1540s, or simply his closest supporter in the Texcocan government.

What was the significance of the year 1538 to Don Antonio and his claims? As estimated from testimony at Don Carlos's trial, Don Pedro of Texcoco, the legitimate tlahtoani since 1535, died in late February or early March of 1539. His death coincided with the end of the indigenous year 7 Rabbit, which began around February–March 1538 and ended in February–March 1539. The end of the year 7 Rabbit was a transitional point when the "legitimate" line of the royal family ended and rulership moved to the natural sons of Nezahualpilli (see figure 2). In the Boban document, Don Antonio is in effect claiming himself, rather than Don Carlos, as heir to Don Pedro in the year 7 Rabbit.

The facts, of course, are quite different. We know from the trial that Don Pedro named Don Carlos Ometochtli as tlahtoani, and Don Carlos, not Don Antonio, took office in late February or early March 1539. Even the Spanish acknowledged Don Carlos as ruler, referring to him at his arrest on July 2, 1539, as Texcoco's "cacique," the word the Spanish used for tlahtoani. When Don Carlos was arrested, Texcoco's town council apparently named Don Lorenzo de Luna as governor so they would have a leader who could deal with the many demands the bishop placed on the community that summer. Only after Don Carlos's execution on December 1, 1539, did Texcoco's town council elect Don Antonio as governor. If Don Antonio were interested in the facts, he would have marked the beginning of his rule as 1539 or 1540. But the Boban Calendar Wheel served larger purposes. As one historian has noted, indigenous codices and documents were "less perceptions of reality than assertions about reality."[15] Cartographic historian Dana Liebsohn notes that early colonial maps "responded to tangential desires, thwarted possessions, birds-not-in-the-hand."[16] The "quiet, sensible" Don Antonio, who had a "special interest in collecting and writing," used Texcocan historical documentary tradition to expunge Don Carlos from the Boban Calendar Wheel and also from the Texcocan royal chronology that appears in the Mapa Tlotzin, because his version of history served Texcoco (and his lawsuit) better in 1540.[17]

However, the Boban Calendar Wheel has an even more ambitious goal than asserting an earlier date for Don Antonio's reign and eliminating Don Carlos from the historical record. A visual comparison of the leaders Don Hernando and Don Antonio with the prehispanic figures below them shows that Don Antonio defined the nature of his rule by blending Spanish and prehispanic Texcocan symbols of authority. Later additions to the illustration make the message even more explicit. Robertson notes that the Boban Calendar Wheel was illustrated by two different scribes.[18] The more sophisticated Hand A painted the glyphs around the periphery and the three historical vignettes. Hand B added the sun in the lower right quadrant as well as the line drawings of buildings next to the prehispanic and colonial leaders. Since the sun is tightly surrounded by Nahuatl writing, it appears that the writing was added after the pictures. Many codices and documents of the period had additions immediately after the production of the original or much later. In this case, I suggest that Don Antonio commissioned the first scribe, Hand A, to compose the document, possibly for the long trial he was involved in with Riverol and Vergara. The simple line drawings of Hand B, including the architecture and the smiling sun, were added in the course of the trial to further explain the proposed historical interpretation. And, as was seen in Mateo's illustration in chapter 4 of this book, the Nahuatl gloss was added to further clarify the pictographs for the Spanish (who were more accustomed to text). The Boban Calendar Wheel is a classic example from a crucial stage of colonial history in the 1540s when prehispanic pictorial writing was being Europeanized to help indigenous leaders speak to two audiences—their native subjects and the Spanish authorities.[19]

What fundamental message was Don Antonio trying to clarify by adding more pictographs and alphabetized Nahuatl words? The parallel construction of the Boban Calendar Wheel suggests that, in the Texcocan writing tradition of presenting aspirations rather than reality, Don Antonio was describing a new phase in Texcocan governance starting in 1538. On the top level, the colonial, Christian phase, Don Hernando sits next to a governing palace with a European arch, suggesting Spanish influence. Don Antonio presides next to a convento with a great arch, possibly representing its open chapel. Below them are Nezahualcoyotl on the left with a line drawing of his governing palace and Itzcoatl on the right with a temple of the prehispanic gods. To further blend the prehispanic and colonial symbols for this new vision of Texcocan leadership, the colonial leaders, Don Hernando and Don Antonio, are both dressed in colonial hats with prehispanic robes and carry the long staffs that are most often seen in pictures of friars. They sit on woven thrones elevated like European-style chairs, while the prehispanic leaders below them sit on traditional icpalli on woven mats. Each of these modifications combines prehispanic and Spanish motifs of leadership and more or less sanitizes the vestiges of prehispanic religion while maintaining and asserting prehispanic political values important to Don Antonio and Texcoco.

The message is that Don Hernando supported Spanish justice and rule in the altepetl of Texcoco, just as Nezahualcoyotl, directly below him, established prehispanic Texcocan justice and rule in the Acolhua area. Don Antonio supported and defended the Christian faith and the alliance with the Christians, just as Itzcoatl, the Mexica ruler, headed the alliance and served the prehispanic gods. Thus, Don Antonio tried to erase from Texcocan history the unhealthy and unpleasant chapter of Don Carlos's kingship, which had put the Texcocans dangerously at odds with Spanish power and Franciscan authority. In its place, he presented an alternative view that was deferential to the new colonial realities but asserted his historic right to rule Texcoco. Like his predecessors and other native leaders, Don Antonio was responding to the intensive intrusions of Bishop Zumárraga's Inquisition by shifting back and forth as needed across the arc between resistance and collaboration. He presented his own plan for the arbitration of avoidance, a kind of negotiation for himself and his successors about how to fit into Spanish rule on indigenous terms. Like his predecessors, Don Antonio used the values, language, and visual genres of prehispanic culture to express the new proposed paradigm, and he took advantage of the occasion of the lawsuit in Spanish courts to make his case. In a further show of alliance to inoculate Texcoco from trouble, he raised large indigenous armies to march with Viceroy Mendoza to put down the native rebels in the Mixtón War in 1541.[20] In these moves, Don Antonio necessarily brought Texcocan leaders far more to the collaboration side of the range of leadership responses than his predecessors had done.

NOTES

INTRODUCTION

1. Pomar, Relación de Tezcoco, 3–4; Alva Ixtlilxóchitl, Obras históricas, 1:33–34; Alva Ixtlilxóchitl, Ally of Cortés, 33–34. I cite both Spanish and English language sources when available.

2. García Icazbalceta, Don Fray Juan de Zumárraga (1947), 2:304; Medina, Biblioteca hispanoamérica, 1:181.

3. "Relación de la genealogía y linaje," 3:241. All notes in brackets are by the author unless otherwise specified.

4. D. Carrasco, Daily Life of the Aztecs, 14. Pomar, Relación de Tezcoco, 4, writes that many Texcocans burned transcripts for fear of the bishop's actions.

5. Greenleaf, Zumárraga and the Mexican Inquisition, chap. 3 and 4. Greenleaf also expresses these opinions and generously shares sources and information with colleagues in further publications: "Historiography of the Mexican Inquisition," 248–76; "Inquisition and the Indians of New Spain," 138–66; "Mexican Inquisition and the Indians," 315–44; and "Persistence of Native Values," 351–76. Greenleaf, Mexican Inquisition of the Sixteenth Century, also deals with the non-indigenous trials; see also Porras Muñoz, Personas y lugares de la ciudad de México, 80.

6. While a few trials were held before this episode, Zumárraga's Inquisition is considered the first systematic use of the institution in Mexico. Most of the trials that made up Zumárraga's Inquisition were transcribed and published by the Archivo General de la Nación (hereafter AGN) in Mexico nearly a century ago. The author has consulted both the original and published versions; however, only the page numbers of the published versions are cited here. The trial evidence includes the most famous trial, that of Don Carlos of Texcoco, published by AGN as "Proceso inquisitorial del cacique de Tetzcoco," 1–85, also located in AGN, Inquisición. The trials of an additional 21 men and 2 women are published by AGN as "Procesos de indios idólatras y hechiceras," also located in AGN, Inquisición. Proceso de Don Pedro, cacique de

Totolapa, y su hermano, Antón, is in AGN, Inquisición, and is unpublished; for Ana of Xochimilco, see "Proceso del Santo Oficio contra una india curandera," 211–14. Because of the cryptic record-keeping in some of the trials, the definitive number of trials and accused is not always clear in trials involving multiple witnesses and accused. See Greenleaf, "Inquisition and the Indians of New Spain," 139, where he lists 19 trials and 75 accused, but my reading of the transcripts suggests a more conservative number in both categories, as I count episodes of multiple accused as one trial and include in the accused only those against whom judgments were rendered.

7. The saying paraphrased here, "Wherever they burn books they will also, in the end, burn human beings," comes from Heinrich Heine's play *Almansor* (1821), in which he writes about the burning of the Qur'an in Granada after the defeat of the Muslims in 1492.

8. "Procesos de indios," 207.

9. Dedieu, "Inquisition and Popular Culture in New Castile," 130; Haliczer, "First Holocaust," 10.

10. See chapter 1 for estimates of population and baptism in the Valley of Mexico in the 1530s.

11. Clendinnen, *Ambivalent Conquests*, makes the case for an emotional response by the friars; Greenleaf, *Zumárraga and the Mexican Inquisition*, 131, provides a limited interpretation of native trials; Timmer, "Providence and Perdition," 477–88, suggests the apocalypse thesis.

12. Traslosheros, "El tribunal eclesiástico y los indios," 485–516; Grunberg, *L'Inquisition apostolique au Mexique*.

13. Klor de Alva, "Colonizing Souls," 10.

14. Moreno de los Arcos, "New Spain's Inquisition for Indians," 23.

15. See Kamen, *Inquisition and Society in Spain*, 7, 55, and especially 165, for Ferdinand's statement (after it is suggested that a decision should be applied through the Vatican): "In fact, it [the Spanish Inquisition] is all ours."

16. Beinart, *Conversos on Trial*; Contreras, *Sotos contra Riquelmes*; and *Santo Oficio de la Inquisición en Galicia*; Monter, *Frontiers of Heresy*; Haliczer, *Inquisition and Society in the Kingdom of Valencia*; see also note 20. See Starr-LeBeau, *In the Shadow of the Virgin*, for a very good example of this regional process.

17. I am thinking here particularly of Wood, *Transcending Conquest*, and Restall, *Seven Myths of the Spanish Conquest*; see also Lockhart, *Nahuas After the Conquest*.

18. Taylor, "Two Shrines of the Cristo Renovado," 971.

19. Ibid., 971–72. I would emphasize that this is not adding new typologies, a strategy to which microhistorians would be highly resistant; it is describing a range of patterned behavior that colonial actors learned from each other and duplicated or chose not to duplicate in their own lives.

20. Karttunen opened up this discussion in less systematic ways with her *Between Worlds*; more recent works that delve deeper into the phenomenon include Yannakakis, *Art of Being In-between*, and Metcalf, *Go-betweens and the Colonization of Brazil*.

21. My findings are similar to those of Kellogg, *Law and the Transformation of Aztec Culture*, xix–xx: "Hegemony develops not because people collaborate in their own

subjugation but because a dominating power has been able to institute practices and beliefs that rational people choose to adhere to, often because of coercive threats, but that over time come to appear normal, even natural. In Mexico City, hegemony was not something imposed from without. Rather, it was accommodated from within as a product of an intricate process of conflict, negotiation, and dialogue."

22. Readers will note that this approach is a little different from Lockhart's thesis of "double mistaken identity," which he writes about in "Some Nahua Concepts in Postconquest Guise," 477: "Each side in a cultural exchange presumes that a given form or concept is operating in the way familiar within its own tradition and is unaware of or unimpressed by the other side's interpretation." This is a good characterization of the Spanish, but native leaders in these trials were well aware of the threat Spaniards posed to their own power and took measures to avoid or ameliorate the consequences of the decisions they were forced into by Spanish coercion.

23. Marcus, *Mesoamerican Writing Systems*, 54–55, indicates that the technical study of Nahuatl is limited by the paucity of prehispanic sources in comparison with colonial sources.

24. Boone, introduction to *Writing without Words*, 13.

25. Karttunen, introduction to *Analytical Dictionary of Nahuatl*, xvii.

26. The most effective use of this strategy is in the work of historians influenced by James Lockhart, who demonstrates the use of alphabetized Nahuatl documents in *Nahuas After the Conquest*.

27. Cortés, *Letters from Mexico*; Motolinía, *History*; García Icazbalceta, *Don Fray Juan de Zumárraga* (1947), vols. 1–4.

28. See note 6.

29. I have found 43 works that briefly refer to Zumárraga's Inquisition and cite either Greenleaf or the published AGN trial transcripts. Most of these works focus on questions of indigenous identity, but none attempts to revise Greenleaf.

30. For a very good analysis of what microhistorians do, see Ginzburg, "Inquisitor as Anthropologist," 156–64; the classic example of the method in European history is Ginzburg, *Cheese and the Worms*; for a good summary of the method of microhistorians, see Muir and Ruggiero, *Microhistory and the Lost Peoples of Europe*; for some concerns about cultural history in Latin American studies, see "Mexico's New Cultural History" special issue, *Hispanic American Historical Review*, 203–85, especially the article by Eric Van Young, "New Cultural History Comes to Old Mexico," 211–47.

31. This is a significant concern, as some Inquisition manuscripts can be quite prosaic and filled with legal language immaterial to what interests the historian—the life experiences of the accused. Some inquisitors in Spain opened up witnesses by eliciting a type of testimony called *"discurso de su vida,"* long autobiographical accounts. Unfortunately, the indigenous manuscripts here do not contain requests for "discursos," but in many cases the indigenous were more verbose than Spanish peasants, who knew the reputation of the Inquisition and were more reticent in their testimony. In lieu of this autobiographical quality in the transcript, it is best, according to the case-study methodology, to have the longest transcripts one can obtain. For

a discussion of the autobiographical nature of some Inquisition accounts, see Kagan and Dyer, *Inquisitorial Inquiries*.

CHAPTER 1. THE EARLY COLONIAL LEADERSHIP DILEMMA

1. Kamen, *Spanish Inquisition*, 2.
2. Ruiz de Larrinaga, *Don Fray Juan de Zumárraga*, 13, quotes Zumárraga as saying in 1538, "I am around seventy years old."
3. Kamen, *Spanish Inquisition*, 7.
4. Netanyahu, *Origins of the Inquisition*, 162–67, 1014.
5. Netanyahu, 1009, argues that Espina posed a "theory of infidelity rather than allude to the socio-economic advantages that the *conversos* acquired after their conversions," and that the theory was taken up by Franciscans, Dominicans, and Hieronymites.
6. Netanyahu, 1009.
7. Kamen, *Spanish Inquisition*, 7.
8. Ibid., 137.
9. Ibid.
10. Ibid., 178, 57; Parker, "Some Recent Work on the Inquisition," 519.
11. Kamen, *Spanish Inquisition*, 42; Rawlings, *Spanish Inquisition*, 58, estimates that the 75 percent totaled 2,000 victims.
12. Kamen, *Spanish Inquisition*, 178.
13. Kamen, *Spanish Inquisition*, 20, notes that many members of the intelligentsia were opposed on the grounds that the Jews had "not received the sacrament properly" because they were forced.
14. Rummel, *Jiménez de Cisneros*, 116, writes that Cisneros and the Catholic Kings were consistent in their promotion of a religious policy based on the late medieval theory of good government of "one faith, one king."
15. Kamen, *Spanish Inquisition*, 3.
16. Rummel, *Jiménez de Cisneros*, 33.
17. Ibid., 34.
18. Boronat y Barrachina, *Moriscos españoles*, 1:108.
19. Rummel, *Jiménez de Cisneros*, 34; Merton, *Cardinal Ximenes*, 77.
20. L. P. Harvey, *Muslims in Spain*, 56–57.
21. Ibid., 31–32.
22. Kamen, *Spanish Inquisition*, 221.
23. Ibid., 215; L. P. Harvey, *Muslims in Spain*, 70–71.
24. Kamen, *Spanish Inquisition*, 215.
25. Ibid., 105.
26. Rummel, *Jiménez de Cisneros*, 35. According to Rummel, Pietro Martire, a contemporary of Cisneros, argued that "it would have been more to the point to accept their petitions and to impose the new discipline on them gradually."
27. Kamen, *Spanish Inquisition*, 218.

28. See L. P. Harvey, 108–109, on the relative stasis of the middle period, 1520s–60s.

29. Kamen, *Spanish Inquisition*, 223–24.

30. Zavala, *Fray Juan de Zumárraga*, 1:42–43; Abrojo was founded at the beginning of the fifteenth century and was led into the Regular Observant Franciscans by Pedro de Santoya at mid-century.

31. Ibid., 1:43; Iriarte, *Franciscan History*, 351: "Only the most learned were approved as the teachers" in the *studia generalia* of the Franciscans, suggesting that Zumárraga was an unusually well educated member of his province; Holzapfel, *History of the Franciscan Order*, 229, notes that Cisneros should "be reckoned as the most successful promoter of higher studies among the Observants."

32. Zavala, *Fray Juan de Zumárraga*, 1:43.

33. Both quotes are from Kamen, *Spanish Inquisition*, 256–57.

34. Zavala, *Fray Juan de Zumárraga*, 1:23.

35. Ibid., 1:30. The Duranguese elite faithfully served Henry IV of Castile and, when Henry's sister Isabel's succession was challenged at the start of her reign in 1474, one of Zumárraga's relatives supported Ferdinand and Isabel with a privately fitted warship. Another cousin, who was mayor of Durango, greeted the triumphant Isabel when she visited loyal Vizcaya in 1483. In fact, from 1471 forward the province of Vizcaya recognized Isabel, who was still princess elsewhere, as its sovereign; see Lunenfeld, *Keepers of the City*, 20.

36. Moorman, *Sources for the Life of S. Francis of Assisi*, 25–26; Colish, *Medieval Foundations*, 237: "Francis was most anxious that his Fraternity should not become just another Order with a Rule." According to Lambert, *Medieval Heresy*, 226–35, from the time of Saint Francis, there were two ways that the order could interpret itself: "One was to reformulate [the order] philosophically, making it accessible to intellectuals. The second was to popularize it, making it available to lay people, whether learned or unlearned." Holzapfel, *History of the Franciscan Order*, 52–53, writes that the Fraticelli originally came from the Spirituals, who wanted to "popularize" the Franciscan Order.

37. O'Callaghan, *History of Medieval Spain*, 634; Zavala, *Fray Juan de Zumárraga*, 1:82.

38. Zavala, *Fray Juan de Zumárraga*, 1:82–83, 85.

39. Ibid., 1:85.

40. Castañeda, "Fray Juan de Zumárraga," 298.

41. García Icazbalceta, *Don Fray Juan de Zumárraga* (1947), 1:16.

42. Amezúa, introduction to Castañega, *Tratado de las supersticiones* (1946), xii, indicates that Olmos studied with Castañega (whose work is discussed in chapter 2). Castañega believed that the witches were deluded. Kamen, *Spanish Inquisition*, 269–71, states that Inquisitor General Manrique asked for a study that proclaimed the same, thinking that it was a "civil crime" and that "most jurists did not believe in witching." Caro Baroja, *World of the Witches*, 189, says that most educated Spaniards believe it was "a leftover from paganism."

43. Greenleaf, *Zumárraga and His Family*, 37.

44. Pagden, *Fall of Natural Man*, 102.

45. Lea, *Inquisition in the Spanish Dependencies*, 191.
46. For a particularly revealing account, see "Letter of Pedro Vaz de Caminha to King Manuel, Porto Seguro de Vera Cruz, May 1, 1500," 56.
47. Cortés, *Letters from Mexico*, 36.
48. Baudot, *Utopia and History in Mexico*, 25–26.
49. García Icazbalceta, *Don Fray Juan de Zumárraga* (1947), 2:200, 222.
50. Díaz del Castillo, *True History of the Conquest*, 4:155–56.
51. The first organized group of Franciscan missionaries were John de Tecto (Spanish), John Dekkers (Flemish), John de Couvreur (French), Juan de Ayora (Spanish), John van der Auwera (Flemish), Pedro de Gante (Spanish), and Peter de Mura or Muer or Muro (French).
52. Lockhart, *We People Here*, 1:5–6.
53. Gibson, *Tlaxcala in the Sixteenth Century*, 29, also makes this observation.
54. Motolinía, *History*, 48.
55. López Austin, "Núcleo duro," 50.
56. Motolinía, *History*, 48.
57. Ibid., 48–49.
58. Alva Ixtlilxóchitl, *Obras históricas*, 2:484; and *Ally of Cortés*, 62.
59. Gibson, *Tlaxcala in the Sixteenth Century*, 64; Elliott, "Cortés, Velásquez and Charles V," introduction to Cortés, *Letters from Mexico*, xxxv–xxxvi.
60. Alva Ixtlixóchitl, *Obras históricas*, 1:515; and *Ally of Cortés*, 117.
61. Ricard, *Spiritual Conquest of Mexico*, 91; Motolinía, *History*, 80, writes of the Franciscans, "For two years they left the monasteries infrequently because they did not know the language or the land."
62. Alva Ixtlilxóchitl, *Obras históricas*, 1:492; and *Ally of Cortés*, 75–76, where his dating of this event is two years early; Mills, "Limits of Political Coercion," 85–86, writes, "Accustomed as they were to the presence of an undercurrent of force in their efforts at evangelization, many churchmen saw no contradiction between means and end."
63. D. Carrasco, *Religions of Mesoamerica*, 20.
64. Ibid.
65. Edgerton, *Theaters of Conversion*, 41, 49.
66. This and previous quote are from Motolinía, *History*, 128.
67. Ricard, *Spiritual Conquest of Mexico*, 259, gives the example of when Zumárraga moved the entire mission from the city of Mexico to Texcoco in 1530 after incidents in which the friars felt threatened by angry conquerors.
68. Motolinía, *History*, 149.
69. Alva Ixtlilxóchitl, *Obras históricas*, 1:494; and *Ally of Cortés*, 80–81; Motolinía, *History*, 148; H. Cline, "Oztoticpac Lands Map of Texcoco" (1966), 86.
70. Burkhart, *Slippery Earth*, 44.
71. Ibid., 188.
72. Terraciano, *Mixtecs of Colonial Oaxaca*, 276, notes that Spanish conquerors complained that the Franciscans were channeling native resources toward their mission

and away from the *encomienda*; thus, many conquerors opposed the establishment of a convento in their tributary towns.

73. Burkhart, *Slippery Earth*, 70, writes: "The Aztec state cult no longer proclaimed Tenochtitlán the navel of the universe; each community in its own small way was able to order itself around its own sacred and moral center." Over time, the tlahtocayotl was the site of the syncretism that eventually took place in the colonial setting.

74. Motolinía, *History*, 53.

75. García Icazbalceta, *Don Fray Juan de Zumárraga* (1947), 3:102.

76. Ibid., 4:109.

77. Offner, *Law and Politics in Aztec Texcoco*, 260.

78. P. Carrasco, "Social Organization of Ancient Mexico," 369–70; Offner, *Law and Politics in Aztec Texcoco*, 260.

79. Borah and Cook, "Marriage and Legitimacy in Mexican Culture," 955; Mendieta, *Historia eclesiástica indiana*, 1:181, maintains that the friars did not even begin to tackle this complex problem until 1529–30, or after Zumárraga insisted on dealing with it; Archivo General de Indias (hereafter AGI), Mexico, 2555, Memorial of the bishop of Mexico to the king, 1533, is a letter from Zumárraga asking for wider authority to deal with the matrimonial affairs of the Indians.

80. Gante, *Cartas de Fr. Pedro de Gante*, 15.

81. Motolinía, *History*, 7.

82. García Icazbalceta, *Don Fray Juan de Zumárraga* (1947), 4:122; according to Rummel, *Jiménez de Cisneros*, 56, Zumárraga's formation of the houses for *"doncellas"* was similar to Cisneros's founding of similar houses in Granada, which was "unusual for the time."

83. García Icazbalceta, *Don Fray Juan de Zumárraga* (1947), 3:97, 144, 146; AGI, Mexico, 336A, R2, 97, Ecclesiastical junta to king. Zumárraga's correspondence with Madrid throughout the 1530s contains pleas for further "legal advice and research" to help him untangle the web of intrigue that his heavy-handed ways had created. He tends throughout to protest too much about the burden of patrolling native marriages, precisely as he demands more control over them. Zumárraga complains about the incredible "novelties that we find" in matters of indigenous marriage, that the "triumph against the passions costs the missionaries immense work," and that the native unions proved more and more "confusing."

84. Motolinía, *History*, 86, states that there were more conformity and agreement before "more clerics and friars of the other orders came"; Seed, "Are These Not Men," 647.

85. Hanke, *First Social Experiments in America*, 52.

86. Seed, "Are These Not Men," 637–38, 640.

87. According to Seed, "Are These Not Men," 635, and further developed in her *American Pentimento*, 64–67, there were two periods in which mendicants and the church in the New World engaged in this larger debate about the "rational capacity" of indigenous peoples to become Christian: 1511–17 in the Caribbean and 1532–37 in central Mexico. Seed, "Are These Not Men," argues that some Dominican friars raised the

issue of "rational capacity" in Hispaniola in 1511 because they found that the Franciscans had taken the best territories for proselytization, as they would later in New Spain. Seed points out, however, that "in raising the question in this fashion the friars were also provoking a political maelstrom." In 1517, Cardinal Cisneros, a Franciscan and regent for the young Charles V, put an end to the dangerous debate by threatening the Dominicans with expulsion. For a similar interpretation, see Hanke, 19–20.

88. Seed, "Are These Not Men," 644.

89. Baudot, *Utopia and History in Mexico*, 276–77; Seed, "Are These Not Men," 689; see García Icazbalceta, introduction to *Don Fray Juan de* Zumárraga (1947), 1:144, for García Icazbalceta's opinion that the arrival of the other orders "elevated the question of baptism," and 3:160–61, for the "Capítulos de 27 abril 1539," where the orders agreed to the conditions under which baptism could be provided to adults.

90. Motolinía, *History*, 85; according to Holzapfel, *History of the Franciscan Order*, 405, Clement VII gave Charles V permission to send 120 Franciscans, 70 Dominicans, and 10 Hieronymites to New Spain in 1526, "even against the will of their superiors," which seems to have been a serious hindrance to recruitment, as Holzapfel, 193, notes, because the friars needed the permission of the superiors to go to the New World. Though friars technically could not perform sacraments, Cisneros and Charles V allowed the friars in the Caribbean and Mexico to carry out these duties in the absence of priests.

91. Motolinía, *History*, 271.

92. Ibid., 105; Ricard, *Spiritual Conquest of Mexico*, 96; Haskett, *Indigenous Rulers*, 114–15.

93. Ricard, *Spiritual Conquest of Mexico*, 91, reports a doubling of the total number of baptisms in the years 1524–1532 and again in the years 1532–36; Zulaica Gárate, *Franciscanos y la imprenta*, 86, indicates that twenty Franciscan conventos existed by 1530; Motolinía, *History*, 78, says they doubled the number to forty conventos by 1540.

94. Motolinía, *History*, 195, also argues that the Dominicans' lack of success was due to their unwillingness to learn the languages of the natives.

95. Ricard, *Spiritual Conquest of Mexico*, 68, 253.

96. Gibson, *Aztecs under Spanish Rule*, 110; Ricard, *Spiritual Conquest of Mexico*, 242–46, cites many complaints about the competition and lack of coordination, noting that the queen in 1536 asked the bishop to put an end to his constant letters of complaint.

97. Seed, "Are These Not Men," 641; Baudot, *Utopia and History in Mexico*, 276–77, makes a similar argument.

98. AGI, Patronato Real, 1, no. 37, Apostolic declaration of the bull of Pope Paul III, June 22, 1537.

99. Kamen, *Spanish Inquisition*, 262.

100. Reff, "Predicament of Culture," 80, puts the question this way: "Faced with widespread rebellion, they had to accept that the Indians were not strong in their faith. Whose fault?" Naturally, the indigenous leaders became the scapegoats.

101. For larger institutional negotiations, see Schwaller, "Cathedral Chapter of Mexico," 651–74, where he explains the many uncertain jurisdictional problems

between the early bishops and the rest of the church that had to be worked out in the first thirty years; also, see Bowser, "Church in Colonial Middle America," 141, where he says that Sahagún was doubtful early on about the success of the mission, but "total loyalty with the Franciscan Order was prized, and a challenge by one of their own to the myth of the Twelve's success was unthinkable."

102. Greenleaf, *Zumárraga and the Mexican Inquisition*, 37, suggests that Cisneros was Zumárraga's model; Sylvest, *Motifs of Franciscan Mission Theory*, x, tells us that "in certain significant respects, his concern for formal education, the good order of the Church, Franciscan Observance, and his openness to Erasmian Christianity, Zumárraga transported the Cisnerian reform of the Spanish church to New Spain"; Greenleaf, *Zumárraga and the Mexican Inquisition*, 7; Ayllón, *Tribunal de la Inquisición*, 434; Medina, *Primitiva Inquisición americana*, 69, says Cisneros gave Inquisition powers in 1517 to the bishops of Santo Domingo and Darien, who were both Franciscan; see Lea, *Inquisition in the Spanish Dependencies*, 191–92.

103. Rummel, *Jiménez de Cisneros*, 115, suggests that Cisneros's actions were not contradictory; however, "Cisneros was clearly behind the virtues of a centralized government and as regent used a pragmatic mixture of dictatorial moves and strategic retreats to maintain the prerogatives of the king. This included a religious policy promoting national interests and based on the ideal of 'one faith, one king.'"

104. Merton, *Cardinal Ximenes*, 14.

105. Greenleaf, *Mexican Inquisition*, 39–40.

106. Ruiz Medrano, *Reshaping New Spain*, 27–28, says that the Second Audiencia favored Franciscan efforts to physically punish the natives "to maintain effective control" without interfering in crown jurisdiction and was openly hostile at times to the Dominicans.

107. See Greenleaf, *Zumárraga and the Mexican Inquisition*, 19, for the first letter written by Ramírez de Fuenleal, president of the Second Audiencia; and García Icazbalceta, *Colección de documentos*, 1:60–61, for the second quote, from Cortés.

108. García Icazbalceta, *Don Fray Juan de Zumárraga* (1947), 3:64–67; Castañeda, "Fray Juan de Zumárraga," 300–305.

109. Lea, *Inquisition in the Spanish Dependencies*, 195.

110. García Icazbalceta, *Don Fray Juan de Zumárraga* (1947), 3:102–103.

111. Carreño, *Nuevos documentos inéditos*, 67.

112. Ricard, *Spiritual Conquest of Mexico*, 269.

113. Cave, "Inquisition in Mexico," 12.

114. García Icazbalceta, *Don Fray Juan de Zumárraga* (1947), 4:137.

115. Ibid., 4:138.

116. García Icazbalceta, *Don Fray Juan de Zumárraga* (1881), 490; Lea, *Inquisition in the Spanish Dependencies*, 195, confirms that the Spanish tribunal insisted that all trials be conducted in Spain.

117. García Icazbalceta, *Don Fray Juan de Zumárraga* (1881), 490; moreover, as Pope Alexander VI had given the Spanish crown such extensive royal patronage privileges, Zumárraga and the other American bishops found that their correspondence

with the pope was censored; these secret instructions seemed to get around the restrictions of royal patronage.

CHAPTER 2. THE NAHUALLI

1. Lafaye, *Quetzalcóatl and Guadalupe*, 20.
2. Klor de Alva, "Martín Ocelotl," 129–30.
3. Gruzinski, *Man-Gods in the Mexican Highlands*, 41.
4. "Procesos de indios," 27.
5. There has not been much study about historical nahualism and its particular geographic and temporal variations. The best explanation of the characteristics of the nahualli in central Mexico at the time of the conquest is a very old study by Brinton, "Nagualism" (1894).
6. "Procesos de indios," 25.
7. Ibid., 28.
8. Ibid., 47.
9. Ibid., 23.
10. These dates for Ocelotl's presence in Texcoco seem to conform to other facts in evidence. Fray Pedro de Gante claimed to know Martín "quite well," and the friar had resided in Texcoco from 1523 to about 1527, when he moved to the city of Mexico and did not return. Ocelotl occasionally visited Mexico City, but he most likely made the acquaintance of Fray Pedro around 1525 in Texcoco.
11. "Procesos de indios," 25.
12. Adorno, "Depiction of Self and Other," 113.
13. "Procesos de indios," 25.
14. Ibid., 32.
15. Ibid., 33.
16. Ibid., 31.
17. Ibid., 20.
18. Ibid., 23.
19. In other transcripts, the notaries use the term *"naguatato"* (nahuatlahto) to denote a translator in Otomi, which suggests that the Spanish did not understand the meaning of the term.
20. Paso y Troncoso, *Epistolario de Nueva España*, 2:59; why Zumárraga refers to Ocelotl as a nahuatlahto is unclear in the manuscript. Ocelotl's relationships with Spanish encomenderos and the Spanish business community may have been even closer than the transcript suggests, or Zumárraga may simply have called any native who spoke some Spanish a nahuatlahto.
21. "Procesos de indios," 25.
22. Ibid., 23.
23. Burkhart, *Slippery Earth*, 44.
24. "Procesos de indios," 31.
25. Ibid.

26. Ibid., 42.
27. Ibid., 28.
28. Nicholson, "Religion," 431.
29. Berdan, *Aztecs of Central Mexico*, 132–33.
30. Ibid., 132.
31. Nicholson, "Religion," 437.
32. Terraciano, *Mixtecs of Colonial Oaxaca*, 281.
33. Carreño, *Don Fray Juan de Zumárraga*, 65–66, King Charles to Zumárraga and bishops, December 10, 1537.
34. D. Carrasco, "Sacrifice of Tezcatlipoca," 40.
35. Ibid., 40–41, where D. Carrasco argues that prehispanic ritual was more decentralized than we had previously thought.
36. D. Carrasco, introduction to *Aztec Ceremonial Landscapes*, xxiv.
37. "Procesos de indios," 28.
38. Ibid., 30 and 23.
39. Nicholson, "Religion," 436.
40. Berdan, *Aztecs of Central Mexico*, 130; Nicholson, "Religion," 436.
41. "Procesos de indios," 1–16.
42. Nicholson, "Religion," 438.
43. Nutini and Roberts, *Bloodsucking Witchcraft*, 81, state that "the structural discharge of magic and religion are kept separate"; see Berdan, *Aztecs of Central Mexico*, 139, who says that "the realm of magic and sorcery operated alongside the formal religious system, with the two often overlapping."
44. Sahagún, *Florentine Codex*, 10:31.
45. Ibid., 4:42.
46. Berdan, *Aztecs of Central Mexico*, 139.
47. Nicholson, "Religion," 412.
48. Ibid.
49. "Procesos de indios," 25.
50. Nicholson, "Religion," 412.
51. "Procesos de indios," 20–21.
52. Ibid., 29.
53. Lockhart, "Initial Nahua Reactions," 246.
54. Sahagún, *Florentine Codex*, 12:3.
55. "Procesos de indios," 28.
56. Ibid., 26.
57. Ibid., 29. *Ixiptla* and *ixiptlatl* indicate an image, representation, or representative, and historians have used these terms to mean god impersonator. *Teotl ixiptla* and *teixiptla* have also been used. *Ixiptla*, the form most commonly used by historians, is the term used in this book.
58. Cook, *Born to Die*, 132–33.
59. Sahagún, *Florentine Codex*, 6:2–3.
60. "Procesos de indios," 31.

61. Ibid., 17.
62. Ibid., 31.
63. D. Carrasco, "Sacrifice of Tezcatlipoca," 42.
64. Sahagún, *Florentine Codex*, 6:25.
65. "Procesos de indios," 30–31.
66. Ibid., 31.
67. Ibid., 29.
68. Nicholson, "Religion," 426.
69. Ibid.
70. Ibid.
71. Ibid.; Alva Ixtlilxóchitl, *Obras históricas*, 2:208, says that Mixcoatl-Camaxtli was equivalent to Huitzilopochtli, Tezcatlipoca, and Tlaloc.
72. "Procesos de indios," 18.
73. Ibid., 18.
74. Ibid.
75. Ibid.
76. Ibid., 19.
77. Ibid.
78. Ibid.
79. Ibid.
80. Ibid.
81. Nicholson, "Religion," 426.
82. "Procesos de indios," 21.
83. Sahagún, *Florentine Codex*, 4:77.
84. Broda, "Sacred Landscape," 103.
85. López Austin, "Núcleo duro," 325, notes that rulers gave offerings to their ancestors in the month Quecholli.
86. "Procesos de indios," 21.
87. Ibid., 20.
88. Ibid., 17.
89. Ibid., 25.
90. Pou y Martí, "Libro perdido de las pláticas," 304; Rubial García, *Hermana pobreza*, 137, notes that when Fray Antonio de Ciudad Rodrigo was first offered a bishopric, he turned it down (although later he became a bishop in Nueva Galicia). One Christmas, Zumárraga sent a bottle of wine to each of the friars and Ciudad Rodrigo sent it back. Mendieta, *Historia eclesiástica indiana*, 2:160, tells us that Zumárraga also displayed a lot of anger at the indigenous leaders, especially with regard to their taking multiple wives and especially very young girls, see García Icazbalceta, *Don Fray Juan de Zumárraga* (1947), 4:61; Rubial García, *Hermana pobreza*, 147, 164, 174; Mendieta, *Historia eclesiástica indiana*, 2:31, 113.
91. Clendinnen, "Ways to the Sacred," 107, argues that the friars delayed in dealing with Ocelotl because they feared him, "until the bishop took the lead." I disagree and believe that the opportunity of Inquisition and the recent provocative behavior

of Ocelotl were the catalyst. Fray Antonio was clearly the instigator, as Klor de Alva, "Martín Ocelotl," 133, recognizes when he says that Ciudad Rodrigo "cast a shadow" over Ocelotl.

92. Gibson, *Aztecs under Spanish Rule*, 168–69; P. Carrasco, "Royal Marriages in Ancient Mexico," 63.

93. "Procesos de indios," 26.

94. Ibid.

95. AGI, Mexico, 1088 L3, f.142, August 9, 1538; also f.102, May 8, 1538, Queen to royal council, permitting construction of road through Puebla; Paso y Troncoso, *Epistolario de Nueva España*, 2:19, Salmerón to council, February 2, 1531.

96. "Procesos de indios," 25.

97. Ibid., 20.

98. Sahagún, *Florentine Codex*, 8:2; Gruzinski, *Man-Gods in the Mexican Highlands*, 41–42, correctly speculates that the tzitzimime were associated with dreaded goddesses in pre-Columbian ideology and even "latent fear of the mother"; see also Cervantes, *Devil in the New World*, 45, for a similar interpretation; for a more detailed analysis of the female characteristics of the tzitzimime, as well as a clear connection to the god Mixcoatl in Tlaxcala and Puebla, see Klein, "Devil and the Skirt," 1–26.

99. Klor de Alva, "Martín Ocelotl," 135; Nicholson, "Religion," 427.

100. Burkhart, "Mexica Women on the Home Front," 49; [Olmos], *Historia de los mexicanos por sus pinturas*, chap. 2, associates the tzitzimime with the end of an epoch in human history: "there are some women who have no flesh, only bones . . . [and had] another name, *cicinime*; and these then were the ones when the world came to an end that had to eat all of the humans."

101. Terraciano, *Mixtecs of Colonial Oaxaca*, 280.

102. Saunders, "Predators of Culture," 107.

103. "Procesos de indios," 21.

104. Gruzinski, *Man-Gods in the Mexican Highlands*, 42, maintains that the philosophical underpinnings of this statement are in prehispanic elite morality. He claims that we have a "prudish" and false picture of prehispanic religion and moral philosophy because it is wholly based on accounts that Sahagún collected in the *Florentine Codex*. Looking back nostalgically, the elders who provided Sahagún with his information wove an overly rigorous and ascetic vision of elite conduct and practice; Burkhart, *Slippery Earth*, 140, however, argues that what Ocelotl was advocating was inconsistent with native ideology, as we know from many sources, and that he was actually making an "argument against Christianity, not simply an assertion of Nahua ideology." Hedonistic ideas did not have a foundation in indigenous moral principles. As Burkhart explains, lying with your neighbors' wives was entirely contradictory of Texcocan law and most Mesoamerican codes, which would have punished adultery with death for both man and woman.

105. Klor de Alva, "Aztec Spirituality," 191, takes the following position, which makes sense in the Ocelotl context: "The end of Nahuatlized Christianity was to be well off in this life—as healthy, wealthy and wise as the gods permitted."

106. The pattern of anti-Franciscan and anti-monogamy attitudes occurs over and over in the early colonial period. In the Mixtón War of 1541–43 in the western state of Jalisco, pagan priests told their followers that those who fought the Spanish would "become young again and have several wives, not merely one, as the monks order.... Whoever takes only one wife will be killed"; see Ricard, *Spiritual Conquest of Mexico*, 265, for the reference; in New Mexico, according to Gutiérrez, *When Jesus Came*, 76–77, "the friars' control of marriage and their imposition of monogamy were the tyrannies that most angered Pueblo men and became the most pervasive reasons for revolt."

107. "Procesos de indios," 32.
108. Ibid., 36–51.
109. Ibid., 39.
110. Ibid., 40–41.
111. Ibid., 42–44.
112. Ibid., 37–38.
113. Ibid., 39.
114. López Austin, "Núcleo duro," 362.

CHAPTER 3. THE MILLENARIAN

1. Gruzinski, *Man-Gods in the Mexican Highlands*, 53, makes a larger argument about the role of the man-god as a recurring leitmotiv of Mexican history.
2. "Procesos de indios," 56.
3. Sahagún, *Florentine Codex*, 10:175.
4. Lupo, "Cosmovisión de los nahuas," 340.
5. Offner, *Law and Politics in Aztec Texcoco*, 10–12.
6. Ibid., 10.
7. Ibid., 11.
8. López Austin, "Núcleo duro," 50.
9. Gerhard, *Guide to the Historical Geography*, 335.
10. Ibid., 118.
11. Ibid., 336; Oss, "Mendicant Expansion in New Spain," 55, indicates that the Franciscans founded missions in Otumba and Tepeapulco. Tulancingo was founded in 1529–30. There was a thrust into the Puebla region in the 1530s, with conventos in Cholula, Tlalmanalco, and Puebla de los Aacutengeles; we may speculate that some natives were familiar with Christianity simply because they were part of labor drafts that were sent to the city of Mexico from Otumba and Tepeapulco around 1530, according to Paso y Troncoso, *Epistolario de Nueva España*, 1:136, Francisco de Terrazos to Cortés, July 30, 1529.
12. Gerhard, *Guide to the Historical Geography*, 118.
13. Terraciano, *Mixtecs of Colonial Oaxaca*, 265–66, states flatly that the Inquisition trials in the Mixtec area south of the Valley of Mexico were directly related to the more openly practiced spiritual activities that sought to relieve the drought in the area prior to 1548.

14. Acuña-Soto et al., "Megadrought and Megadeath in 16th Century Mexico."
15. "Procesos de indios," 74.
16. Ibid.
17. Ibid.
18. Ibid., 64.
19. In this I disagree with Gruzinski's interpretation in *Man-Gods in the Mexican Highlands*, 59, in which he states that Don Juan of Xicotepec was part of a "Christian party" who "traveled in the Franciscan orbit." There is no clear evidence that these tlahtoqueh were believers or advocates, or that Xicotepec was effectively proselytized. All tlahtoqueh had numerous reasons for taking a middle standpoint in crises and employing arbitration of avoidance strategies.
20. See "Procesos de indios," 78, for the sale of Mixcoatl's goods.
21. Ibid., 75.
22. Nicholson, preface to Sahagún, *Primeros memoriales,*, 4–5, makes the point that *Primeros memoriales* is basically the history of Tepeapulco.
23. "Procesos de indios," 54.
24. Gibson, "Aztec Aristocracy in Colonial Mexico," 173, states than "Christianity, rather than peace alone, became by the late 1530s a recognized criterion for acceptable native conduct. Without it no member of the Indian upper class could thereafter maintain his position."
25. D. Carrasco, *Daily Life of the Aztecs*, 131–32.
26. "Procesos de indios," 72–73.
27. Ibid., 72–74.
28. Ibid., 56.
29. Nicholson, "Religion," 10:442; Lafaye, *Quetzalcóatl and Guadalupe*, 20, makes a similar argument.
30. "Procesos de indios," 73.
31. Ibid., 71.
32. Ibid., 66.
33. Ibid.
34. Ibid.
35. Burkhart, *Slippery Earth*, 70.
36. Ibid., 18–19.
37. López Austin, *Human Body and Ideology*, 362.
38. Farfán Morales, "Nahuas de la Sierra Norte de Puebla," 131–33, notes that in Huauchinango and Xicotepec today, people "communicate with their gods through the person of the local curandero [healer]" and use ceremonies involving mushrooms, copal, and amate, and other sacred ceremonies to reach back to ancient times. According to González Jácome, "Agricultura y especialistas en ideología agrícola," 482, nanahualtin still function in the highlands above Tlaxcala in the Sierra de Puebla and send clouds to other places with their chants and ceremonies.
39. "Procesos de indios," 70.
40. Ibid., 60.

41. Ibid., 61.
42. Ibid., 57, 61.
43. Ibid., 56–57.
44. Ibid., 69.
45. Ibid., 58.
46. Berdan, *Aztecs of Central Mexico*, 140, says that a typical task of the diviner was to "cast grains or beans."
47. "Procesos de indios," 63.
48. Ibid., 61.
49. Ibid., 59.
50. Ibid., 58–59.
51. Ibid., 54.
52. Ibid., 60.
53. Ibid., 61.
54. Ibid., 75; as León-Portilla notes, "Those Made Worthy," 50–51, offerings of all kinds were considered drink and sustenance for the gods: firstfruits, live animals, copal, prepared foods, piled wood.
55. Sahagún, *Primeros memoriales*, 177, mentions that the three most common gifts to the gods were "papers, incense, rubber."
56. Sahagún, *Florentine Codex*, 11:187, says that the copal was grown "in the hotlands," which usually referred to the area from Veracruz south.
57. "Procesos de indios," 66.
58. Sahagún, *Florentine Codex*, 10:88, refers to "pine resin" and "amber" sellers, who would harvest the sap from cuts in the trees, dry it, and grind it up; Sahagún, *Primeros memoriales*, 70, indicates that the copal was usually burned on hot coals that were held in ladles and that these ladles were the stock in trade of prehispanic priests, who carried them next to a pouch that contained the copal (81).
59. "Procesos de indios," 65, 68–69; see note 13 in Sahagún, *Florentine Codex*, 2:69, for information that the amate comes from the *Ficus* tree.
60. "Procesos de indios," 53, 68–69; "Lexical Origin," International Rubber Resource and Development Board, www.irrdb.com/irrdb/NaturalRubber/Lexical Origins.htm (September 22, 2007).
61. Stross, "Mesoamerican Copal Resins."
62. "Procesos de indios," 65.
63. Ibid., 58.
64. Ibid., 69; Báez-Jorge and Gómez Martínez, "Tlacatecolotl," 405, indicate that the papers are used to represent not only gods but sacred concepts associated with weather.
65. "Procesos de indios," 69.
66. Brinton, "Nagualism," 15–18.
67. "Procesos de indios," 58; Sahagún, *Florentine Codex*, 11:130, on nanacatl.
68. "Procesos de indios," 61, 64.
69. Sahagún, *Florentine Codex*, 10:85.

70. Ibid., 11:165.
71. "Procesos de indios," 62, 66.
72. Ibid., 56, 62, 66.
73. Sahagún, *Primeros memoriales*, 210, says that "the sorcerer casts rain with wormwood"; Sahagún spent the middle 1530s in Tepeapulco and completed research there for *Primeros memoriales*, which probably closely reflects the medicinal and divinatory aspects of herbology in the region where Mixcoatl was preaching.
74. See "Procesos de indios," 59–61, for numerous references to Mixcoatl as a god, among many others in the transcript.
75. Since Marmolejo does not appear in the lists of friars who came before 1529 and is not specifically listed in Ricard, *Spiritual Conquest of Mexico*, I assume he was one of the thirty friars that Fray Antonio de Ciudad Rodrigo recruited in Spain in 1529 and that he may have returned to Spain or died before gaining any notoriety; see also Grass, "America's First Linguists," 60.
76. Gruzinski, *Man-Gods in the Mexican Highlands*, 22.
77. For a good description of this ceremony, see D. Carrasco, "Sacrifice of Tezcatlipoca," 31–57.
78. Sahagún, *Florentine Codex*, 2:68.
79. "Procesos de indios," 62.
80. Ibid., 66.
81. Ibid., 69.
82. Ibid., 70; see D. Carrasco, "Sacrifice of Tezcatlipoca," 35–36, for the manner in which Tezcatlipoca's ixiptla was feted.
83. "Procesos de indios," 70.
84. Ibid., 60.
85. Ibid., 61.
86. Ibid., 55.
87. Ibid., 62.
88. Ibid., 60.
89. Ibid., 65.
90. Ibid., 72.
91. Both quotes are from "Procesos de indios," 67.
92. Burkhart, "Moral Deviance," 107–39.
93. "Procesos de indios," 68.
94. Ibid., 67.
95. Ibid., 57–58.
96. Ibid.
97. Ibid., 75.
98. Sahagún, *Primeros memoriales*, 64, emphasizes Mixcoatl as an important god more than in the *Florentine Codex*, and in his preface to the former, Nicholson suggests this is because *Primeros memoriales* reflects the local version of religion around Tepeapulco.
99. Sahagún, *Florentine Codex*, 2:25.
100. Ibid., 2:126–28.

101. Broda, "Sacred Landscape," 103–104.
102. "Procesos de indios," 58.
103. Ibid., 65.
104. Sahagún, *Florentine Codex*, 11:89; in *Primeros memoriales*, 175, Sahagún states that when someone "encountered a beetle on the road or saw it [in] the house, it was said that perhaps somewhere he would be reprehended before people, he would be shamed."
105. Sahagún, *Florentine Codex*, 5:169.
106. "Procesos de indios," 71.
107. Ibid., 78.
108. Ibid., 70–71.

CHAPTER 4. THE KEEPERS OF THE HUITZILOPOCHTLIS

1. Motolinía, *History*, 275–76.
2. See Díaz del Castillo, *True History of the Conquest*, 4:161, 176, for just two examples of the Spaniard's common use of the word "Huitzilobos" to mean representations of the gods.
3. Illustration in Greenleaf, *Zumárraga and the Mexican Inquisition*, between 52 and 53; see also Nuttall, "L'évêque Zumárraga," 156, for an interpretation that the illustration is by Mateo.
4. "Procesos de indios," 116.
5. Karttunen, *Analytical Dictionary of Nahuatl*, 229.
6. Ibid., 191.
7. In trial texts, we have contradictory identifications of these bundles from other witnesses. "Procesos de indios," 124, says that two bundles represented Huitzilopochtli and two represented Tezcatlipoca. The same source, 179, has another witness saying that two of the bundles were "Tezcatlipoca and de Topilci"; see also 189. Nuttall, "L'évêque Zumárraga," 156, identifies the fifth bundle as Quetzalcoatl.
8. Boone, "Incarnations of the Aztec Supernatural," 26; Boone and Cummins, *Native Traditions in the Postconquest World*, 167.
9. León-Portilla, *Broken Spears*, 146.
10. "Procesos de indios," 116.
11. Ibid., 117.
12. Ibid.
13. Ibid.
14. Ibid.
15. Padden, *Hummingbird and the Hawk*, 257.
16. Boone, *Stories in Red and Black*, 24–27, describes the occupations as primarily "hereditary" and that some *tlacuiloqueh* were also *tlamatinime* (priest-philosophers).
17. Berdan and Anawalt write in their introduction to *Essential Codex Mendoza*, xii, "Throughout the document, the hand of a single master painter is evident; other skilled natives worked with him."

18. "Procesos de indios," 119.
19. Ibid., 99–108.
20. Ibid., 115.
21. Boone, "Incarnations of the Aztec Supernatural," 34, suggests that the dough god was not a feature of Toxcatl and that Sahagún was in error in his account of May 1520 in the *Florentine Codex*, book 12; Sahagún repeats his inclusion of the dough god at Toxcatl in book 2, and other historians seem to have accepted both his accounts.
22. Boone, "Incarnations of the Aztec Supernatural," 4.
23. López Austin, *Tamoanchan, Tlalocan*, 254.
24. Ibid.
25. See Stenzel, "Sacred Bundles in Meso-american Religion," 347–52, for citations in literature about the widespread phenomenon in all of North American native cultures, including Mesoamerica; Olivier, "Les paquets sacrés," is particularly good on various uses of the tlaquimilloli.
26. López Austin, *Human Body and Ideology*, 1:70.
27. *Codex Borgia*; see plate 36 on page 42.
28. D. Carrasco, *City of Sacrifice*, 45; Smith, *Aztecs*, 198; Haly, "Bare Bones," 301.
29. D. Carrasco, *City of Sacrifice*, 25.
30. López Austin, *Tamoanchan, Tlalocan*, 254.
31. Olivier, "Hidden King and the Broken Flutes," 110; Gillespie, *Aztec Kings*, 147, notes that the four brother gods were also imagined as a "quadripartite Tezcatlipoca born of the supreme male-female deity" and names them: Red Tezcatlipoca = Mixcoatl-Camaxtli; Black Tezcatlipoca = Tezcatlipoca; White Tezcatlipoca = Quetzalcoatl; Blue Tezcatlipoca = Huitzilopochtli; López Austin, *Hombre-dios*, 107–109, suggests that Tezcatlipoca, Camaxtli, and Huitzilopochtli were "actually men who were either the leaders of pilgrimages or great warrior heroes."
32. Sahagún, *Florentine Codex*, 2:69.
33. Ibid., 2:73.
34. Ibid., 2:66.
35. Olivier, "Hidden King and the Broken Flutes," 124–26.
36. "Procesos de indios," 121.
37. Ibid., 122.
38. Ibid., 123.
39. Ibid., 123–24; Padden, *Hummingbird and the Hawk*, 266, describes Don Pedro as a cacique near Tula.
40. "Procesos de indios," 124.
41. Ibid., 125.
42. Ibid., 177–78.
43. The interrogations and strategies of the various leaders are reminiscent of incidents that Terraciano, *Mixtecs of Colonial Oaxaca*, 263, found in the later Yanhuitlan Inquisition, when the lords near Coatlan said that in 1536 a priest demanded their idols and they "gave him the lesser ones but kept the main ones," later trying to reason with the gods by sacrificing a female slave.

44. "Procesos de indios," 139.
45. Ibid.
46. Ibid., 140.
47. For a comparative account of Zumárraga's hesitance to use torture as an interrogation technique, see Greenleaf, "Francisco de Millán," 193–94, in which the bishop ordered the mock torture of a Jew but declined to authorize actual torture. The "torturer" in that case was Juan de Rebollo and the official torture witnesses were Pedro de Medinilla and Cristóbal de Cañego, the same three as in Pochtecatl Tlaylotla's torture.
48. Cortés, *Letters from Mexico*, 106.
49. "Procesos de indios"; the witnesses were Mateo, 116, Don Baltasar of Culhuacan, 181, and Don Andrés of Culhuacan, 179; for the death of Pitzotzin, see *Anales de Tlatelolco y Códice de Tlatelolco*, 76.
50. Olivier, "Hidden King and the Broken Flutes," 115–16, writes that Diego Holguín, a conqueror, saw Alvarado's imprisonment of the two ixiptla.
51. Sahagún, *Florentine Codex*, 12:47.
52. "Procesos de indios," 179, 182.
53. Ibid., 179.
54. Sahagún, *Florentine Codex*, 2:68.
55. P. Carrasco, *Tenochca Kingdom of Ancient Mexico*, 99–101, says that Mexica princes ruled Xilotepec, Xaltocan, and Azcapotzalco.
56. "Procesos de indios," 124.
57. Sahagún, *Florentine Codex*, 12:79–80.
58. See Robert McCaa, "Spanish and Nahuatl Views," 408, for the death of Cuitlahuac.
59. "Procesos de indios," 180; interestingly, Pomar, Relación de Texcoco, 13, says of the sacred bundles kept in Texcoco: "Two very important and divine bundles with many rich and very white blankets were kept, one of Tezcatlipoca and the other of Huitzilopochtli. In the one of Tezcatlipoca was a mirror of crystal the size of a moderately large orange."
60. Cortés, *Letters from Mexico*, 251–53.
61. Ibid., 264.
62. León-Portilla, *Broken Spears*, 142–44.
63. "Procesos de indios," 124.
64. Gibson, *Aztecs under Spanish Rule*, 68.
65. *Codex Chimalpahin*, 2:171; P. Carrasco, "Royal Marriages in Ancient Mexico," 63; Gibson, *Aztecs under Spanish Rule*, 168–69; Aiton, *Antonio Mendoza*, 55.
66. Klor de Alva, "Colonizing Souls," 66.
67. Baudot, *Utopia and History in Mexico*, 274, points to the chapter meeting of the order at Easter in 1536 as critical for revitalizing the mission: "It was simultaneously a certificate of maturity and an urgent call to better diversify the effort to conquer souls and to organize better and more efficiently the means of achieving this end." See

also Reff, "Predicament of Culture," 72, who writes that the missionaries "were much more comfortable using logic and reason to identify supernatural agency—to discover God's secretly transmitted signs—rather than culturological constraints on human behavior."

68. Ruiz Medrano, *Reshaping New Spain*, 26; Baudot, *Utopia and History in Mexico*, 28–33.
69. Baudot, *Utopia and History in Mexico*, 276.
70. Ibid., 171.
71. Ibid.
72. Wilkerson, "Ethnographic Works of Andrés de Olmos," 71.
73. Ibid., 72.
74. Ibid., 71–72.
75. Baudot, *Utopia and History in Mexico*, 194–95.
76. [Olmos], *Historia de los mexicanos por sus pinturas*, chap. 1.
77. Ibid.
78. Ibid.
79. Ibid.
80. Ibid., chap. 11.
81. Ibid.
82. Ibid., chap. 16.
83. Ibid.
84. Mendieta, *Historia eclesiástica indiana*, 2:79–80.
85. Wilkerson, "Ethnographic Works of Andrés de Olmos," 65.
86. Ibid., 75.
87. "Proceso inquisitorial del cacique de Tetzcoco," 27.
88. Mendieta, *Historia eclesiástica indiana*, 2:4, identifies "Lorenzo" in Texcoco as one of Olmos's most important informants for the legends he describes in his early work.
89. "Proceso inquisitorial del cacique de Tetzcoco," 15–16.
90. Ibid., 22–23.
91. Ibid.
92. Ibid., 25.
93. Ibid., 26.
94. Ibid., 29.
95. Ibid., 30.
96. Ibid., 31.
97. Ibid.
98. Ibid.
99. "Procesos de indios," 141–44.
100. Ibid., 158–59.
101. Ibid., 150–52.
102. Ibid., 180.

CHAPTER 5. THETLAHTOANI

1. Don Carlos also bore the name Chichimecateuctli. Greenleaf writes about the case in *Zumárraga and the Mexican Inquisition*. The first notice of the trial in the historical literature is in Suárez de Peralta, *Noticias históricas de la Nueva España* (1878), 275–80.

2. "Proceso inquisitorial del cacique de Tetzcoco," 67.

3. Ibid., 32.

4. Gillespie, *Aztec Kings*, 13–19; Offner, *Law and Politics in Aztec Texcoco*, 207.

5. P. Carrasco, "Royal Marriages in Ancient Mexico," 47.

6. According to Gillmor, *King Danced in the Marketplace*, 3, Nezahualcoyotl's mother was Matlalcihuatzin, the daughter of Huitzilihuitzin of Mexico; see P. Carrasco, "Royal Marriages in Ancient Mexico," 47–55, for the innovations of Nezahualcoyotl; Offner, *Law and Politics in Aztec Texcoco*, 231–32.

7. Offner, *Law and Politics in Aztec Texcoco*, 238.

8. *Codex Chimalpahin*, 2:237–38.

9. Ibid., 2:120–21, 221; Offner, *Law and Politics in Aztec Texcoco*, 238–39.

10. Offner, *Law and Politics in Aztec Texcoco*, 94; Gibson, *Aztecs under Spanish Rule*, 18.

11. See Cortés, *Letters from Mexico*, 96–97, for his account of Cacama in the wars and page 176 for his kidnapping of Cacama in the "noche triste."

12. See *Codex Chimalpahin*, 2:187, for the split in the family.

13. Gibson, *Aztecs under Spanish Rule*, 19; *Codex Chimalpahin*, 2:187.

14. See Gibson, "Aztec Aristocracy in Colonial Mexico," 191, for the discussion of the suits and disputes over the question of "legitimacy" in inheritance. See Cortés, *Letters from Mexico*, 173, on alliance with Texcoco. The sources are rather contradictory about the order of the very early colonial inheritance. Cortés, *Letters from Mexico*, 178, explains the decision to replace Tecocoltzin with Cohuanacoch; Sahagún, *Florentine Codex*, 8:9–10, gives a slightly revised colonial inheritance pattern, listing Cohuanacoch before Tecocoltzin, while *Codex Chimalpahin*, 2:199, suggests that Cortés installed a Don Carlos Ahuachpitzactxin and then Cohuanacoch. Most indigenous accounts indicate very brief reigns for these two non-Mexica rulers and then a return to the rule of the Mexica brothers. H. Cline, "Oztoticpac Lands Map of Texcoco" (1966), 83, reports that both Mapa Tlotzin and the Oztoticpac Map make it very clear that the inheritance of Texcoco went first to Cacama in 1517–19 and then very briefly to Don Fernando Tecocoltzin, a non-Mexica brother, in 1520–21. On the whole, the most reliable source is probably the Oztoticpac Map, and this chapter follows its order of inheritance.

15. Alva Ixtlilxóchitl, *Obras históricas*, 1:492.

16. P. Carrasco, "Social Organization of Ancient Mexico," 370–71. See Cortés, *Letters from Mexico*, 220, where he estimates Don Fernando's age in 1520 as twenty-four; also see P. Carrasco, "Social Organization of Ancient Mexico," 369, for his estimation that marriage in the eastern Valley of Mexico was typically at the age of thirty.

17. *Codex Chimalpahin*, 2:211.

18. Ibid., 2:203.

19. It should be noted that Gibson, *Aztecs under Spanish Rule*, 170, is one of the few historians who understood that the brief reference in a part of *Codex Chimalpahin*— that Don Carlos ruled from 1531, which ignores both Don Jorge's and Don Pedro's reigns—was inaccurate. He cites AGI, Inquisition, vol. 2, no. 10, f.262, to support his chronology of the inheritance. See also Gibson, *Aztecs under Spanish Rule*, 155, for his discussion of *tecuhtli*, which denoted a close advisor to the tlahtoani or a kind of military governor.

20. Don Carlos was married in 1535, which, according to Texcocan custom, would have happened when he was about thirty years old. We also know that he had a child eight years before, which would have been when he was about twenty-two. Therefore, he could not have been a very young child at the time of the conquest, as has been suggested by Luis González Obregón, preface to "Proceso inquisitorial del cacique de Tetzcoco," x–xi.

21. P. Carrasco, "Social Organization of Ancient Mexico," 354.

22. Sahagún, *Florentine Codex*, 8:71–72.

23. "Proceso inquisitorial del cacique de Tetzcoco," 56; a couple of Franciscan friars fit this description, but the possibilities were friars Juan de Tecto and Juan de Aora, Flemish Franciscans who accompanied Fray Pedro de Gante to New Spain in 1523 ahead of the famous Franciscan Twelve and founded the convent school at Texcoco; both died shortly after; see Aiton, *Antonio Mendoza*, 106; Cruces Carvajal, *Pedro de Gante*, 21–24; Cuevas, *Historia de la iglesia en México*, 1:116, also indicates that Fray Juan Díaz, a priest, baptized the leaders of Tlaxcala and Texcoco along with Fray Bartolomé de Olmedo; both died in 1524 on Cortés's expedition to Honduras.

24. P. Carrasco, "Social Organization of Ancient Mexico," 369, states that young nobles were allowed many concubines and illegitimate children.

25. González Obregón, preface to "Proceso inquisitorial del cacique de Tetzcoco," x, is incorrect when he speculates that Don Carlos stayed with Cortés until 1531 and that he took over the crown of Texcoco in the same year. See Mendieta, *Historia eclesiástica indiana*, 2:40, for the guidelines of placing a hundred youths of 10–12 years old, two from each cabecera, in the college when it was first founded; Zumárraga writes in García Icazbalceta, *Don Fray Juan de Zumárraga* (1947), 1:361, that they used six years of tribute from Texcoco for the building and support of the monastery and college at Tlatelolco; Estarellas, "College of Tlatelolco," 239, makes the strong argument that the myth of Don Carlos attending the college was formed by Gerónimo López, a Spanish settler who was very much against the education of indigenous youth at Tlatelolco and wrote letters to the court denouncing the college and the Franciscan effort there. He used the Don Carlos case "as an example of the harm that could be done by giving the Indians higher education." However, there is no direct or indirect proof that Don Carlos was educated at the college other than López's claim; see García Icazbalceta, *Colección de documentos*, 2:149–50, for the López letter to the emperor dated October 20, 1541; Baudot, *Utopia and History in Mexico*, 110, citing AGI, Mexico, 68, 2, Carta del obispo Fuenleal al emperador de México, August 8, 1533, says that

Ramírez de Fuenleal confirmed that unofficial instruction at Santa Cruz Tlatelolco had already begun in 1533, but Don Carlos was too old at that time.

26. H. Cline, "Oztoticpac Lands Map of Texcoco" (1966), 86.
27. Ibid., 106.
28. Haskett, *Indigenous Rulers*, 145, notes that "marriage marked one's entry into adult society and bachelors were considered unsuitable for governorship."
29. *Codex Chimalpahin*, 2:223.
30. Ibid., 2:225.
31. H. Cline, "Oztoticpac Lands Map of Texcoco" (1966), 96.
32. *Codex Chimalpahin*, 2:191.
33. Felipe Fernández Armesto, in discussion with the author at the John Carter Brown Library, Providence, Rhode Island, September 2004. His current research demonstrates the financial fragility of the prehispanic "empires." See also Hassig, *Trade, Tribute and Transportation*, 93–94, for an explanation of the hegemonic empire.
34. It is quite telling that the ruler of Texcoco after Don Carlos's death, his half brother and successor, Don Antonio Pimentel Tlahuitoltzin, reported that he made much effort to give land from the frontiers of the Texcocan community to his brothers and nephews, as well as other nobles and his sisters, in the next years, probably trying to engage their support and allegiance; see Horcasitas, "Descendientes de Nezahualpilli," 151.
35. Brumfiel, "Aztec State Making," 268.
36. K. Read, "Sacred Commoners," 52.
37. "Proceso inquisitorial del cacique de Tetzcoco," 60; P. Carrasco, "Social Organization of Ancient Mexico," 369.
38. "Proceso inquisitorial del cacique de Tetzcoco," 56, where Don Carlos says that he "married four years ago in Guaxutla, subject of Texcoco."
39. Burkhart, *Slippery Earth*, 71.
40. Sahagún, *Florentine Codex*, 10:15–16.
41. Gibson, "Aztec Aristocracy in Colonial Mexico," 173–74, notes that "Christianity, rather than peace alone, had become by the late 1530s a recognized criterion for acceptable native conduct. Without it no member of the indigenous upper class could thereafter maintain his position."
42. León-Portilla, "Testimonios nahuas sobre la conquista espiritual," 32–33, uses certain Spanish and Nahuatl terms to refer to this kind of middle cultural and political position. "Whenever and wherever Spanish activity had significantly altered native routines but not enough time elapsed for new ways to be properly assimilated, those who found themselves *sin rumbo* (without direction) considered the possibility of remaining *nepantla*, in the middle."
43. "Proceso inquisitorial del cacique de Tetzcoco," 38.
44. Ibid.
45. S. Cline, "Spiritual Conquest Re-examined," 466.
46. "Proceso inquisitorial del cacique de Tetzcoco," 11–13.
47. Burkhart, "Mexica Women on the Home Front," 45–52.

48. Gibson, *Aztecs under Spanish Rule*, 243, states that the viceroy owned weaving factories in Texcoco.
49. Ricard, *Spiritual Conquest of Mexico*, 111.
50. Offner, *Law and Politics in Aztec Texcoco*, 260.
51. "Procesos de indios," 88–89, 202, 209.
52. Ibid., 95, 205–206, 202–203.
53. Kellogg, *Weaving the Past*, 71–75; see also Tuñón Pablos, *Women in Mexico*, 26–27.
54. Offner, *Law and Politics in Aztec Texcoco*, 10–11, 16; or about 8 percent of a total Texcoco population of about 70,000; see also Ivanhoe, "Diet and Demography in Texcoco," 143, who estimates the count at 10 percent of a total Texcoco population of 180,000.
55. Offner, *Law and Politics in Aztec Texcoco*, 10–11.
56. Don, "Franciscans, Indian Sorcerers, and the Inquisition," 27–49.
57. "Proceso inquisitorial del cacique de Tetzcoco," 38.
58. Ibid., 2–3, for Francisco's original statement made on June 22; 4–5, for Cristóbal's substantial confirmation of it on July 2, the same day that Don Carlos was arrested; and 44–47, for Don Alonso's testimony that corroborates what Francisco said on June 22 but not what he added in his amplified testimony of July 11.
59. "Proceso inquisitorial del cacique de Tetzcoco," 55.
60. Vaillant, *Aztecs of Mexico*, 182; Gillmor, *Flute of the Smoking Mirror*, 29–30, 85.
61. Taylor, *Drinking, Homicide, and Rebellion*, 35.
62. Himmerich y Valencia, *Encomenderos of New Spain*, for stonemasonry in Chiconautla.
63. Offner, *Law and Politics in Aztec Texcoco*, 93; according to Gerhard, *Guide to the Historical Geography*, 100, Chiconautla had a dependent relationship with Texcoco during colonial times as well; Hodge, "Land and Lordship in the Valley of Mexico," 135, notes that unlike the Tepaneca area, where the Tenochca interfered constantly with the relationship between tlahtoani and dependent city-states, Texcoco was reasonably independent of the Tenochca. See Kubler, "Architects and Builders in Mexico," 18, who writes that "certain districts, such as Texcoco, were maintained as sources of building labor." See also Gibson, "Llamamiento General, Repartimiento, and the Empire of Acohuacan," 2, who reports that as late as 1558, Texcoco was responsible for calling up labor drafts to build a bridge in Chiconautla.
64. Offner, *Law and Politics in Aztec Texcoco*, 93; Gibson, *Aztecs under Spanish Rule*, 264.
65. "Proceso inquisitorial del cacique de Tetzcoco," 2, 5, 45, 51.
66. Cañizares-Esguerra, *How to Write the History of the New World*, 92–129, explains some of the characteristics of the indigenous sources.
67. "Proceso inquisitorial del cacique de Tetzcoco," 5.
68. Ibid., 52.
69. Díaz Balsera, *Pyramid under the Cross*, 15–50, suggests that the colloquies published later but recording dialogues that took place in Texcoco in 1524 are evidence

of the ongoing discussions and the elaborate speech patterns of the priests and tlahtoqueh, which were still in use in the colonial period; see also Klor de Alva, "Aztec-Spanish Dialogues of 1524," 52–193.

70. [Olmos], *Huehuehtlahtolli. Testimonios de la antigua palabra*, 377–95; Sahagún, *Florentine Codex*, 6:57–83, for the speeches between tlahtoani and nobles; Karttunen and Lockhart, preface to *Art of Nahuatl Speech*, 10–11, 45–47; see also Marcus, *Mesoamerican Writing Systems*, 52, who indicates that there were actually three typical speech patterns—*techpillatolli*, lordly or courteous speech among nobles, *huehuehtlahtolli*, ancient or historic speech of the tlahtoani, and *macehuallatolli*, rustic or common speech of the common people.

71. According to Sahagún, *Florentine Codex*, 8:71–72, the young noble of the household began his training in speech and proper conduct at age six. He was placed in a priest's house at about ten years old in order to learn religious practice and at fifteen learned arms.

72. "Proceso inquisitorial del cacique de Tetzcoco," 40.
73. Ibid., 54.
74. Burkhart, *Slippery Earth*, 111–12.
75. "Proceso inquisitorial del cacique de Tetzcoco," 40.
76. Gruzinski, 65–66; Ricard, *Spiritual Conquest of Mexico*, 96; Haskett, *Indigenous Rulers*, 114–15.
77. Motolinía, *History*, 14.
78. "Proceso inquisitorial del cacique de Tetzcoco," 2.
79. Ibid., 40–41.
80. Offner, *Law and Politics in Aztec Texcoco*, 66–67.
81. "Proceso inquisitorial del cacique de Tetzcoco," 42.
82. Ibid.
83. Ibid., 2.
84. Ibid.
85. Ibid., 3.
86. Carreño, *Don Fray Juan de Zumárraga*, 50–52.
87. For the hunt for votive objects, see "Proceso inquisitorial del cacique de Tetzcoco," 16–31; for Don Carlos's wife, 38.
88. "Proceso inquisitorial del cacique de Tetzcoco," 38; the wife of Don Carlos notes that Inés came to the house when Don Carlos was ill (about 140 days before the wife gave her testimony on July 10), about the beginning of March. Don Pedro then disappears from this and other transcripts, suggesting that he had died in March, probably from the same illness, and that Don Carlos was recovering in April and ascending to the throne at the same time.
89. The leaders Don Carlos refers to in this speech range from the well known to the obscure. The best known, Tlacahuapantli, is most certainly Don Pedro Motecuhzoma Tlacahuepantli, son of Motecuhzoma and Doña María Miahuasuchitl of Tula. Cortés gave the inheritance of Tula to Don Pedro, whom the people of Tula readily accepted, as his mother was a royal princess of the Tollan dynasty (see Gibson, *Aztecs*

under Spanish Rule, 164). "Tezapilli, señor of Tacuba" may refer to Don Antonio Totoquihuatzin, son of Tetlepanquetzatzin, the tlahtoani of Tlacopan (the prehispanic name of Tacuba) whom Cortés killed in Honduras in 1526. Cortés gave the encomienda of Tacuba to Isabel Motecuhzoma, daughter of Motecuhzoma, but the Spanish continued to recognize the descendants of Tetlepanquetzatzin as political rulers in Tacuba. Don Antonio, the most legitimate heir, disputed with several other claimants in the family until he obtained uncontested rule in 1550 (Ibid., 171). "Tezapilli" may refer to Don Antonio or one of the other claimants. The most difficult to identify is "señor of Mexico, Yoanize." Viceroy Mendoza named Don Diego Huanitzin governor of the indigenous communities of the city of Mexico in 1538. "Yoanize" may be Huanitzin. An alternative candidate is Anahuacaca, who directed the safeguarding of the Huitzilopochtlis after 1526. The Spanish regarded Anahuacaca as a rebellious lord, and he died sometime in 1539 (see Padden, *Hummingbird and the Hawk*, 257).

90. Ibid., 47–48.

91. "Procesos de indios," 122–23, records that on October 14, 1539, in the case of Miguel Pochtecatl Tlaylotla, Francisco was brought in to name the leading prehispanic priests of Motecuhzoma that still lived in the city and listed seven men, which helped Zumárraga begin a new round of inquiries and prosecutions.

92. "Relaxation" was the term for turning the convicted over for execution, usually burning at the stake. "Reconcile" meant the convicted accepted his sins, remained in the Church, and received a lighter sentence. In both the Ocelotl case and the Don Carlos case, Zumárraga announced sentences only after consulting with the viceroy and Audiencia; see references in the transcripts, "Procesos de indios," 32, and "Proceso del cacique," 81; Greenleaf, *Zumárraga and the Mexican Inquisition*, 72.

EPILOGUE. THE LEGACY OF THE INQUISITION IN CENTRAL MEXICO

1. Carreño, *Nuevos documentos inéditos*, 81; García Icazbalceta, *Don Fray Juan de Zumárraga* (1947), 2:170–73, "Cédula al obispo Zumárraga recomendándole que no se apliquen castigos rigurosos a los indios, Madrid, 22 de noviembre de 1540," and "Cédula al obispo Zumárraga reprobando la ejecución del cacique Don Carlos, Madrid, 22 de noviembre de 1540"; see García Icazbalceta, *Don Fray Juan de Zumárraga* (1947), 3:263, where Zumárraga in a letter to Fray Marcos de Niza in 1546 says that Nava, the bishop of Badajoz, was then the president of the royal council, one of the highest offices in the Spanish court.

2. García Icazbalceta, *Don Fray Juan de Zumárraga* (1947), 2:170–71.

3. Ibid., 2:172.

4. Cuevas, *Historia de la iglesia en México*, 1:378.

5. Evidence that the attorney also represented the Spaniard is provided in the Humboldt Fragment VI, interpreted in H. Cline, "Oztoticpac Lands Map of Texcoco" (1972), 13–18.

6. "Proceso inquisitorial del cacique de Tetzcoco," 83.

7. "Good lesson" is how the Inquisition secretary describes Don Carlos's confession in the trial transcript; see "Proceso inquisitorial del cacique de Tetzcoco," 83.

8. García Icazbalceta, *Don Fray Juan de Zumárraga* (1947), 2:167, "Carta de Don Fray Juan de Zumárraga de la Orden de San Francisco, primer obispo de México, escrita a Suero del Aacuteguila, México, 17 de septiembre de 1538."

9. "Procesos de indios," 136–38.

10. See Clendinnen, *Ambivalent Conquests*, 76–77, for the comparison with Zumárraga.

11. Greenleaf, "Inquisition and the Indians," 140–41.

12. See Moreno de los Arcos, "New Spain's Inquisition."

13. See Kamen, *Spanish Inquisition*, 152–53, for the crown's concern that Inquisition would be "driven by financial need"; Haliczer, "First Holocaust," 10, about the constant and early problems of the 1530s and '40s with runaway and abusive local tribunals in Spain.

14. Cuevas, *Historia de la iglesia en México*, 1:380.

15. "Procesos de indios," 207.

16. A fragment of the "Manual de adultos" is in the John Carter Brown Library, with a colophon that states that it was printed "at the expense" of Zumárraga in the house of Juan Cromberger in the city of Mexico on December 13, 1540; García Icazbalceta, *Don Fray Juan de Zumárraga* (1947), 1:173, tells us that the "Manual de adultos" was used into the late sixteenth century; see also Carreño, "Books of Fray Juan de Zumárraga," 311–30.

17. Caro Baroja, *World of the Witches*, 188; Kamen, *Spanish Inquisition*, 271; Lea, *Inquisition in the Spanish Dependencies*, 211; Levack, *Witch-hunt in Early Modern Europe*, 8; Henningsen and Tedeschi, *Inquisition in Early Modern Europe*, 22; unlike many in Europe, the Spanish Inquisition and the Spanish elite maintained a healthy skepticism about the reality of witchcraft, but Spaniards believed fervently that there was a devil and that the devil inspired followers to the practice of witchcraft, or diabolism. In 1526, a tribunal of the Inquisition confirmed that the practice of diabolism was a legitimate area of Inquisition jurisdiction but warned the tribunals to tread carefully.

18. Interestingly, Zumárraga seems to have supported Olmos's ideas and efforts by publishing a work by John Gerson of the University of Paris, a foremost expert in the subject of witchcraft; for Castañega's theories, see Darst, "Witchcraft in Spain," 300: "Moreover, the tone of Castañega was skeptical and designed to dissuade belief in witchcraft, to prove that diabolical intervention does not exist."

19. Castañega, *Tratado de las supersticiones* (1994), 44–45.

20. Olmos, *Tratado de hechicerías y sortilegios* (1990), 55.

21. Ibid., 51, 57.

22. Ibid., 17.

23. Mendieta, *Historia eclesiástica indiana*, 2:109.

24. Baudot, *Utopia and History in Mexico*, 244.

25. Mendieta, *Historia eclesiástica indiana*, 2:95.

26. Olmos, *Tratado de hechicerías y sortilegios*, 43.

27. Sahagún, *Florentine Codex*, 1:38.

28. Sousa, "Devil and Deviance in Native Criminal Narratives," 165, says that the friars later called the devil *tzitzimitl* or *colelectli*, terms unfamiliar to them at the time of Ocelotl's trial.

29. As Cervantes demonstrates in *Devil in the New World*, the friars' campaign backfired in the long run because the indigenous conscience did not distinguish good from evil, just power from lack of power. The more the friars presented Tezcatlipoca as a powerful evil, the more the natives admired the powerful Tezcatlipoca; see Cervantes, 25, for his discussion of Olmos as the first to make the theological transition.

30. Cervantes, *Devil in the New World*, 40–74.

31. See Elliott, "Discovery of America," 23.

32. According to H. R. Harvey, "Oztoticpac Lands Map," 179, the amount of land in the palace complex was 27 to 42.5 hectares, or 66.5 to 105 acres. According to Hicks, "Rotational Labor and Urban Development," 151, the total number of acres in Texcoco was 1,111; therefore, the Oztoticpac palace represented around 10 percent of the land.

33. According to Boone, "Pictorial Documents and Visual Thinking," 19, these codices were "an elite enterprise directed upward toward, or used by, those in authority."

34. H. Cline, "Oztoticpac Lands Map of Texcoco" (1972).

35. Douglass, "Figures of Speech," 281–309, establishes that all three codices were produced in the period 1540–45.

36. Two accounts of how geography allowed native communities to adapt more slowly are contained in Haskett, "Living in Two Worlds," 34–59; and Poole, "Some Observations on Mission Methods," 337–49; see Ricard, *Spiritual Conquest of Mexico*, 265, for an example of an alternative resistance scenario that was about to rage in the lightly settled western frontier of the colony. Native Mixtec priests had encouraged native leaders to rise up against the few Spanish garrisons and the handful of Franciscans who had intrepidly gone into the hostile area to proselytize the native subjects. Reflecting the "religious nature of the uprising," the rebels told their followers that whoever joined them "will become young again and have several wives, not merely one as the monks order. . . . Whoever takes only one wife will be killed."

37. AGI, Mexico, Mexico, 68, R12, N31, Tello de Sandoval to Prince Philip, March 28, 1545, where the visitador reports that 160–70 natives were dying each day in the city of Mexico; see Gibson, *Aztecs under Spanish Rule*, 179, for the way clerics manipulated native elections, even forcing them to be held in churches.

38. *Codex Chimalpahin*, 2:203.

39. Horcasitas, "Descendientes de Nezahualpilli," 150–51, 152, also states that Fray Juan de San Francisco was the one who arranged the inheritance at Don Antonio's deathbed.

40. Baudot, *Utopia and History in Mexico*, 284.

41. Gibson, *Tlaxcala in the Sixteenth Century*, 101, indicates that the Pimentel descendants engaged in a marriage policy that took over several other noble houses

even in Tlaxcala; in a "complete breakdown of legitimate succession," the Tlaxcalan line came under the Texcocan nobility. For example, Don Fernando's granddaughter Francisca Pimentel Maxixcatzin consolidated the family fortunes when she married Don Diego Muñoz Camargo, heir to the fortune of Ocotelulco and son of the historian by the same name (author of the *Historia de Tlaxcala*).

42. Gibson, *Aztecs under Spanish Rule*, 51–52, says that Don Fernando argued in letters of 1550–51 that all formerly subject Acolhua towns should continue to be subject, which they of course were not by then.

43. Wood, "Testaments and Títulos," 85–111, suggests that primordial wills that related the family history seemed over time to emphasize less the community history and welfare and more the history and welfare of an individual elite family.

44. See Orozco y Berra, *Historia antigua y de la conquista de México*, 2:201–203, for the complete contents of the letter; another letter is in Cuevas, *Historia de la iglesia en México*, 1:468.

45. Horcasitas, "Descendientes de Nezahualpilli," 154.

APPENDIX. BOBAN CALENDAR WHEEL

1. The John Carter Brown Library image reproduced here is a lithograph that Colonel Doutrelaine made of the original document in 1866, when he brought the Boban Calendar Wheel to the attention of Eugène Boban. The original document changed hands several times in the early twentieth century and had deteriorated when the John Carter Brown Library acquired both original and lithograph in 1950.

2. See the John Carter Brown Library catalog description that accompanies the online images of the document at www.lunacommons.org.

3. Glass and Robertson, "Census," 96.

4. Robertson, *Mexican Manuscript Painting*, 149.

5. Dibble, "Boban Calendar Wheel," 173–82.

6. Ibid., 176; see Douglass, "Figures of Speech," for the dating of *Mapa Quinatzin* and other codices of the early 1540s and their connection to Don Carlos's trial.

7. Robertson, *Mexican Manuscript Painting*, 147.

8. Ibid., 148–49; Boone, *Stories in* Red and Black, 194, notes that the Texcocan scribes use "foundation events as a springboard for the rest of the story."

9. Robertson, *Mexican Manuscript Painting*, 147; Barnes, "Secularizing Survival," 338, also notes that each pair of figures indicates "the beginning of an epoch in Texcoco's history."

10. Dibble, "Boban Calendar Wheel," 177.

11. See Barnes, "Secularizing Survival," 322–23, on the equality of rulers facing each other in manuscripts.

12. "Proceso inquisitorial del cacique de Tetzcoco," 19–20.

13. Dibble, "Boban Calendar Wheel," 176.

14. Ibid., both translations.

15. Douglass, "Figures of Speech," 289; see Seler, "Alexander von Humboldt's Picture Manuscripts," 194, concerning Don Antonio.

16. Liebsohn, "Mapping after the Letter," 127.

17. McAfee and Barlow, "Titles of Tetzcotzinco," 119–20, brought forward a document that asserts that Don Antonio was governor in 1537, but H. Cline, "Oztoticpac Lands Map of Texcoco" (1966), demonstrates that the Nahuatl date on the document corresponds with 1540 rather than 1537; thus, the earlier translation is wrong. While Don Antonio was governor, he distributed lands in the Tetzcotzingo area to members of the Texcoco royal family with the help of Fray Juan de Alameda on Monday, January 4, which would have fallen in the year 1540 rather than 1537.

18. Robertson, *Mexican Manuscript Painting*, 147–48.

19. See Barnes, "Secularizing Survival," 340–41, for his investigation of this and various other documents and codices of the 1540s that demonstrate the same middle transition from pictorial to combined pictorial and alphabetized and finally, fully alphabetized documents in the latter half of the sixteenth century.

20. Alva Ixtlilxóchitl, *Obras históricas*, 1:392, says he took four thousand Texcocans with him.

Glossary

NAHUATL

achcauhtli (achcauhtin)	barrio leader(s)
altepetl (altepemeh)	community(ies), city-state(s)
amate	ceremonial paper
calmecac	school for elite children
calpanpilli	house son or illegitimate son
calpulli (calpultin)	kin and trade network(s) in an *altepetl*
huehuetlahtolli	formal speech
hueytlahtoani	great leader; usually, *tlahtoani* of Mexico
icpalli	throne woven of reeds
ixiptla	god impersonator
iztauhyatl	Mexican wormwood
macehualli (macehualtin)	commoner(s)
nahualli (nanahualtin)	native priest(s) believed to have supernatural powers
nahuatlahto	interpreter
nanacatl	hallucinogenic mushrooms
popochcomitl	incense burner, *sahumeria*
quetzalcoatl	high priest from the nobility
teocalli	temple
teotl	god
tepehua	lord
tlacuilo (tlaquiloqueh)	scribe(s)

tlahtoani (*tlahtoqueh*)	speaker(s), leader(s)
tlahtocayotl	ceremonial center or square
tlahuitzin	cult priest from commoner class
tlaquimilloli	sacred bundle containing relics of a god
tlazopilli	esteemed or legitimate son
tzitzimime	demons of darkness, flesh-eating women spirits
ulli	rubber

SPANISH

alcalde	council member
alcalde mayor	mayor
alfaquí	Muslim religious leader
alguacil	sheriff
Audiencia	legislative and judicial tribunal
bruja/o	witch
cabecera	independent principal town
cabildo	council
canuto de color	tube of color
colegio	secondary school
concordia	agreement
convento	monastery
converso	baptized Jew
corregidor	local crown official, governor
Cortes	regional parliament
cue	sacrificial pyramid
curandero	healer
encomendero	recipient of an *encomienda*
encomienda	Spanish grant of tribute and labor
gobernador	governor
mandón	native neophyte who instructs others
manta	cape, blanket
mástel	loincloth
morisco	baptized Muslim
mudéjar	unbaptized Muslim

núcleo duro	persistent core cultural capital of rituals and beliefs
oidor	*Audiencia* judge
papa	priest
plática	talk
principal	leader
proceso	trial proceeding
pueblo de visita	town visited infrequently by friars to administer the sacraments
regidor	crown representative
rogativa	Christian religious procession
sahumeria	incense burner, *popochcomitl*
señor	leader
señoridad	rule of a leader
veintena	native twenty-day month
visita	inspection
visitador	inspector

Bibliography

PRIMARY SOURCES

Alva Ixtlilxóchitl, Fernando de. *Ally of Cortés*. Translated by Douglass K. Ballentine. [El Paso]: Texas Western Press, 1969.

———. *Obras históricas*. Edited by Edmundo O'Gorman. 2 vols. Mexico: Universidad Nacional Autónoma de México, 1975.

Anales de Tlatelolco y Códice de Tlatelolco. Edited by Heinrich Berlin. Mexico: Antigua Librería Robredo, 1948.

Archivo General de Indias, Mexico, 336A, R2, 97, Ecclesiastical junta to king.

Archivo General de Indias, Mexico, 2555, Memorial of the bishop of Mexico to the king, 1533.

Archivo General de Indias, Mexico, 1088 L3, f.142, August 9, 1538, and f.102, May 8, 1538, Queen to royal council, permitting construction of road through Puebla.

Archivo General de Indias, Mexico, 68, R12, N31, Tello de Sandoval to Prince Philip, March 28, 1545.

Archivo General de Indias, Patronato Real, 1, no. 37, Apostolic declaration of the bull of Pope Paul III, June 22, 1537.

Carreño, Alberto María, ed. *Don Fray Juan de Zumárraga: Teólogo y editor, humanista e inquisidor; documentos inéditos*. Mexico: Editorial Jus, 1950.

———, ed. *Nuevos documentos inéditos de d. fr. Juan de Zumárraga y cédulas y cartas reales en relación con su gobierno*. Mexico: Ediciones Victoria, 1942.

Castañega, Fray Martín de. *Tratado de las supersticiones y hechicerias*. Introduction by Agustín G. de Amezúa. Madrid: Sociedad de Bibliófilos Españoles, 1946.

———. *Tratado de las supersticiones y hechizerias y de la posibilidad y remedio dellas, 1929*. Edited by Juan Robert Muro Abad. 3rd ed. Logroño, Spain: Gobierno de La Rioja, Instituto de Estudios Riojanos, 1994.

Codex Borgia: A Full-Color Restoration of the Ancient Mexican Manuscript. Edited by Gisele Díaz and Alan Rodgers. New York: Dover, 1993.

Codex Chimalpahin: Society and Politics in Mexico Tenochtitlan, Tlatelolco, Texcoco, Culhuacan, and Other Nahua Altepetl in Central Mexico. Edited by Arthur J. O. Anderson and Susan Schroeder. 2 vols. Norman: University of Oklahoma Press, 1997.

Cortés, Hernán. *Letters from Mexico*. Translated and edited by Anthony Pagden. Introduction by John H. Elliott. New Haven: Yale University Press, 1986.

Díaz del Castillo, Bernal. *The True History of the Conquest of New Spain*. Edited by Genaro García. Translated by Alfred Percival Maudsley. 5 vols. Wiesbaden, Germany: Hakluyt Society, 1916. Reprint, Nendeln, Liechtenstein: Krause, 1967.

Gante, Fray Pedro de. *Cartas de Fr. Pedro de Gante, O. F. M., primer educador de América*. Edited by Fidel de J. Chauvet. Mexico: Talleres Fr. Junípero Serra, 1947.

García Icazbalceta, Joaquín, ed. *Colección de documentos para la historia de México*. 2 vols. Mexico: M. Andrade, 1858.

———, ed. *Don Fray Juan de Zumárraga, primer obispo y arzobispo de México*. Mexico: Andrade y Morales, 1881.

———, ed. *Don Fray Juan de Zumárraga: Primer obispo y arzobispo de México. Colección de Escritores Mexicanos*. 4 vols. Mexico: Editorial Porrúa, 1947.

———, ed. *Nueva coleccio'n de documentos para la historia de Me'xico*. Vol. 3. Mexico: Salvador Chávez Hayhoe, 1941.

Greenleaf, Richard, ed. *Zumárraga and His Family: Letters to Vizcaya, 1536–1548*. Washington, D.C.: Academy of American Franciscan History, 1979.

"Letter of Pedro Vaz de Caminha to King Manuel, Porto Seguro de Vera Cruz, May 1, 1500." In *Colonial Latin America: A Documentary History*. Edited by Kenneth Mills, William B. Taylor, and Sandra Lauderdale Graham. Wilmington, Del.: Scholarly Resources, 2002.

"Manual de adultos." Mexico: Juan Cromberger, 1540.

Mendieta, Fray Gerónimo de. *Historia eclesiástica indiana*. 2 vols. Mexico: Salvador Chávez Hayhoe, 1945.

Motolinía (Fray Toribio de Benavente). *History of the Indians of New Spain*. Translated by Elizabeth Andros Foster. Berkeley: Cortés Society, 1950.

[Olmos, Fray Andrés de]. *Historia de los mexicanos por sus pinturas. Histoire des mexicains par leurs peintures: Manuscrit espagnol anonyme du XVI siècle*. Translated by Paule Obadia-Baudesson. Paris: Association Oxomoco y Cipactomal, 1988.

———. *Huehuehtlahtolli. Testimonios de la antigua palabra*. Edited by Miguel León-Portilla and Librado Silva Galeana. Madrid: Edición de Miguel León-Portilla, 1990.

Olmos, Fray Andrés de. *Tratado de hechicerías y sortilegios de Fray Andrés de Olmos*. Translated by Georges Baudot. Mexico: Universidad Nacional Autónoma de México, 1990.

Paso y Troncoso, Francisco del, ed. *Epistolario de Nueva España, 1505–1818*. Vols. 1–2. Mexico: Antigua Librería Robredo de J. Porrúa e hijos, 1939–42.

Pomar, Juan Bautista. Relación de Tezcoco. In García Icazbalceta, *Nueva colección de documentos para la historia de México*, vol. 3.

Proceso de Don Pedro, cacique de Totolapa, y su hermano, Antón. Archivo General de la Nación, Inquisición, vol. 212, exp. 7.

"Proceso del Santo Oficio contra una india curandera." *Boletín del Archivo General de la Nación* 12 (1941): 211–14.

"Proceso inquisitorial del cacique de Tetzcoco." Preface by Luis González Obregón. In *Publicaciones del Archivo General de la Nación*. Vol. 1. Mexico: Eusebio Gómez de la Puente, 1910. Original in Archivo General de la Nación, Inquisición, tomo 2, exp. 10.

"Procesos de indios idólatras y hechiceras." In *Publicaciones del Archivo General de la Nación*. Vol. 3. Mexico: Tipográfico Guerrero, 1912. Originals in Archivo General de la Nación, Inquisición, tomo 23, exp. 1; tomo 30, exp. 9; tomo 37, exp. 1–4; tomo 38, exp. 1A; tomo 40, exp. 1, 7, and 8; tomo 42, exp. 17–18.

"Relación de la genealogía y linaje de los señores que han señoreado esta tierra de la Nueva España." In García Icazbalceta, *Nueva colección de documentos para la historia de México*, vol. 3.

Sahagún, Fray Bernardino de. *Florentine Codex: General History of the Things of New Spain*. Edited by Charles E. Dibble and Arthur J. O. Anderson. 12 vols. Salt Lake City: University of Utah Press, 1952–80.

———. *Primeros memoriales*. Preface by H. B. Nicholson. Translated by Thelma D. Sullivan. Norman: University of Oklahoma Press, 1997.

SECONDARY SOURCES

Acuña-Soto, Rodolfo, David W. Stahle, Malcolm K. Cleaveland, and Matthew D. Therrell. "Megadrought and Megadeath in 16th Century Mexico." *Emerging Infectious Diseases* 8, no. 4 (April 2002). www.cdc.gov/ncidod/eid/vol8no4/01-0175.htm

Adorno, Rolena. "The Depiction of Self and Other in Colonial Peru." *Art Journal* 49, no. 2 (Summer 1990): 110–18.

Aiton, Arthur S. *Antonio Mendoza, First Viceroy of New Spain*. Durham, N.C.: Duke University Press, 1927.

Ayllón, Fernando de. *El tribunal de la Inquisición: De la leyenda a la historia*. Lima, Peru: Ediciones del Congreso de la República del Perú, 1999.

Báez-Jorge, Félix, and Arturo Gómez Martínez. "*Tlacatecolotl, señor del bien y del mal (La dualidad en la cosmovisión de los nahuas de Chicotepec).*" In Broda and Báez-Jorge, *Cosmovisión, ritual e identidad de los pueblos indígenas de México*.

Barnes, William L. "Secularizing Survival: Changing Depictions of Central Mexican Native Rule in the Early Colonial Period." In Painted Books and Indigenous Knowledge in Mesoamerica: Manuscript Studies in Honor of Mary Elizabeth Smith. Edited by Elizabeth Hill Boone. New Orleans: Middle American Research Institute, 2005.

Baudot, Georges. *Utopia and History in Mexico: The First Chroniclers of Mexican Civilization, 1520–1569*. Niwot: University Press of Colorado, 1995.

Beinart, Haim. *Conversos on Trial: The Inquisition in Ciudad Real*. Jerusalem: Magnes Press, Hebrew University, 1981.

Berdan, Frances F. *The Aztecs of Central Mexico: An Imperial Society*. New York: Holt, Rinehart and Winston, 1982.

Berdan, Frances F., and Patricia Rieff Anawalt. Introduction to *The Essential Codex Mendoza*. Berkeley: University of California Press, 1997.

Boone, Elizabeth Hill. "Incarnations of the Aztec Supernatural: The Image of Huitzilopochtli in Mexico and Europe." *Transactions of the American Philosophical Society*, n.s., 79, no. 2 (1989): 1–107.

———. "Pictorial Documents and Visual Thinking in Postconquest Mexico." In *Native Traditions in the Postconquest World*. Edited by Elizabeth Hill Boone and Tom Cummins. Washington, D.C.: Dumbarton Oaks, 1998.

———. *Stories in Red and Black: Pictorial Histories of the Aztecs and Mixtecs*. Austin: University of Texas Press, 2000.

———. Introduction to *Writing without Words: Alternative Literacies in Mesoamerica and the Andes*. Edited by Elizabeth Hill Boone and Walter D. Mignolo. Durham: University of North Carolina Press, 1994.

Boone, Elizabeth Hill, and Tom Cummins, eds. *Native Traditions in the Postconquest World: A Symposium at Dumbarton Oaks, 2nd through 4th October 1992*. Washington, D.C.: Dumbarton Oaks, 1998.

Borah, Woodrow, and Sherbourne Cook. "Marriage and Legitimacy in Mexican Culture." *California Law Review* 54, no. 2 (1966): 946–1008.

Boronat y Barrachina, Pascual. *Los moriscos españoles y su expulsión*. 2 vols. Valencia: Francisco Vives y Mora, 1901.

Bowser, Frederick P. "The Church in Colonial Middle America: *Non Fecit Taliter Omni Nationi*." *Latin American Research Review* 25, no. 1 (1990): 137–56.

Brinton, Daniel G. "Nagualism: A Study in Native American Folk-Lore and History." *Proceedings of the American Philosophical Society* 33, no. 144 (January 1894): 11–73.

Broda, Johanna. "Sacred Landscape of Aztec Calendar Festivals: Myth, Nature and Society." In D. Carrasco, *Aztec Ceremonial Landscapes*.

Broda, Johanna, and Félix Báez-Jorge, eds. *Cosmovisión, ritual e identidad de los pueblos indígenas de México*. Mexico: Consejo Nacional para la Cultura y las Artes, 2001.

Brumfiel, Elizabeth. "Aztec State Making: Ecology, Structure, and the Origins of the State." *American Anthropologist*, n.s., 85, no. 2 (June 1983): 261–84.

Burkhart, Louise M. "Mexica Women on the Home Front: Housework and Religion in Aztec Mexico." In *Indian Women of Early Mexico*. Edited by Susan Schroeder, Stephanie Wood, and Robert Haskett. Norman: University of Oklahoma Press, 1997.

———. "Moral Deviance in Sixteenth-Century Nahua and Christian Thought: The Rabbit and the Deer." *Journal of Latin American Lore* 12 (1986): 107–39.

———. *The Slippery Earth: Nahua–Christian Moral Dialogue in Sixteenth-Century Mexico*. Tucson: University of Arizona Press, 1989.

Cañizares-Esguerra, Jorge. *How to Write the History of the New World: Histories, Epistemologies, and Identities in the Eighteenth-Century Atlantic World*. Stanford: Stanford University Press, 2001.

Caro Baroja, Julio. *The World of the Witches*. Translated by O. N. V. Glendinning. Chicago: University of Chicago Press, 1965.

Carrasco, Davíd, ed. *Aztec Ceremonial Landscapes*. Niwot: University Press of Colorado, 1999.

———. *City of Sacrifice: The Aztec Empire and the Role of Violence in Civilization*. Boston: Beacon, 1999.

———. *Daily Life of the Aztecs: People of the Sun and the Earth*. Westport, Conn.: Greenwood Press, 1998.

———. *Religions of Mesoamerica: Cosmovision and Ceremonial Centers*. San Francisco: Harper, 1990.

———. "The Sacrifice of Tezcatlipoca: To Change Place." In D. Carrasco, *Aztec Ceremonial Landscapes*.

Carrasco, Pedro. "Royal Marriages in Ancient Mexico." In *Explorations in Ethnohistory: Indians of Central Mexico in the Sixteenth Century*. Edited by H. R. Harvey and Hanns J. Prem. Albuquerque: University of New Mexico Press, 1984.

———. "Social Organization of Ancient Mexico." In *Handbook of Middle American Indians*. Vol. 10. Edited by Gordon F. Elkholm and Ignacio Bernal. Austin: University of Texas Press, 1971.

———. *The Tenochca Empire of Ancient Mexico: The Triple Alliance of Tenochtitlan, Tetzcoco, and Tlacopan*. Norman: University of Oklahoma Press, 1999.

Carreño, Alberto María. "The Books of Fray Juan de Zumárraga." *The Americas* (Academy of American Franciscan History) 5 (1949): 311–30.

Castañeda, Carlos E. "Fray Juan de Zumárraga and Indian Policy in New Spain." *The Americas* (Academy of American Franciscan History) 5 (1949): 296–310.

Cave, Berneice Bergman. "The Inquisition in Mexico." Master's thesis, University of California, Berkeley, 1928.

Cervantes, Fernando. *The Devil in the New World: The Impact of Diabolism in New Spain*. New Haven: Yale University Press, 1994.

Clendinnen, Inga. *Ambivalent Conquests: Maya and Spaniard in Yucatan, 1517–1570*. 2nd ed. Cambridge: Cambridge University Press, 2003.

———. "Ways to the Sacred: Reconstructing 'Religion' in Sixteenth-Century Mexico." *History and Anthropology* 5 (1990): 105–41.

Cline, Howard. "The Oztoticpac Lands Map of Texcoco, 1540." In *A la Carte: Selected Papers on Maps and Atlases*. Edited by Walter W. Ristow. Washington, D.C.: Library of Congress, 1972.

———. "The Oztoticpac Lands Map of Texcoco, 1540." *Quarterly Journal of the Library of Congress* 23 (1966): 76–116.

Cline, Sarah. "The Spiritual Conquest Re-examined: Baptism and Church Marriage in Early Colonial Mexico." *Hispanic American Historical Review* 73, no. 3 (1993): 453–80.

Colish, Marcia. *Medieval Foundations of the Western Intellectual Tradition, 400–1400*. New Haven: Yale University Press, 1997.

Contreras, Jaime. *El Santo Oficio de la Inquisición en Galicia, 1560–1700: Poder, sociedad y cultura*. Madrid: Akal, 1982.

———. *Sotos contra Riquelmes: Regidores, inquisidores y criptojudías*. Madrid: Anaya and Mario Muchnik, 1992.

Cook, Noble David. *Born to Die: Disease and New World Conquest, 1492–1650.* Cambridge: Cambridge University Press, 1998.
Cruces Carvajal, Ramón. *Pedro de Gante: Su presencia en Texcoco.* Texcoco, Mexico: Talleres de Imprenta Catedral, 1987.
Cuevas, Mariano. *Historia de la iglesia en México.* 3rd ed. Vol. 1. El Paso, Tex.: Editorial "Revista Católica," 1928.
Darst, David H. "Witchcraft in Spain: The Testimony of Martín de Castañega's Treatise on Superstition and Witchcraft (1529)." *Proceedings of the American Philosophical Society* 123, no. 5 (October 1976): 298–322.
Dedieu, Jean-Pierre. "The Inquisition and Popular Culture in New Castile." In *Inquisition and Society in Early Modern Europe.* Edited and translated by Stephen Haliczer. Totowa, N.J.: Barnes & Noble, 1987.
Díaz Balsera, Viviana. *The Pyramid under the Cross: Franciscan Discourses of Evangelization and the Nahua Christian Subject in Sixteenth-Century Mexico.* Tucson: University of Arizona Press, 2005.
Dibble, Charles. "The Boban Calendar Wheel." *Estudios de Cultura Nahuatl* 20 (1990): 173–82.
Don, Patricia Lopes. "Carnivals, Triumphs, and Rain Gods: A Civic Festival in the City of México-Tenochtitlan, 1539." *Colonial Latin American Review* 6, no. 1 (June 1997): 17–40.
———. "The 1539 Inquisition and Trial of Don Carlos of Texcoco: Religion and Politics in Early Mexico." *Hispanic American Historical Review* 88, no. 4 (November 2008): 573–606.
———. "Franciscans, Indian Sorcerers, and the Inquisition in New Spain, 1536–1543." *Journal of World History* 17, no. 1 (March 2006): 27–50.
Douglass, Eduardo de J. "Figures of Speech: Pictorial History in the *Quinatzin Map* of about 1542." *Art Bulletin* 85, no. 2 (June 2003): 281–309.
Edgerton, Samuel Y. "The Discovery of America and the Discovery of Man" (Raleigh Lecture on History). *Proceedings of the British Academy.* Vol. 58. London: Oxford University Press, 1972.
———. *Theaters of Conversion: Religious Architecture and Indian Artisans in Colonial Mexico.* Albuquerque: University of New Mexico Press, 2001.
Estarellas, Juan. "The College of Tlatelolco and the Problem of Higher Education for Indians in 16th-Century Mexico." *History of Education Quarterly* 2, no. 4 (December 1962): 234–43.
Farfán Morales, Olimpia. "Los nahuas de la Sierra Norte de Puebla: El chamanismo entre los nahuas." In *Estudios nahuas.* Edited by María Suárez y Farías. Mexico: Instituto Nacional de Antropología, 1988.
Gerhard, Peter. *A Guide to the Historical Geography of New Spain.* Cambridge: Cambridge University Press, 1972.
Gibson, Charles. "The Aztec Aristocracy in Colonial Mexico." *Comparative Studies in Society and History* 2 (1960): 169–96.

———. *Aztecs under Spanish Rule: A History of the Indians of the Valley of Mexico, 1519–1810*. Stanford: Stanford University Press, 1964.
———. "Llamamiento General, Repartimiento, and the Empire of Acolhuacan." *Hispanic American Historical Review* 36, no. 1 (1956): 1–27.
———. *Tlaxcala in the Sixteenth Century*. New Haven: Yale University Press, 1952.
Gillespie, Susan D. *The Aztec Kings*. Tucson: University of Arizona Press, 1989.
Gillmor, Frances. *Flute of the Smoking Mirror: A Portrait of Nezahualcoyotl, Poet-King of the Aztecs*. Tucson: University of Arizona Press, 1949.
———. *The King Danced in the Marketplace*. Tucson: University of Arizona Press, 1964.
Ginzburg, Carlo. *The Cheese and the Worms: The Cosmos of a Sixteenth-Century Miller*. Translated by John Tedeschi and Anne C. Tedeschi. Baltimore: Johns Hopkins University Press, 1980.
———. "The Inquisitor as Anthropologist." In *Clues, Myths, and the Historical Method*. Translated by John Tedeschi and Anne C. Tedeschi. Baltimore: Johns Hopkins University Press, 1989.
Glass, John B, and Donald Robertson. "A Census of Native Middle American Pictorial Manuscripts." *Handbook of Middle American Indians*. Vol. 14. Edited by Howard F. Cline. Austin: University of Texas Press, 1975.
González Jácome, Alba. "*Agricultura y especialistas en ideología agrícola: Tlaxcala, México*." In *Graniceros: Cosmovisión y meteorología indígenas de Mesoamérica*. Edited by Beatriz Albores and Johanna Broda. Mexico: Universidad Autónoma de México, 1997.
Gossen, Gary H., ed. *South and Meso-American Native Spirituality: From the Cult of the Feathered Serpent to the Theology of Liberation*. New York: Crossroad, 1997.
Grass, Roland. "America's First Linguists: Their Objectives and Methods." *Hispania* 48, no. 1 (March 1965): 57–66.
Greenleaf, Richard E. "Francisco de Millán before the Mexican Inquisition, 1538–39." *The Americas* (Academy of American Franciscan History) 21 (1964): 184–95.
———. "Historiography of the Mexican Inquisition: Evolution of Interpretations and Methodologies." In Perry and Cruz, *Cultural Encounters*.
———. "The Inquisition and the Indians of New Spain: A Study in Jurisdictional Confusion." *The Americas* (Academy of American Franciscan History) 22 (1965): 138–66.
———. "The Mexican Inquisition and the Indians: Sources for the Ethnohistorian." *The Americas* (Academy of American Franciscan History) 34, no. 3 (January 1978): 315–44.
———. *The Mexican Inquisition of the Sixteenth Century*. Albuquerque: University of New Mexico Press, 1969.
———. "Persistence of Native Values: The Inquisition and Indians of Colonial Mexico." *The Americas* (Academy of American Franciscan History) 50, no. 3 (January 1994): 351–76.
———. *Zumárraga and the Mexican Inquisition, 1536–1543*. Washington, D.C.: Academy of American Franciscan History, 1961.

Grunberg, Bernard. *L'Inquisition apostolique au Mexique: Histoire d'une institution et de son impact dans une société coloniale (1521–1571)*. Paris: Editions L'Harmattan, 1998.

Gruzinski, Serge. *Man-Gods in the Mexican Highlands: Indian Power and Colonial Society, 1520–1800*. Stanford: Stanford University Press, 1989.

Gutiérrez, Ramón. *When Jesus Came, the Corn Mothers Went Away: Marriage, Sexuality, and Power in New Mexico, 1500–1846*. Stanford: Stanford University Press, 1991.

Haliczer, Stephen. "The First Holocaust: The Inquisition and the Converted Jews of Spain and Portugal." In *Inquisition and Society in Early Modern Europe*. Edited and translated by Stephen Haliczer. Totowa, N.J.: Barnes & Noble, 1987.

———. *Inquisition and Society in the Kingdom of Valencia, 1478–1834*. Berkeley: University of California Press, 1990.

Haly, Richard. "Bare Bones: Rethinking Mesoamerican Divinity." *History of Religions* 31, no. 3 (February 1992): 269–304.

Hanke, Lewis. *The First Social Experiments in America: A Study in the Development of Spanish Indian Policy in the Sixteenth Century*. Cambridge: Cambridge University Press, 1936.

Harvey, H. R. "The Oztoticpac Lands Map: A Reexamination." In *Land and Politics in the Valley of Mexico: A Two Thousand Year Perspective*. Edited by H. R. Harvey. Albuquerque: University of New Mexico Press, 1991.

Harvey, L. P. *Muslims in Spain, 1500–1614*. Chicago: University of Chicago Press, 2005.

Haskett, Robert S. *Indigenous Rulers: An Ethnohistory of Town Government in Colonial Cuernavaca*. Albuquerque: University of New Mexico Press, 1991.

———. "Living in Two Worlds: Cultural Continuity and Change among Cuernavaca's Colonial Indigenous Elite." *Ethnohistory* 35, no. 1 (Winter 1988): 34–59.

Hassig, Ross. *Trade, Tribute, and Transportation: The Sixteenth-Century Political Economy of the Valley of Mexico*. Norman: University of Oklahoma Press, 1985.

Henningsen, Gustav, and John Tedeschi. *The Inquisition in Early Modern Europe: Studies on Sources and Methods*. DeKalb: North Illinois University Press, 1986.

Hicks, Frederic. "Rotational Labor and Urban Development in Prehispanic Tetzcoco." In *Explorations in Ethnohistory: Indian Mexico in the Sixteenth Century*. Edited by Hanns J. Prem and H. R. Harvey. Albuquerque, University of New Mexico Press, 1978.

Himmerich y Valencia, Robert. *The Encomenderos of New Spain, 1521–1555*. Austin: University of Texas Press, 1991.

Hodge, Mary G. "Land and Lordship in the Valley of Mexico: The Politics of Ancient Provincial Administration." In *Land and Politics in the Valley of Mexico: A Two Thousand Year Perspective*. Edited by H. R. Harvey. Albuquerque: University of New Mexico Press, 1991.

Holzapfel, Heribert. *The History of the Franciscan Order*. Translated by Antonine Tibesar and Gervase Brinkman. Teutopolis, Ill.: St. Joseph Seminary, 1948.

Horcasitas, Fernando. "Los descendientes de Nezahualpilli: Documentos del cacicazgo de Tetzcoco (1545–1855)." *Estudios de Historia Novohispana* (Mexico) 6 (1978): 145–85.

Iriarte, Fray Lázaro. *Franciscan History: The Three Orders of Saint Francis of Assisi*. Translated by Patricia Ross. Chicago: Franciscan Herald Press, 1983.

Ivanhoe, Frances. "Diet and Demography in Texcoco on the Eve of the Spanish Conquest: A Semiquantitative Reconstruction from Selected Ethnohistorical Texts." *Revista Mexicana de Estudios Antropológicos* 24 (1978): 137–46.

Kagan, Richard L., and Abigail Dyer, eds. and trans. *Inquisitorial Inquiries: Brief Lives of Secret Jews and Other Heretics*. Baltimore: Johns Hopkins University Press, 2004.

Kamen, Henry. *Inquisition and Society in Spain in the Sixteenth and Seventeenth Centuries*. Bloomington: University of Indiana Press, 1985.

———. *The Spanish Inquisition: A Historical Revision*. New Haven: Yale University Press, 1997.

Karttunen, Frances. *An Analytical Dictionary of Nahuatl*. Norman: University of Oklahoma Press, 1991.

———. *Between Worlds: Interpreters, Guides, and Survivors*. New Brunswick, N.J.: Rutgers University Press, 1994.

Karttunen, Frances, and James Lockhart. Preface to *The Art of Nahuatl Speech: The Bancroft Dialogues*. Los Angeles: UCLA Latin American Center Publications, 1987.

Kellogg, Susan. *Law and the Transformation of Aztec Culture, 1500–1700*. Norman: University of Oklahoma Press, 1995.

———. *Weaving the Past: A History of Latin America's Indigenous Women from the Prehispanic Period to the Present*. Oxford: Oxford University Press, 2005.

Klein, Cecelia F. "The Devil and the Skirt: An Iconographic Inquiry into the Prehispanic Nature of the *Tzitzimime*." *Ancient Mesoamerica* 11 (2000): 1–26.

Klor de Alva, J. Jorge. "The Aztec-Spanish Dialogues of 1524." *Alcheringa* 4, no. 2 (1980): 52–193.

———. "Aztec Spirituality and Nahuatlized Christianity." In Gossen, *South and Meso-American Native Spirituality*.

———. "Colonizing Souls: The Failure of the Indian Inquisition and the Rise of Penitential Discipline." In Perry and Cruz, *Cultural Encounters*.

———. "Martín Ocelotl: Clandestine Cult Leader." In *Struggle and Survival in Colonial America*. Edited by David G. Sweet and Gary B. Nash. Berkeley: University of California Press, 1981.

Kubler, George. "Architects and Builders in Mexico, 1521–1550." *Journal of the Warburg and Courtauld Institutes* 7 (1944): 7–19.

Kubler, George, and Charles Gibson. *The Tovar Calendar: An Illustrated Mexican Manuscript, circa 1585*. New Haven: Yale University Press, 1951.

Lafaye, Jacques. *Quetzalcóatl and Guadalupe: The Formation of Mexican National Consciousness, 1531–1813*. Translated by Benjamin Keen. Chicago: University of Chicago Press, 1974.

Lambert, Malcolm. *Medieval Heresy: Popular Movements from the Gregorian Reform to the Reformation*. 3rd ed. Oxford: Blackwell, 2002.

Lea, Henry Charles. *The Inquisition in the Spanish Dependencies: Sicily, Naples, Milan, the Canaries, Mexico, Peru, and New Granada*. New York: Macmillan, 1908.

León-Portilla, Miguel, ed. *The Broken Spears: The Aztec Account of the Conquest of Mexico*. Foreword by J. Jorge Klor de Alva. Boston: Beacon Press, 1990.

―――. "Testimonios nahuas sobre la conquista espiritual." *Estudios de Cultura Náhuatl* 11 (1974): 11–36.

―――. "Those Made Worthy by Divine Sacrifice: The Faith of Ancient Mexico." In Gossen, *South and Meso-American Native Spirituality*.

Levack, Brian P. *The Witch-hunt in Early Modern Europe*. New York: Longman, 1987.

Liebsohn, Dana. "Mapping after the Letter: Graphology and Indigenous Cartography in New Spain." In *The Language Encounter in the Americas, 1492–1800: A Collection of Essays*. Edited by Edward G. Gray and Norman Fiering. New York: Berghahn Books, 2000.

Lockhart, James. "Initial Nahua Reactions to Spanish Culture." In *Implicit Understandings: Observing, Reporting, and Reflecting on the Encounter Between Europeans and Other Peoples in the Early Modern Era*. Edited by Stuart B. Swartz. Cambridge: Cambridge University Press, 1994.

―――. *The Nahuas after the Conquest: A Social and Cultural History of the Indians of Central Mexico, Sixteenth through Eighteenth Centuries*. Stanford: Stanford University Press, 1992.

―――. "Some Nahua Concepts in Postconquest Guise." *History of European Ideas* 6, no. 4 (1985): 465–82.

―――, ed. and trans. *We People Here: Nahuatl Accounts of the Conquest of Mexico*. Berkeley: University of California Press, 1993.

López Austin, Alfredo. *Hombre-dios: Religión y política en el mundo náhuatl*. Mexico: Universidad Nacional Autónoma de México, 1973.

―――. *The Human Body and Ideology: Concepts of the Ancient Nahuas*. Translated by Thelma Ortíz de Montellano and Bernard R. Ortíz de Montellano. Vol. 1. Salt Lake City: University of Utah Press, 1980.

―――. "*El núcleo duro, la cosmovisión y la tradición mesoamericana*." In Broda and Báez-Jorge, *Cosmovisión, ritual e identidad de los pueblos indígenas de México*.

―――. *Tamoanchan, Tlalocan: Places of Mist*. Translated by Bernard R. Ortíz de Montellano and Thelma Ortíz de Montellano. Niwot: University Press of Colorado, 1997.

Lunenfeld, Marvin. *Keepers of the City: The Corregidores of Isabella I of Castile (1474–1504)*. Cambridge: Cambridge University Press, 1987.

Lupo, Alessandro. "*La Cosmovisión de los nahuas en la Sierra de Puebla*." In Broda and Báez-Jorge, *Cosmovisión, ritual e identidad de los pueblos indígenas de México*.

Marcus, Joyce. *Mesoamerican Writing Systems: Propaganda, Myth, and History in Four Ancient Civilizations*. Princeton: Princeton University Press, 1992.

McAfee, Byron, and Robert H. Barlow. "The Titles of Tetzcotzinco (Santa María Nativitas)." *Tlalocan* 2, no. 2 (1946): 110–27.

McCaa, Robert. "Spanish and Nahuatl Views on Smallpox and Demographic Catastrophe in Mexico." *Journal of Interdisciplinary History* 25, no. 3 (Winter 1995): 397–431.

Medina, José Toribio. *Biblioteca hispanoamérica (1493–1810)*. Vol 1. Santiago de Chile: Fondo Histórico y Bibliográfico José Toribio Medina, 1958.

———. *La primitiva Inquisición americana, 1493–1569*. Santiago de Chile: Imprenta Elzeviriana, 1914.

Merton, Reginald. *Cardinal Ximenes and the Making of Spain*. Edinburgh, Scotland: Kegan Paul, 1934.

Metcalf, Alida C. *Go-betweens and the Colonization of Brazil, 1500–1600*. Austin: University of Texas Press, 2005.

"Mexico's New Cultural History: Una lucha libre." Special issue, *Hispanic American Historical Review* 79, no. 2 (May 1999).

Mills, Kenneth. "The Limits of Political Coercion in Mid-Colonial Peru." *Past and Present* 145 (November 1994): 84–121.

Monter, E. William. *Frontiers of Heresy: The Spanish Inquisition from the Basque Lands to Sicily*. Cambridge: Cambridge University Press, 1990.

Moorman, John R. H. *The Sources for the Life of S. Francis of Assisi*. [Manchester]: Manchester University Press, 1940.

Moreno de los Arcos, Roberto. "New Spain's Inquisition for Indians from the Sixteenth to the Nineteenth Century." In Perry and Cruz, *Cultural Encounters*.

Muir, Edward, and Guido Ruggiero, eds. *Microhistory and the Lost Peoples of Europe*. Translated by Eren Branch. Baltimore: Johns Hopkins University Press, 1991.

Netanyahu, Benzion. *The Origins of the Inquisition in Fifteenth Century Spain*. New York: Random House, 1995.

Nicholson, Henry B. "Religion in Pre-Hispanic Central Mexico." In *Handbook of Middle American Indians*. Vol. 10. Edited by Gordon F. Elkholm and Ignacio Bernal. Austin: University of Texas Press, 1971.

Nutini, Hugo G., and John M. Roberts. *Bloodsucking Witchcraft: An Epistemological Study of Anthropomorphic Supernaturalism in Rural Tlaxcala*. Tucson: University of Arizona Press, 1993.

Nuttall, Zelia. "L'évêque Zumarraga et les idoles principales du grand temple de Mexico." *Journal de la Société des Americanistes* 8, no. 1 (1911): 153–69.

O'Callaghan, Joseph F. *A History of Medieval Spain*. Ithaca, N.Y.: Cornell University Press, 1975.

Offner, Jerome A. *Law and Politics in Aztec Texcoco*. Cambridge: Cambridge University Press, 1983.

Olivier, Guilhem. "The Hidden King and the Broken Flutes: Mythical and Royal Dimensions of the Feast of Tezcatlipoca in Toxcatl." In *Representing Aztec Ritual: Performance, Text, and Image in the Work of Sahagún*. Edited by Eloise Quiñones Keber. Niwot: University Press of Colorado, 2002.

———. "Les paquets sacrés ou la mémoire cachée des Indiens du Mexique central (XV–XVI siècles)." *Journal de la Société des Américanistes* 81 (1995): 105–41.

Orozco y Berra, Manuel. *Historia antigua y de la conquista de México*. Vol. 2. Mexico: G. A. Esteva, 1880.

Oss, Adriaan C. van. "Mendicant Expansion in New Spain and the Extent of the Colony." *Boletín de Estudios Latinoamericanos y del Caribe* 21 (1976): 32–56.
Padden, R. C. *The Hummingbird and the Hawk.* New York: Harper & Row, 1970.
Pagden, Anthony. *The Fall of Natural Man: The American Indian and the Origins of Comparative Ethnography.* Cambridge: Cambridge University Press, 1987.
Parker, Geoffrey. "Some Recent Work on the Inquisition in Spain and Italy." *Journal of Modern History* 54 (1982): 519–32.
Perry, Mary Elizabeth, and Anne J. Cruz, eds. *Cultural Encounters: The Impact of the Inquisition in Spain and the New World.* Berkeley: University of California Press, 1991.
Poole, Stafford. "Some Observations on Mission Methods and Native Reactions in Sixteenth-Century New Spain." *The Americas* (Academy of American Franciscan History) 50, no. 3 (January 1994): 337–49.
Porras Muñoz, Guillermo. *Personas y lugares de la ciudad de México, siglo XVI.* Mexico City: Universidad Nacional Autónoma de México, Instituto de Investigaciones Histo'ricas, 1988.
Pou y Martí, José María. "El libro perdido de las pláticas o coloquios de los doce primeros misioneros de México." *Miscellanean Francesca Ehrte* 3 (1924): 281–333.
Rawlings, Helen. *The Spanish Inquisition.* Malden, Mass.: Blackwell, 2006.
Read, Kay. "Sacred Commoners: The Motion of Cosmic Powers in Mexica Rulership." *History of Religions* 34, no. 1 (August 1994): 39–69.
Reff, Daniel T. "The Predicament of Culture and the Spanish Missionary Accounts of the Tepehuan and Puebla Revolts." *Ethnohistory* 42, no. 1 (Winter 1995): 63–90.
Restall, Matthew. *Seven Myths of the Spanish Conquest.* Oxford: Oxford University Press, 2004.
Ricard, Robert. *The Spiritual Conquest of Mexico: An Essay on the Apostolate and the Evangelizing Methods of the Mendicant Orders in New Spain, 1523–1572.* Translated by Lesley Byrd Simpson. Berkeley: University of California Press, 1966.
Robertson, Donald. *Mexican Manuscript Painting of the Early Colonial Period: The Metropolitan Schools.* New Haven: Yale University Press, 1959.
Rubial García, Antonio. *La hermana pobreza: El franciscanismo de la Edad Media a la evangelización novohispana.* Mexico: Universidad Nacional Autónoma de México, 1996.
Ruiz de Larrinaga, Fray Juan. *Don Fray Juan de Zumárraga, primer obispo y arzobispo de Méjico, durangués, franciscano y servidor de la patria al márgen de su pontificado.* Bilbao, Spain: n.p, 1948.
Ruiz Medrano, Ethelia. *Reshaping New Spain: Government and Private Interests in the Colonial Bureaucracy, 1531–1550.* Translated by Julia Constantino and Pauline Marmasse. Boulder: University Press of Colorado, 2006.
Rummel, Erika. *Jiménez de Cisneros: On the Threshold of Spain's Golden Age.* Tempe: Arizona Center for Medieval and Renaissance Studies, 1999.
Saunders, Nicholas J. "Predators of Culture: Jaguar Symbolism and Mesoamerican Elites." *World Archaeology* 36, no. 1 (June 1994): 104–17.
Schwaller, John Frederick. "The Cathedral Chapter of Mexico in the Sixteenth Century," *Hispanic American Historical Review* 61, no. 4 (1981): 651–74.

Seed, Patricia. *American Pentimento: The Invention of Indians and the Pursuit of Riches.* Minneapolis: University of Minnesota Press, 2001.

———. "'Are These Not Men Also?': The Indians' Humanity and Capacity for Spanish Civilization." *Journal of Latin American Studies* 25, no. 3 (October 1993): 629–52.

Seler, Edward. "Alexander von Humboldt's Picture Manuscripts in the Royal Library at Berlin." In *Mexican and Central American Antiquities: Calendar Systems and History.* Translated by Charles P. Bowditch. Washington, D.C.: Government Printing Office, 1904.

Smith, Michael E. *The Aztecs.* Oxford: Cambridge University Press, 1996.

Sousa, Lisa. "The Devil and Deviance in Native Criminal Narratives from Early Mexico." *The Americas* (Academy of American Franciscan History) 59, no. 2 (October 2002): 161–79.

Starr-LeBeau, Gretchen. *In the Shadow of the Virgin: Inquisitors, Friars, and Conversos in Guadalupe, Spain.* Princeton: Princeton University Press, 2003.

Stenzel, Werner. "The Sacred Bundles in Meso-american Religion." *Verhandlungen des XXXVIII Internationalen Amerikanisten-Kongresses, Stuttgart-München 12–18 August 1968.* Vol. 2 (1968): 347–52.

Stross, Brian. "Mesoamerican Copal Resins." www.utexas.edu/courses/stross/papers/copal.htm (September 10, 2007).

Suárez de Peralta, Juan. *Noticias históricas de la Nueva España.* Madrid: Imp. de M. G. Hernández, 1878.

Sylvest, Edwin Edward. *Motifs of Franciscan Mission Theory in Sixteenth Century New Spain, Province of the Holy Gospel.* Washington, D.C.: Academy of American Franciscan History, 1975.

Taylor, William B. *Drinking, Homicide, and Rebellion in Colonial Mexican Villages.* Stanford: Stanford University Press, 1979.

———. "Two Shrines of the Cristo Renovado: Religion and Peasant Politics in Late Colonial Mexico." *American Historical Review* 110, no. 4 (October 2005): 945–74.

Terraciano, Kevin. *The Mixtecs of Colonial Oaxaca: Ñudzahui History, Sixteenth through Eighteenth Centuries.* Stanford: Stanford University Press, 2001.

Timmer, David E. "Providence and Perdition: Fray Diego de Landa Justifies His Inquisition Against the Yucatecan Maya." *Church History* 66, no. 3 (September 1997): 477–88.

Traslosheros, Jorge E. "*El tribunal eclesiástico y los indios en el arzobispado de México, hasta 1630.*" *Historia Mexicana* 5, no. 3 (January–March 2002): 485–516.

Tuñón Pablos, Julia. *Women in Mexico: A Past Unveiled.* Translated by Alan Hynds. Austin: University of Texas Press, 1987.

Vaillant, George C. *Aztecs of Mexico: Origin, Rise and Fall of the Aztec Nation.* Garden City, N.Y.: Doubleday, 1962.

Van Young, Eric. "The New Cultural History Comes to Old Mexico." In "Mexico's New Cultural History: Una Lucha Libre." Special issue, *Hispanic American Historical Review* 79, no. 2 (May 1999): 211–47.

Wilkerson, Jeffrey K. "The Ethnographic Works of Andrés de Olmos, Precursor and Contemporary of Sahagún." In *Sixteenth-Century Mexico: The Work of Sahagún*. Edited by Munro S. Edmonson. Albuquerque: University of New Mexico Press, 1974.

Wood, Stephanie. "Testaments and Títulos: Conflict and Coincidence of Caciques and Community Interests in Central Mexico." In *Dead Giveaways: Indigenous Testaments of Colonial Mesoamerica and the Andes*. Edited by Susan Kellogg and Matthew Restall. Salt Lake City: University of Utah Press, 1998.

———. *Transcending Conquest: Nahua Views of Spanish Colonial Mexico*. Norman: University of Oklahoma Press, 2003.

Yannakakis, Yanna. *The Art of Being In-between: Native Intermediaries, Indian Identity, and Local Rule in Colonial Oaxaca*. Durham: Duke University Press, 2008.

Zavala, Vicente. *Fray Juan de Zumárraga*. 2 vols. Colección Kurutzeaga 7–8. Durango, Vizcaya, Spain, 1985.

Zulaica Gárate, Román. *Los franciscanos y la imprenta en México en el siglo XVI*. Mexico: Robredo, 1939.

INDEX

Abrojo (convent of), 28, 30
Acatepec, 70
Acatepec, Don Juan of, 56, 69, 71
Achacatl, Don Pedro of, 123, 132–33, 145
Achcauhtin, 88, 94, 103–104
Acolhua, 70, 86, 88, 123, 148, 162, 164–65, 168
Ahuitzol (tlahtoani of Mexico), 142
Alcalde, 197–98
Alexander VI (pope), 26, 42
Alfaquies, 24, 27, 31
Alguaciles, 197–98
Alpujarras: First Revolt of, 26–27; Second Revolt of, 28
Altepemeh, 7, 35–36, 43, 60, 70, 84, 86, 90–91, 93, 96, 98, 103, 107, 109, 117, 120–21, 131, 133, 139, 148, 155, 162–63, 180, 185, 197
Alvarado, Pedro de, 126–27
Amancebamiento, 40
Amaranth seeds, 118
Amate, 92, 96–97, 99–100, 103–104, 142
Ambivalent Conquests (Clendinnen), 8
Anahuacaca, 116–17, 131, 132
Anti-Christian (or -Franciscan), 11, 76, 79, 83, 96, 101, 106, 164
Antonio (son of Don Carlos), 159
Apipilhuaxco, 96, 104
Aragon, 21–22, 24

Aragonese nobles, 27, 31, 42
Arbitration of avoidance, 13–14, 38, 39, 51, 53, 58, 84, 90, 133, 143, 146–47, 157–59, 163, 186–90, 201
Archivo General de la Nación, 15
Arrows and arrowheads, 72, 107–108, 196
Arte de la lengua mexicana (Olmos), 137
Artisans, 164
Ash, 116
Asientos, 97
Atlixtaca, 96, 98
Audiencia, 47–48, 57, 79, 134, 178, 180, 182, 186
Augustinians, 44, 87
Auto de fé, 147, 177
Avila, 28
Axayaca (son of Mohtecuhzoma), 127–28
Azcapotzalco, 112, 113, 115–16, 118, 128, 130–32, 196
Aztec ceremonial landscapes, 38, 60
Aztec state cults, 94
Aztlan, 120, 137

Bailiffs, 79–80
Banishment, 17, 59, 70, 73
Baptism, 5, 35, 38, 117, 123, 151; mass (or forced), 3, 5–6, 17, 22–23, 40, 42–45, 51, 143, 153, 159, 178, 182
Basque, 28, 30

Baudot, Georges, 137, 184
Beatas, 75
Beatriz, Doña. *See* Papantzin, Doña Beatriz
Benavente, Count of. *See* Pimentel (Spanish noble family)
Benavente, Fray Toríbio de (Motolinía), 15, 33–38, 41, 43, 59, 111–12, 118, 135–36, 143–44, 179, 190
Berdan, Frances, 63
Betanzos, Fray Domingo de, 42
Bigamy. *See* Polygamy
Bishops, 22–23, 30, 44, 46, 48–49, 60, 62, 140, 179
Black Death, 21
Blankets. *See* Mantas
Blasphemies, 35, 76, 78
Boban Calendar Wheel, 188, 193–201, 203n1
Bundles. *See* Tlaquimilloli
Burkhart, Louise, 37, 58, 94–96, 106, 157
Burning of books (or manuscripts), 3–5, 14, 26
Burro, 125
Bursera, 99

Cabeceras, 190
Cacama, 149, 151
Cachula, Don Gonzalo of, 71
Caciques, 41, 176, 184, 198
Cactus, 71–72
Calmecac, 36, 59, 61–62
Calpanpilli, 153
Calpultin, 59–60, 74
Camaxtli, 72, 138
Campos, Martín de, 56
Canutos de colores, 71–72
Carlos of Texcoco, Don. *See* Texcoco, Don Carlos Ometochtli (Chichimecateuchtli) of
Carrasco, David, 38, 60–61
Castañega, Fray Martín de, 183, 185
Castile, 21, 24, 26, 28, 50, 105–107; fruit, 79, 177
Catechisms, 134, 182
Catholic kings. *See* Ferdinand and Isabel

Cervantes, Fernando, 185
Chalco, 67, 80, 103, 121
Charles V (of Spain), 27–28, 30, 32, 47–50, 60, 74, 105–106, 126, 190
Chia, 142
Chiautla, 88–91
Chichimec, 60, 75, 84, 86, 106, 108, 138, 196
Chichimicli, 76
Chiconautla, 112, 148, 163, 165, 168, 169, 170–72
Chiconautla, Don Alonso of, 164–65, 167, 169, 172
Chinantla, 54, 61, 65–66, 70
Cholula, 70
Christians and Christianity, 3–8, 11, 19–23, 26–27, 30–32, 34–38, 40–42, 51–52, 56–57, 75, 77–79, 82, 87, 89–91, 93–95, 106–107, 110, 112, 117, 119, 129–30, 133, 141–42, 157, 159, 162, 167–70, 181, 200
Cihuacoatl (domestic ruler), 115
Cihuacoatl (goddess), 113, 121, 127–28, 138–39
Cisneros, Cardinal Francisco Jiménez de, 3, 4, 24, 26–28, 32, 46
Cisneros, Cristóbal de, 58, 65, 69
Ciudad Rodrigo, Fray Antonio de, 37, 41, 54, 56–58, 64, 73–74, 76, 79, 135–36, 154, 164–165
Clandestine religion, 39, 60, 89
Clendinnen, Inga, 8
Coacalco, 120
Coatepec, 36, 58–59, 70, 72, 78
Coatlinchan, 123
Coatopilli, 115
Cocolitzli, 189
Codex Borgia, 120
Codex Mendoza, 117
Codex Tudela, 136–37
Codex Xolotl, 188
Codices, 4, 14, 188, 196, 199
Cohuanacoch, 35, 115, 130, 149, 151, 152, 190
Colegios, 135, 168, 191
Commoner men. *See* Macehualtin
Concordia, 27, 181

Concubines, 40, 52, 148, 151, 153, 167
Consanguinity, 146, 157–58, 160, 162
Contreras, Alonso de, 187
Convento, 36, 43–44, 83, 87, 183, 200
Converso, 22, 26–27, 31, 51
Converso problem, 22–23, 32
Convibia fecho, 72
Convivencia, 21
Copal, 92, 96–97, 99, 103–104, 142
Copila, 91, 95, 98–99, 101
Córdoba, Fray Pedro de, 42
Corregidor, 35, 56, 58, 65, 69, 87, 91
Cortés, Hernán, 3, 13, 15, 32–34, 37, 47, 48, 87, 115, 118, 126–32, 149, 151–53, 194; trip to Honduras, 34–35, 190
Cortes (parliament), 24, 27
Cosmic warfare, 102, 108
Council of the Indies, 4–5, 32, 39, 41, 46, 48, 175–76
Coyoacan, 153
Coyoci, 117
Cristóbal (noble of Chiconautla), 165, 173
Crypto-Islamists, 26
Crypto-Judaism, 22–23
Cuba, 126
Cuauhtemoc (leader of Mexico), 35, 75, 115, 117, 129–32
Cuauhtitlan, 103
Cuauhtlahtoani, 75
Cue, 34, 118, 121, 130
Cuenca, Spain, 137
Cuernavaca, 184
Cuitlahuac (leader of Mexico), 129
Culhua, 121, 127–28, 139
Culhuacan, 121, 123, 127–28, 131–32, 138
Culhuacan, Don Andrés of, 125, 127–30, 139
Culhuacan, Don Baltasar of, 125, 127–30, 139, 179
Culoa Tlaspique (noble of Mexico), 123, 125, 128, 132–33, 139, 145
Curanderos, 75, 100

Dance, 100, 121, 127, 184
Demon, 76–77, 111, 118, 123, 140, 163

Depopulation, 88
Devil, 15, 34, 38, 69, 100, 143, 177, 182–84
Diabolism, 18, 182–83, 185
Díaz, Diego, 144
Dibble, Charles, 194, 196
Divination, 82–63, 67, 69, 94
Dogmatizer. *See* Native dogmatizer
Dominicans, 42–47, 60
Drought, 71, 88, 163
Durango, Spain, 29–30

Ecatepec, Don Diego Huanitzin of, 132
Emperor. *See* Charles V (of Spain)
Encomenderos, 39–40, 57, 60, 81, 198
Encomienda, 48, 87
Epidemic, 43, 68
Espina, Fray Alonso de, 22–23
Ethnographic studies, 9, 18, 134, 136
Ethnoplural communities, 17, 23, 51
Evangelical gap, 94
Eytacli (mother of Ocelotl), 54, 62

Fatal feminine, 78
Ferdinand and Isabel (of Spain), 3, 9, 22–24, 42
Ferdinand (of Aragon), 23, 26–28, 151
Festivals and feasts, 38, 40, 118, 120–21
Florentine Codex, 63, 65–67. 76, 101, 118–19, 127, 129, 134, 157, 166, 184
Franciscans, 7–10, 13, 16, 18, 20, 29, 34–36, 51, 74, 90, 95, 153, 164, 167, 172, 176, 181–82, 201; conventos, 36, 38, 43–44, 83, 87, 93, 110, 190–91; correspondence, 4, 5, 15, 45, 62; detractors, 6, 19, 42–43, 81, 179; education, 6, 11, 28, 43, 134–35, 182, 191; ethnographic project, 14, 112–13, 134, 140–41, 173; Franciscan Twelve, 15, 33, 37; leadership, 5, 41, 182, 186, 190; meetings, 49, 135; mission, 5, 13, 18, 32, 43, 74, 84, 87, 89, 94, 105, 135, 185–86; native relations, 35, 38, 52, 88, 91–92, 117, 151, 189; Observants, 29–30, 46; regulation of natives, 4, 19, 41, 58, 79, 106, 157, 159, 160, 162, 168, 198

Francisco (of Chiconautla), 112, 123, 133, 148, 164–65, 167–70, 172–73
Fraticelli, 29–31
Fueros, 188
Funeral rites, 122

Gante, Fray Pedro de, 125
Gárces, Fray Juan de (Bishop of Tlaxcala), 42
Gibson, Charles, 194
Gift exchange, 70, 81, 100
Glass, John B., 194
Glyphs, 195, 199
Go-between, 12, 17, 56–57
Gods, 23, 59, 65–66, 68, 77, 88, 94, 97–100, 102, 104, 106, 109, 118–23, 128, 138–139, 141–42, 156, 168, 171, 183, 186 199; local and tutelary, 36, 59, 111, 113; of fire, 103, 108, 139
Gods, impersonator of. *See* Ixiptla
Golden Age of tlahtoque. *See* Tlahtoani (tlahtoqueh)
Gonzáles, Juan, 144
Grammars, 134
Granada, 3, 24, 26, 35, 41, 51
Greenleaf, Richard, 46, 146, 173
Green stones, 53, 75, 120, 140
Gruzinski, Serge, 83, 90, 93, 102
Guatemala, 35, 53
Gulf of Mexico, 76

Hassig, Ross, 33
Hallucinogens, 99–100
Hedonism, 39
Hegemony, 33
Hendo (the witch), 30–31
Henry IV (of Castile), 22
Herbs, 23, 101
Heresy, 30, 40, 147
Heretical dogmatism, 5, 18–19, 52, 146
Hidalgo, 84
Hispaniola, 42
Historia de los mexicanos por sus pinturas (Pinturas), 136–39, 184
Historia eclesiástica indiana, 136, 139
History of the Indians of New Spain, 15, 111, 135

Holy Offices. *See* Inquisition
Honduras, 35, 115–16, 131–32, 151
Hongos, 100
Huanitzin, Don Diego Alvarado (leader of Mexico), 132–33, 145, 179
Huauchinango, 84, 86–88, 90, 93–94, 96–97, 103
Huehuetlahtolli, 137, 166, 168, 172
Huehuetlahtolli (Olmos), 166
Huehuexoxtl, 153
Huexocingo, 70, 138, 142
Huexotla, 157
Hueytlalpan, 140
Hueytlatoani, 121, 142
Huitzilobos. *See* Huitzilopochtlis
Huitzilopochtli, 34, 64–65, 70, 73, 100, 108, 111, 118, 120–22, 127, 130–31, 133, 138–39, 170
Huitzilopochtlis (god bundles of Huitzilopochtli), 18, 108, 112–13, 118, 122–23, 132, 137–39, 141, 144–45, 173, 176–77
Huitzli, 92, 97
Human sacrifice. *See* Sacrifice
Humboldt Fragment VI, 186
Hummingbird, 115
Hypogamous marriage, 148, 159

Icpalli, 40, 196
Idolatry, 33, 40, 49, 52, 142, 146, 170, 177
Idols, 34, 39, 111, 113, 116–18, 122–23, 125–26, 140, 142–43, 145, 171, 179, 182
Iguala, Don Juan of, 160–61
Immigration, 165, 189
Incense, 65, 99
Indigenous leaders. *See* Native leaders
Inés (mistress of Don Carlos of Texcoco), 157–58, 171–72, 185, 191
Inquisition, 3, 5, 7, 8, 10, 15, 19, 26–27, 30–31, 46, 50, 93, 101, 117, 122–23, 125, 137, 139, 146, 153, 174, 185, 187, 190; alliance with local elite, 9–10, 41, 46, 49–50, 59, 74, 81, 139, 153, 171, 176, 178–81; Apostolic, 46–49, 180; confiscations, 19, 60, 80–81, 105, 111, 143, 175–79, 181, 186, 189, 193; Holy

Offices, 10, 23, 27, 46–48, 50, 80, 178, 180; interrogations, 134, 141–42, 172; relaxation (execution), 23, 107, 146, 176–77; Roman, 22–23; in Spain, 8–9, 17, 21–22, 45, 50, 176, 183; trials, 4, 8, 12, 18, 52, 64, 93, 111–12, 134, 140, 145, 148, 164, 179, 180; transcripts, 7, 11, 14–16, 41, 52, 58, 68, 76, 79, 91, 99, 109, 115–19, 137, 144, 152, 178, 197; tribunals, 10, 46,
Intlapial, 120
Isabel (wife of Charles V), 48, 57
Islam, 181
Itzcoatl, 196, 200
Ixiptla, 67–69, 97, 102–104, 107, 119,121–22, 127
Ixtlilxochitl, Don Fernando, 32, 39, 86–87, 133, 146, 149, 152–55, 158, 186; challengers of, 35, 37, 151; and Cortes, 32–33, 35, 115; and Franciscans, 33–34, 36–38
Iztapaluca, 59, 70, 76
Iztauhyatl (Artemesia mexicana), 100–101
Izúcar, 125

Jaguar, 64, 77–78, 115, 120, 140
Jews, 20–22, 28, 32, 180
Jiménez de Cisneros, Cardinal Francisco. See Cisneros, Cardinal Francisco Jiménez de

Kamen, Henry, 9–10, 21, 45
Kartunnen, Frances, 113, 166
Kellogg, Susan, 161
Kubler, George, 194

La Concepción (Franciscan province), 28
Ladino, 56
Landa, Diego de, 179, 181
Larizes, 29
Las Casas, Fray Bartolomé de, 42, 136, 137
Legitimacy, 147–49, 151, 156–57, 159
Letters from Mexico (Cortés), 15
Liebsohn, Dana, 199

Lintorne, Fray Francisco de, 92–93, 105
Lockhart, James, 33, 66, 166
Logroño, 30–31, 45, 83
Loisa, Francisco de, 80
López, Catalina, 66, 74, 75
López Austin, Alfredo, 34, 82, 119
Luna, Don Lorenzo de, 142–43, 171, 189, 197, 199

Macehualtin, 35, 40, 81, 83–84, 88, 91, 94, 100, 143, 160–62, 167–69, 183
Madrid, 19, 176, 181
Magic, 62–63, 65, 88, 91
Mal de ojo, 100
Mamol, 116
Maña (or tricks), 73–74, 119
Mandones, 87, 165, 168
Manrique, Alonso de, 27, 31, 45
Mantas, 71–72, 76, 97, 103
Mapa Quinatzin, 188, 193–94, 196
Mapa Tlotzin, 188, 193–94, 196
María, Doña (wife of Don Alonso of Chiconautla), 164, 167, 169
María, Doña (wife of Don Carlos of Texcoco), 157–58, 161, 171
María, Doña (half-sister of Don Carlos of Texcoco), 147
Marmolejo, Fray Francisco de, 83–84, 90–94, 97, 99, 101–103, 109
Massacre, 127
Mástel y manta, 138–39
Mateo (the scribe), 112–13, 115–19, 121–22, 128, 131, 138–41, 144, 170, 200
Matlatlan, 5
Matlatlan, Don Juan of, 160
Mayor. *See* Alcalde
Medicine, 53, 95, 100–101
Megadrought, 88
Melchior (noble of Chiconautla), 165, 172
Mella, Fray Alonso de, 29–30
Mendieta, Fray Gerónimo de, 136, 139, 184
Mendoza, Antonio de (viceroy of New Spain), 47, 79, 132–33, 170, 173, 182, 186, 198, 201

Meneses, Pedro de, 58, 69
Metepec, 96
Mexica, 16, 37, 65–67, 70, 86, 120–22, 127–29, 130–31, 138–39, 149, 151–52, 155–56, 196, 200
Mexico, 3, 11–12, 14–15, 17, 33, 42–45, 50, 52, 54, 59, 66, 72, 78, 84, 86, 88, 99, 103, 111, 116–17, 130, 132, 137–38, 156, 168, 170, 172, 177, 179, 183–85, 189, 196; city of, 4–5, 15, 18, 19, 33, 46–47, 49, 51, 62, 71, 74–76, 87, 108, 112, 117–18, 123, 131–32, 135, 140, 145, 164, 172, 173, 178–80
Mexico, Valley of, 5, 9, 18, 33, 43–44, 51, 61, 65–66, 70, 72, 74, 84, 103, 112, 115, 120–23, 148, 158, 170, 178, 185, 189, 190, 196; eastern, 13, 16, 38, 54, 76; northeastern, 83, 89–90, 93, 107, 111, 112, 117; southeastern, 59, 64, 67, 70, 90
Microhistory, 16
Mistress, 160
Mixcoatl, Andrés, 17, 84, 89, 102, 112, 135, 163, 184; and commoners, 88, 93–94, 96–98, 103–104; and drugs, 99–101, 104; millennial ideas, 83, 105–110; and nanahualtin, 90, 92, 95, 98, 101, 103, 106–107; and Ocelotl, 105–107; relations with frontier leaders, 90–91, 93–94, 96
Mixcoatl-Camaxtli (god), 64, 70–73, 78, 106, 108, 113, 127, 138–39
Mixtec, 175
Mixton War, 15, 41–43, 201
Mocahuque, 92
Mocihuaquetque, 78
Molina, Fray Alonso de, 134, 136
Monogamy, 78, 162
Morisco problem, 26
Moriscos, 24, 26–28, 32, 40, 43, 51, 181
Motecuhzoma, 63, 65–67, 75, 91, 116–18, 121–23, 125, 127, 129, 132, 142, 149, 151–52, 164
Motolinía. *See* Benavente, Fray Toríbio de (Motolinía)
Mudéjares, 23, 26–28, 41
Muntxaraxes, 29

Murders, child, 168, 170
Muslim problem, 24
Muslims, 3, 20–21, 24, 26–28, 32

Nahual, 53
Nahualli, 17, 51, 53–54, 62–63, 65, 69, 71, 81–82, 92, 95, 97, 105
Nahuas, 37, 102, 137
Nahuatl, 11, 14, 84, 86, 102, 117, 137, 141, 170, 177, 183, 194, 196–97, 199–200
Nahuatlized Christianity, 94–96, 148
Nahuatlahto, 56–57, 102
Nahuatl-speaking Toltecas, 84
Nahueca, 116, 131
Nanacatl, 100
Nanahualtin, 4, 17–18, 51, 53, 61, 65, 82, 84, 88, 90–93, 95, 101, 103–104, 106, 110, 144, 182, 184–86; corporate ethos of, 97–98; relations with naive leaders, 63–64
Nanahuanci. *See* Anahuacaca
Naolli tlamatine, 63
Narváez, Pánfilo, 126
Native leaders, 5, 7, 11–12, 14, 17–19, 33, 40–41, 63, 75, 82, 91–92, 94, 97, 104, 110, 112–13, 116, 118, 130, 132–33, 143–44, 154–55, 160–61, 166, 169, 172, 174–76, 181–82, 185, 194, 200; challengers, 13, 133, 154, 160, 162; and devil, 182–85; factions, 90, 146; and Franciscans, 145, 160, 171, 178, 182, 190, 194; resistance, 6–7, 11–12, 50, 78, 131, 144, 156, 159, 178, 183, 201; sex and marriage, 12, 19, 40–41, 76, 78–79, 146, 151, 158–63, 173, 184, 190; and Spanish relations, 12–13; tactics and strategies, 11–13, 16, 84, 145, 201
Native/natives, 11, 14, 44, 46, 148, 163, 173, 189; capacity for Christianity, 42, 45, 47; dogmatizers, 45 112, 146, 171; marriage, 35, 37, 40–41, 48, 151–52, 159; neophytes, 6, 18, 36, 43, 88, 112, 133, 148, 154, 176, 182–83; priesthood, 59–61, 93–94, 110, 120, 127, 133; recidivism, 5–6, 45, 74; religion, 12, 18, 53, 60, 70, 79, 82, 89, 92, 95, 102,

113, 118, 122, 134–35, 137, 140–42, 183, 185; values, 11, 146, 159, 162, 168, 189, 191, 195, 201
Native problem, 41, 51, 32, 182
Native scribes. *See* Tlacuilo
Naualtezcatl, 130
Nava, Francisco de, 175–76
Neophytes. *See under* Native/natives
New Fires ceremony, 77
New Spain, 37, 42, 44, 47–49, 62, 79–80, 102, 130, 134, 145, 171, 179, 180–81
New World, 10, 42–43, 137, 188
Nezahualcoyotl (leader of Texcoco), 86, 143, 146, 148, 152, 155, 162, 165, 168, 188, 190, 198
Nezahualpilli (leader of Texcoco), 63, 86, 143, 146, 148, 152, 168, 190, 198
Nicholson, H. B., 62, 64, 93
"Noche triste," 129, 131
"Núcleo duro," 34, 70, 72, 88, 93–95, 99, 102, 104, 110

Oaxaca, 60
Oaxtepec, 58–59, 70, 76, 81
Oaxtepec, Don Juan of, 81
Obregón, Luis González, 153
Obsidian, 196
Ocelotl, Martín, 17, 52–54, 57, 59, 60–61, 70, 81, 86, 88–89, 91, 98, 108, 112, 154, 157, 163, 183; banishment, 17, 58–59, 70, 73, 79, 83, 90, 96, 101, 105, 108, 110; business, 54, 56, 79; and Franciscans, 54, 57–58, 74, 82; and native leaders, 58, 64, 70–73, 79, 81, 96, 132; and noble servants, 56–57, 71; properties, 59, 79–80, 90, 179; representations of, 64–69, 76–79, 97, 101–102, 119, 163, 184; and Spanish, 56–57, 75, 79–80
Ocuituco, 48, 125, 144
Ocuituco, Don Cristóbal of, 144, 177
Offner, Jerome, 168
Oidor, 80, 105
Old Christians, 29, 33, 45, 181
Olivier, Guilhem, 122
Olmos, Fray Andrés de, 6, 30, 41, 90, 92, 160; correspondence, 5, 7, 182; and

ethnographic project, 134–41, 166; and witchcraft, 30, 182–85
Omens, 66–67, 77, 130
Ometochtli. *See* Texcoco, Don Carlos Ometochtli (Chichimectecuhtli) of
Oquitzin, 115–16, 130–32
Ortíz, Fray Tomás de, 42
Otomi, 62, 84, 86, 108
Otumba, 36, 86, 90, 149
Oztoticpac Map, 188
Oztoticpac palace, 37, 153, 155, 177, 186–88

Padden, R. C., 117
Pagan rituals, 29
Pahuatlan, 86
Pajas, 97
Palencia, 28
Panache, 115, 120
Pantheon, 112, 115, 121
Pánuco, 86
Papalotl, Cristóbal, 105–106, 109, 184
Papantzin, Doña Beatriz, 35, 152
Paper. *See* Amate
Parrot, 115
Paul III (pope), 45, 50
Pedro (Mateo the scribe's brother), 113, 115–18, 122, 170
Pehua, 115
Peñol, El, 128, 139
Philip II (of Spain), 9, 28, 119, 180–81
Philip III (of Spain), 28
Pimentel (Spanish noble family), 190
Pimentel Velásquez, Don Fernando (leader of Texcoco), 190
Pinauiztli, 109
Pinturas. See Historia de los mexicanos por sus pinturas
Pitzotzin, 127
Plague, 68
Pláticas, 166
Plaza Mayor of Mexico, 129–30, 173
Pochtecatl Tlaylotla, Miguel, 18, 112, 116, 120, 122, 123, 125, 133, 134, 136, 140, 145, 170, 176, 178
Pogroms, 20, 22, 24
Polygamy, 112, 146, 160–62, 171

Pomar, Gerónimo de, 143
Popochcomitl, 99–100
Primeros memoriales (Sahagún), 101
Prophets and prophecy, 101, 105, 123, 168, 173
Provisorato del Ordinario, 179–80
Puebla, Sierra de, 83–87, 108
Puebla de los Angeles, 59, 69–73, 75–76, 84, 86
Puebla (province), 54, 72
Pueblos de visita, 87
Pulque, 164
Punishment, 6, 17, 21, 45, 48–50, 93, 109, 133, 141, 174, 176, 180, 182
Pyramid. *See* Cue

Quahtliztactzin, Don Juan, 152
Qualli-tlahtolli, 166
Quecholli, 73, 108
Quetzal (bird), 115, 196
Quetzalcoatl (god), 121, 127–28, 137–38
Quetzalcoatl (priest), 61, 123
Quiyauhtlazqui, 65
Qur'an, 3

Rabbits and deer prophecy, 105–106, 197–98
Ramada, 103
Ramírez de Fuenleal, Sebastián (Bishop of Santo Domingo), 47, 135, 137
Red Tezcatlipoca, 108, 113, 138–39
Reed, Kay, 156
Regidor, 197–98
Relaxation (for execution), 132, 173, 175, 178, 182, 197, 199
Relics (reliquias), 112, 118–21, 138
Resurrection, 67
Rhetoric, 36, 76, 91, 101, 156, 160, 166, 169, 182
Riverol, Vicente, 177–78, 186, 193, 199
Robertson, Donald, 194, 196
Rogativas, 165, 167–69
Rome, 49

Sacred precincts. *See* Tlahtocayotl
Sacrifice, 33–34, 40, 59, 62, 67, 99, 103, 107, 115, 118–19, 121–22, 126, 139, 171

Sahagún, Fray Bernardino de, 63, 65–66, 68, 74, 100–101, 109, 119, 134, 136, 139, 141, 184
Sahumeria, 99
San Antonio, Juan (nephew of Don Carlos), 154–55
Sánchez de Muñón, Sancho, 131
San Francisco, Fray Juan de, 189
San Francisco de Avila (convent of), 28
San Francisco de Valladolid (convent of), 28
San Francisco (monastery of), 125
Santa Cruz de Tlatelolco, Colegio de, 112, 117, 134–35, 141, 165, 168
Santiago, Fray Alonso de, 118–19, 141
Santiago de Tlatelolco, 135, 170
Segovia, 28
Segura de la Frontera, 76
Seville, 47–49, 73, 175
Sheriffs. *See* Alguaciles
Shield, 196
Sixtus VI (pope), 23
Slaves and slavery, 43, 160
Snakes and snakeskin, 120, 140
Sorcerer, 61, 64
South Pacific, 74
Spain, 17, 20, 22, 44, 48–49, 75, 175, 180, 190; councils in, 49, 137, 175, 177; elite in, 30–31, 46, 72–73, 105, 118
Spanish, 3, 3, 7, 9–11, 13–16, 19, 26, 31, 56, 60, 66, 75, 78, 81–82, 86, 88, 91, 94, 99, 105–106, 138, 152, 161, 167, 175–81, 185, 188, 190, 195–96, 201; conquerors, 32, 128–33, 169; and indigenous armies, 32, 127, 130, 201; settlers in New Spain, 33, 39, 42, 56, 76, 87, 111–12, 119, 137, 143, 145, 155, 159, 181, 187; violence, 14, 18, 37, 122, 126, 158, 179, 189, 190–91
Statue, 112, 118–19, 141–43, 186
St. Francis, 129
St. Isabel (convent of), 75
Subaltern studies, 12
Sublimis Deus, 45
Suma (Olmos), 136, 139

INDEX 261

Supernatural, 17, 62–63, 66, 75, 78, 89, 91, 107
Suprema (Supreme Council of the Holy Inquisition), 5, 23, 48
Syncretism, 37

Tacatetl, 62
Tacuba, 130, 172
Talavera, Hernando de, 24
Tanixtetl, 62
Taylor, William, 12, 16
Teacalco, 70, 73, 78
Tecamachalco, 70, 76
Tecamachalco, Don Juan of, 70–71
Teixiptla. *See* Ixiptla
Tello de Sandoval, Fray Francisco de, 175–76, 179–80
Telpochtli, 64, 69, 104–105, 107, 113
Temascaltitlan, 123
Temples, 3–4, 33, 39, 60, 68, 77, 120, 139, 143, 200
Templo Mayor, 118, 120–21, 126, 129, 132
Tenancatl, 92
Tenancaxhuantizin, 149
Tenancingo, 128
Tenayuca, 74, 128, 139
Tendilla, Count of, 26
Tenochtitlan, 32, 33, 70, 84, 112, 115, 120–21, 123, 126–31, 137, 148–49, 151, 154, 165, 196
Tenonotzaliztli, 166
Teocallis, 34, 36
Teonanacatl, 100
Teotihuacan, 86, 119, 138, 149
Teotl, 102–103, 107, 119
Tepaneca, 148, 152, 196
Tepanquetzal, 130
Tepeaca, 70, 72, 76
Tepeaca, Don Luís of, 72, 76
Tepeapulco, 36, 86–87, 90, 92, 103, 135
Tepehua, 86, 113, 115, 128
Tepetepec, 62
Tepetlaoztoc, 90
Tepeyahualco, 90
Tepezcuco, 90
Tepuchcalco, 123

Tepuele, 64, 67
Terrazas, Francisco de, 87
Territorial empires, 155
Tetzcocingo, 142–43
Texcoco, 3–4, 16–18, 52, 54, 57–59, 64, 75, 89, 96, 103, 105, 107, 123, 135, 153–54, 159–62, 165–66, 168, 170–73, 184–85, 189–90, 193–94, 196, 198–201; council members, 141–44, 187, 189, 194, 197–99; leaders, 58, 90, 133, 142, 146–47, 152, 154, 158–59, 161–64, 168–69, 171, 188–90, 195, 197–201; regional power, 32–33, 70, 84, 86, 88; religion, 34, 36–37, 68, 148; royal family, 19, 36, 141, 143, 147–49, 151–52, 155–56, 162, 184, 186, 188, 190; succession, 147–49, 151, 154–56, 168, 177, 189
Texcoco, Don Carlos Ometochtli (Chichimecateuchtli) of, 5, 15, 18, 19, 37, 112, 123, 141–43, 148, 161–63, 170–71, 177, 188, 190, 193–94, 197–99; anti-Franciscan ideas, 159–60, 163–65, 168–69, 172; biography, 36, 152–54, 157; execution, 5, 19, 133, 173, 175, 182; legacy of trial of, 145–46, 176, 178–81, 186, 189, 199–200; male-female relations, 156–60, 167; and nobles, 147, 156, 159, 164, 166, 168–69, 174; succession, 152, 154–56
Texcoco, Don Pedro Tetlahuehuetzquititzin of, 58–59, 80, 90, 130, 132, 143, 147, 152, 154–58, 161, 163, 171, 177, 186, 188, 198
Texcoco, Lake, 65, 79, 128, 148, 164
Texuantocatl, 109
Tezcatlipoca, 64–65, 67–68, 70, 72, 78, 102–104, 107–108, 119, 121, 127
Theocracy, 29
Tlacapehua, 121
Tlaclauque Tezcatlipoca, 137–38
Tlacopan, 32, 148, 196
Tlacuilo, 117, 122, 140, 197
Tlacuxcalcatl, 116
Tlahquimilloli, 112–13, 115–21, 123, 125–29, 130–34, 136–40, 144
Tlahtoani (tlahtoqueh), 4, 14–15, 18, 35, 38, 41, 57, 62–63, 70–72, 76, 80–82, 90–

91, 93–95, 98, 108–109, 117, 120, 122, 125, 131, 142, 147, 152, 157, 163–67, 169, 178, 185–86, 188, 198
Tlahtocayotl, 36, 91–92, 98, 101, 103–104, 126–27, 142–43
Tlahuitoltzin, Don Antonio (Pimentel), 142, 186–89, 193–94, 196–201
Tlahuitzin, 61–62
Tlalmanalco, 80, 140
Tlaloc, 34, 91–92, 98, 101, 103–104, 142–43
Tlalocatepetl (Mount Tlaloc), 142
Tlaolchayauhquih, 65
Tlapalli, 97
Tlapanaloa, Don Diego of, 160
Tlatelolco, 80, 131, 170
Tlatolatl, 113, 115, 117, 131
Tlaxcala, 3, 73, 75, 85, 90, 108, 129, 135, 138
Tlazopilli, 117, 153
Tlilantzin, 115–16, 131
Tlilatzin, 115–16, 131
Tlylancalqui, 97
Toca, 125
Toledo, 8, 175–76
Toltec, 84, 86, 116, 128, 138
Toltectlahtoani, 116
Toluca, 117, 131
Tonalpohualli,
Topilci, 128
Toral, Fray Francisco de, 179
Tortillas, 116
Torture, 125, 127, 131–32, 145
Totonaca, 84, 86
Totoquihhuatzin (leader of Tlacopan), 196
Toxcatl, 67, 103, 119, 121–22, 126–29
Tratado de hechicerías y sortilegios (Olmos), 137, 183–85
"Tratado muy sotil y bien fundado de las supersticiones," 183–84
Tribute, 14, 33, 60, 86–87, 128, 149, 155, 160–62, 165, 169, 190, 196
Tridentine reforms, 180
Triple Alliance, 32, 70, 86, 148–49, 155, 196–97
Tula, 62, 84, 128, 131, 138–39, 172

Tulancingo, 36, 83–84, 86–87, 90–93, 95–96, 105, 109
Tulancingo, Don Julian de, 109
Tutotepec, 86–87, 92, 97
Tzitzimime, 76–78

Ulli, 96–97, 99
Unbeliever populations, 7, 20–21, 24, 28, 31, 50–51, 154, 180–81
Urban legends, 66

Valencia, 8, 27, 41, 43, 51
Valladolid, 28
Vargas, Alonso de, 56
Vatican, 22–23, 45, 49, 51
Veintena, 108, 121, 128, 195
Veracruz, 75–76, 84, 86, 99, 126
Vergara, Pedro de, 154, 177–78, 185, 193, 199
Villanueva, Alonso de, 87
Visita, 68, 77, 87, 93
Visitador, 3, 5, 40, 60, 62, 175
Vizcaya (province of Spain), 21, 28–29, 183
Votive objects, 13, 71, 112, 118, 171, 174

Weather, 34, 53, 72, 88, 91, 98, 102
Wilkerson, Jeffrey K., 136–37
Witches (brujos), 29–31, 54, 137, 144, 183–84
Wives, 148, 161, 174
Women, 78, 97, 101, 103, 159–63, 167, 169, 173, 184

Xaltocan, 128
Xaltocan, Lake, 164
Xicotepec, 84, 91–92, 96, 128
Xicotepec, Don Juan of, 33, 87, 91, 93, 95–97, 101, 104, 107–109
Xilotepec, 128
Xochiles, 72
Xochiquentzin, Don Pablo (leader of Mexico), 74–75, 132
Xoxul (sister of Don Carlos of Texcoco), 157
Xucupan, 97, 105, 108

Yanhuitlan, 60
Yanualiuhcan, 154
Yayanque Tezcatlipoca, 138
Yoyotzin, Don Jorge, 37, 152, 154–55
Yucatan, 79, 179, 186
Yxcuecueci, 116–17

Zacatepec, 96, 104
Zan calpizcapilli, 74
Zoomorphic, 77
Zumárraga, Archbishop Fray Juan de, 4–5, 9, 13, 16–17, 20, 30–31, 80, 90, 112–13, 116–19, 133, 135, 144, 146–47, 175–76, 180; biography, 21, 28–30; correspondence, 15, 32, 40, 47–48, 50, 182; as judge, 8, 54, 56, 61–62, 74, 93, 98, 107, 109, 123, 125, 148, 161, 163, 186; jurisdiction, 10, 41, 44, 47; leadership, 19, 134, 136, 140–41, 154, 182–83; and native leaders, 39–40, 81–82, 134, 142–45, 171–72, 175, 177, 189, 191, 197, 201; and Spanish, 46, 79, 87, 173, 178–79, 186
Zumpango, 140

www.ingramcontent.com/pod-product-compliance
Lightning Source LLC
Chambersburg PA
CBHW031432160426
43195CB00010BB/703